Pepys's
London

About the Author

Stephen Porter, until his recent retirement, worked for over seventeen years for the Survey of London, a century-old project devoted to the history of London's built environment. He is a Fellow of the Society of Antiquaries and of the Royal Historical Society, has held research posts at the University of Oxford and lectured on London's history at the Museum of London. After 25 years living in the capital he now lives in Stratford-Upon-Avon.

Pepys's London

Everyday Life in London 1650-1703

STEPHEN PORTER

AMBERLEY

Cover Illustrations

Cover illustrations: Front: Top: The Great Fire of London. © Jonathan Reeve JR588b30fp90 16501700; middle left; A Londoner from Laroon's The Cryes of the City of London (1687) © Jonathan Reeve JR1968b24p1581 16501700; middle right; A Londoner from Laroon's The Cryes of the City of London (1687) © Jonathan Reeve JR1966b24p1579 16501700; bottom: The Great Plague of London © Jonathan Reeve JR371b21p213 16001650. Back: Top: St Pauls. © Stephen Porter; bottom left: A Londoner from Laroon's The Cryes of the City of London (1687) © Jonathan Reeve JR1973b24p1589B 16501700; bottom right: A Londoner from Laroon's The Cryes of the City of London (1687) © Jonathan Reeve JR1971b24p1588T 16501700.

This edition first published 2012

Amberley Publishing
The Hill, Stroud
Gloucestershire, GL5 4EP

www.amberley-books.com

British Library Cataloguing in Publication Data.
A catalogue record for this book is available from the British Library.

ISBN 978-1-4456-0980-5

Typesetting and Origination by Amberley Publishing.
Printed in Great Britain.

Contents

1

Imperial Chamber & Chief Emporium

Samuel Pepys was a Londoner. Born in the city in 1633, he died at Clapham seventy years later, having lived most of his life in the great metropolis. The London which he knew was a big, busy and growing city that had emerged from civil war and political upheaval. Its expanding overseas trade and range of industries underpinned a prosperous economy that attracted a ceaseless flow of incomers. The metropolis held a pre-eminent position within England, as by far and away the largest city, the focus for national politics, the law, aristocratic society, scientific enquiry and culture, and as both consumer and distributor of a wide range of goods and luxuries. And it provided a large and ever-increasing market for food, drink and fuel. The bustling activity in the city's streets, the many shops and the number of vessels on the Thames, which so impressed visitors from abroad, provided visible manifestations of its vibrant economy and lively society. As the national capital it played a significant political role, with its citizens being not only keen observers but also occasional participants in the intermittent crises that punctuated the period.

The civil wars of the 1640s culminated in the execution of Charles I in January 1649. This was followed by the abolition of the monarchy and establishment of a republic, designated the Commonwealth, and the church underwent fundamental changes to its organisation and liturgy. London was at the centre of those events, and had given its support and considerable financial resources to the parliamentarian cause. When the political wheel was spun again, the monarchy and church were restored, and Charles II paraded through the city's streets to the acclamations of its populace. Within a few years of the Restoration, London endured both the greatest plague epidemic in its history and the most destructive fire hitherto experienced by any European city, while naval wars against the Dutch and French hindered its trade. The king's peaceful foreign policy after the mid-1670s ameliorated the commercial problems, but his failure to produce an heir, with his Roman Catholic brother James, Duke of York, set to succeed him, generated more political turmoil. Whig and Tory partisans clashed in

London's streets, which provided the setting for political demonstrations, as first one side and then the other seemed to be in the ascendant.

Charles II re-asserted his authority and after his death in 1685 James duly came to the throne, without disturbances. But he soon lost the support of many senior politicians and churchmen; his son-in-law William of Orange – his daughter Mary's husband – landed in the West Country with a Dutch army and six weeks later London was occupied by his troops. James fled and William and Mary took the throne jointly. William's wars against the French in the 1690s required government expenditure on an unprecedented scale. London's financiers responded with innovations that included the beginnings of the national debt and the establishment, in 1694, of the Bank of England. The change of monarch and political settlement in 1688–9 came to be described as the Glorious Revolution, the new methods of public credit adopted to meet the government's growing requirements as a financial revolution, and the expansion and structural changes of overseas trade from the mid-century as a commercial revolution. As the capital and a great trading city, London played an integral role in those far-reaching developments.

Samuel Pepys witnessed those changes. He was born in February 1633 in a house in Salisbury Court, off the south side of Fleet Street. His father, John Pepys, had come to London from Cambridgeshire when he was about fourteen and had been apprenticed to a tailor in St Bride's parish, perhaps in the house where Samuel was born. John married Margaret Kite in 1626; Samuel was the fifth of their eleven children, only four of whom survived childhood. He lived with his parents until he was about eleven, when he went to the grammar school at Huntingdon, where he studied for perhaps two years before returning to London and attending St Paul's School. Samuel was among the crowd outside the Banqueting House of Whitehall Palace to see the execution of the king; after the Restoration he was concerned in case his old school friends remembered his republican views. In 1652 he went to Magdalene College, Cambridge, with an exhibition. After he graduated in 1654 he took a post with a distant relative, Edward Mountagu, created Earl of Sandwich in 1660, who proved to be a first-rate patron. Samuel was well enough established to marry, in December 1655, the fifteen-year-old Elizabeth St Michel. Most of the remainder of his life was spent in London. Until the end of James II's reign he held senior posts responsible for the Navy's administration, and he had many interests, including music and science; he was elected president of the Royal Society in 1684. Elizabeth died in 1669 and he remained a widower for thirty-four years, until his death in May 1703. Pepys had known, indeed had experienced, London's life and the dramatic events which punctuated the second half of the turbulent seventeenth century.

Pepys's London impressed visitors who arrived there around the middle of the century, with its size, its setting on the Thames and its role as the capital of a prosperous country. Lodewijck Huygens was among the entourage of the Dutch ambassadors who disembarked at Tower Wharf in December 1651. They then travelled to Westminster, 'crossing almost the entire length of the city, which is an immense distance'.[1] The French philosopher and historian Samuel Sorbière visited London in 1663, and wrote that he was, 'surprized with the Vastness of this City', speculating that 'it requires a Year's time to live in it before you can have a very exact Idea of the Place'.[2] Lorenzo Magalotti, secretary to Cosmo III of Tuscany, arrived six years later and observed that, 'from its size, the richness of its commerce, and the number of its inhabitants, it may with justice be ranked among the principal cities of Europe'. He described it as 'the metropolis of the whole island, [it] stands on the banks of the Thames, and, mounting a gently rising eminence, spreads over it in the shape of a half-moon'. He judged it to be 'longer than it is broad, by many miles'.[3]

The royalist writer James Howell, in his *Londinopolis*, written in the mid-1650s, thought that, 'Touching the form and shape of London, it may be aptly compared to a Lawrel leaf, which is far more long than broad.' John Evelyn described the City's position as being 'upon a sweet and most agreeable Eminency of Ground, at the North-side of a goodly and well-conditioned River'.[4] Some visitors referred to this area within the old city walls, which curved around the core from Blackfriars to the Tower, as Old London, and it has become commonly referred to as 'the City'. The merchants were based there, trading from their substantial houses and warehouses. This was so densely built up that there was no quay along the Thames, 'the houses are built to the very water-side'.[5]

On the south side of the Thames was the substantial suburb of Southwark, larger than many provincial cities. It was connected to the City by London Bridge – the only crossing between Kingston and the sea – which prevented sea-going vessels from sailing further upstream. To the west a ribbon of development linked the City to Westminster, which contained the principal palace and the meeting place of parliament, the courts of law and the administrative apparatus of government. There, too, stood the great abbey, which 'hath bin alwayes held the greatest Sanctuary, and randevouze of devotion of the whole Iland'. Westminster could also claim the social distinction of having, in Howell's phrase, 'most of the Nobility and Gentry residing in, or about her Precincts'.[6]

Around the city, on both sides of the Thames, were large and growing suburbs. Less salubrious than the City and Westminster, their inhabitants were poorer and, it was feared, less orderly. They were mostly beyond the control of the corporation, which administered the City. Howell admitted that 'the Suburbs of London are larger than the Body of the City, which make some compare her to a Jesuites Hat, whose brims are far larger than the Block'. He repeated an anecdote which described the Spanish ambassador, the Count Gondomar, telling the queen, on his return to Spain in 1622, that 'I believe there will be no City left shortly, for all will run out at the Gates to the Suburbs'.[7]

Estimates were made of the size of this metropolis, which on the north side of the Thames ran from Stepney to Westminster. Howell thought it five Italian miles long and about half that from north to south (the Italian mile was about 150 yards shorter than the English one).[8] A visitor in 1654 wrote that, 'This city is very long; and certainly from the end of one suburb to the other at least six miles, but it is narrow', while Peter Heylyn, in his *Cosmography* of 1652, described the built-up area as about eight miles in circumference.[9]

The fortifications constructed around the city to defend it against the royalist armies during the Civil War were eleven miles long. Known as the Lines of Communication, they stood well away from the buildings, except in the east, where they cut through the suburbs beyond Whitechapel. After the war they were levelled, although parts of them remained visible until the eighteenth century. They came to form a definition of London for administrative purposes, with the capital specified as the area 'within the Lines of Communication'. The parishes for which the Bills of Mortality were issued also came to be regarded as those constituting the city. The Bills were weekly statistics with the numbers, causes and locations of deaths, and numbers of baptisms. They had been devised in the sixteenth century to provide data about the incidence and distribution of plague. The area which they covered was enlarged from time to time, with the parishes divided into three groups: those within the walls, those outside the walls but within the jurisdiction of the City of London, and the 'out parishes', which from 1626 included Westminster and from 1636 Islington, Hackney, Stepney, Rotherhithe, Newington and Lambeth as well. By 1647 the Bills contained returns from 130 parishes.

They provided a source for estimating the size of the population, and some of its characteristics. Howell was aware that, 'one way to know the populousness of a great City is, to observe the Bills of Mortality, and Nativities every week'. He noted that the number of births and deaths combined were roughly 300 per week, with deaths being twice the number of births. For 1647–56, the ten years following the end of the first Civil War, the average number of deaths and baptisms per week was 345 and there were 179 deaths per 100 baptisms. So Howell's figures were not too wide of the mark, although his estimate of 1.4 million inhabitants was ridiculously high. Heylyn also produced an unrealistically large figure, of 'well nigh 600,000 people', and Magalotti included a figure of 450,000 in his account.[10]

Such speculative attempts were superseded by the pioneering work of John Graunt, who skilfully manipulated the figures from the Bills to produce an estimate for the population of London c.1660 of 384,000.[11] Modern historians put the city's population at roughly 400,000 in 1650, having doubled since 1600, and it continued to rise, to 575,000 by the end of the seventeenth century. The population of England was 5.2 million in 1650 and a long period of growth then came to an end; indeed the population fell slightly, to 5.05 million in 1700. As London had continued to expand, the proportion of the national total living in the metropolis increased during the second half of the century, from under 8 per cent to over 11 per cent.

Almost forty years before he published *Londinopolis*, Howell had visited Amsterdam and Paris, the two cities with which London was most often compared. He used the figures from the Bills to estimate the size of Amsterdam, which he conceded to be 'one of the greatest marts of Europe'. But he concluded that the city 'notwithstanding her huge trade, is far inferior to London for populousness', for its Bills recorded a half or less baptisms and deaths than did those of London. By the time that he wrote *Londinopolis*, he thought that the Bills showed that 'London is five times more populous' than Amsterdam. He was more cautious when summarising Paris, where the compilation of Bills did not begin until 1670. In 1620 he had written that, 'I believe this city is not so populous as she seems to be', and in the 1650s, although admitting that Paris 'is more capacious', he claimed that London had more inhabitants. Its elongated shape 'makes London appear less populous than she is indeed', whereas Paris, 'being round ... the passengers wheel about, and meet oftener than they use to do in the long continued streets of London'. Born in Wales and educated at Oxford, Howell lived most of his life in London and developed a great affection for the city, having 'breath'd air and slept in her bosom, now near upon forty years'. He proudly described it as, 'The Imperial Chamber, and chief Emporium of Great Britain.' And so he approached his task of comparing London with other cities in a spirit of competitiveness, rather than detached assessment.[12]

By the middle of the seventeenth century London was in fact more than twice as big as Amsterdam, yet somewhat smaller than Paris, which had become the touchstone against which London was assessed. Heylyn summarised the comparisons that were made; London was 'the richer, the more populous, and more ancient; Paris is greater, more uniform, and better fortified'. His own judgement was that, 'I do not think that London is the more populous; so neither can I grant that Paris is the greater city'.[13] When the Venetian ambassador Giovanni Sagredo arrived from Paris in 1656 his impression was that London was, 'a city not inferior to Paris in population, the wealth of its merchants, in extent and what is more important access to the sea'. Sorbière also knew Paris well and so was able to give a considered opinion when comparing it with London, which was that, 'I shall not stick to say that it is larger, and has more Houses in it, than Paris; tho' I must add, it has not so many People'. Magalotti drew a similar conclusion, that London, 'contains more houses than Paris, but not so numerous a population'.[14]

The striking difference between the two cities was London's position on the Thames; it could be reached by the largest vessels and yet was far enough upriver to be secure from attack. In 1654 a visitor wrote that, 'There is nothing so pleasant about it, as the shore upon the Thames, and the view of all the ships there'.[15] Visitors were tempted to estimate the numbers of ships which they saw, which represented the city's trade and prosperity. Sagredo wrote that: 'Ships frequent it in such numbers that on my arrival more than 2,000 were counted up and down the famous River Thames.' When the Dutch artist William Schellinks arrived in 1661 there was, 'a great throng of all kinds of craft'.[16] Magalotti, too, saw the river crowded with ships, 'of large size, and of every description' and so busy that, 'it is said, that there are more than one thousand four hundred betwixt Gravesend and London Bridge, a distance of twenty miles ... to which are added the other smaller ships and boats, almost without number, which are passing and repassing incessantly, and with which the river is covered'. Some of them were engaged in the trade upstream, bringing produce and raw materials to the city, and there was also a busy overland trade, geared to supplying the citizens' needs. When Lodewijck Huygens travelled to Chelsea, in 1652, he noted that, 'we met numerous horses and carts going in the direction of London. They sometimes put eight or nine horses in a row to one cart and an outrider to manage them.'[17]

Large numbers of livestock were driven into the city, to satisfy the Londoners' appetite for meat. Howell included an anecdote which related that, 'A knowing Spaniard said, that he thought Eastcheape Shambles alone, vends more flesh in the year, than all the Court of Spain.'[18] Magalotti was aware that, despite Paris's size:

> the consumption of butchers' meat is much greater in London, either because there are no abstinence-days, or in consequence of their voracity, the English eating more meat than any thing else; and on this account, there are slaughtered there, every day, besides other animals, three thousand oxen, with large joints of which their tables are covered.

And he admired the supply and distribution arrangements: 'There is no want of any thing whatever in London, because all things go on regularly and in order', and not only with supplying domestic produce, for it, 'abounds in provisions of all kinds, the convenience of navigation conveying thither from the most remote parts every delicacy or expensive luxury that is not produced in the kingdom'. Howell drew attention to the 'large Warehouses, and spacious fair shops she hath of all mercantile Commodities', and Sorbière wrote that, 'perhaps there is no City in the World that has so many, and such Fine Shops'.[19]

Graunt's findings confirm that the production and marketing of supplies for the metropolis were adequate and efficient. He noted that 'few are starved', just 51 of the 229,250 deaths in the Bills for his sample years were attributed to starvation. Moreover, 'the vast number of Beggars, swarming up and down this City, do all live, and seem to be most of them healthy and strong'.[20] His impression was that the city's support for its poor and destitute was effective, and food supplies evidently kept pace with the growing population. So did the provision of water. The wells, springs and conduits that had supplied Tudor London were supplemented by the New River Company's reservoir at Clerkenwell, completed in 1613, from which pipes ran to the western part of the City, and by towers alongside the Thames within which wheels raised water to pipes for distribution. In 1656 Sir Edward Ford was commissioned to construct a wheel that would raise water into the higher streets of the city, a height of 93 feet. This he achieved, building a 'rare engine' within a year.[21] Southwark's supply was increased by the flow from waterwheels in the arches at the southern end of London Bridge, originally built to grind corn, and there was one in the northern arch, according to Lodewijck Huygens: 'the river turns a watermill which provides a large part of the city in this area with water'. But the number of conduits disappointed Sorbière: 'There are but few Publicke Fountains in this City, and those few that are, instead of being an Ornament to those Places and Streets where they are to be met with, do but offend the Sight, for they are nothing but nasty Square Towers, into which there is an Entrance by Two little Doors to draw Water, which goes unobserved by Strangers, without they are informed that they are Water Conduits'.[22]

London was a major consumer of coal, which by the seventeenth century had replaced wood as the principal fuel. In 1653 Lorenzo Paulucci, the Venetian ambassador in England, mentioned 'the immense consumption of coal in this city by persons of every class'. It was brought down the North Sea in colliers, some from the Scottish coalfields, but mostly from those in north-east England, close to the rivers Tyne and Wear. Paulucci's successor, Francesco Giavarina, wrote that nearly all the coal consumed in London came from Newcastle and he reported the anticipated arrival of a convoy of 300 ships carrying 'this essential commodity in general use'. By 1660, roughly 60 per cent of the tonnage of English vessels engaged in the coastal trades and fishing consisted of colliers, and London was the largest market for coal, as for other produce and goods.[23]

The capital also dominated English foreign trade. Roughly three-quarters of imports and exports were shipped to and from London, and for imports alone the proportion was four-fifths. This does not include re-exports, a growing sector of English trade that almost doubled in value during the final third of century, and London was also predominant in that sector. The principal exports were woollens, tin and lead, with woollens contributing three-quarters of London's exports by value. Imports were dyes, raw silk and other goods for use in textile manufacture; linens, cotton and silks; fruit, wine, currants and spices; naval stores from the Baltic; and steadily increasing quantities of sugar from Jamaica and tobacco from Virginia. Manufactures, raw materials, and food and drink each contributed roughly a third of imports. Northern Europe and Iberia remained the principal markets for exports and sources of imports, although trade with the Mediterranean, the East and the New World was expanding. Trade was conducted by the merchants who were members of the trading companies: the Merchant Adventurers, the East India Company, the Levant Company for those trading with the Mediterranean, the Royal African Company and the Russia Company. But their dominance was to come under attack during the second half of the century.[24]

The merchants' focus was the Royal Exchange in Cornhill, erected at Sir Thomas Gresham's expense and opened in 1568. It was both a meeting place for the merchant community and a shopping centre in the heart of the City. Trading was conducted by the merchants in the courtyard during set hours and the galleries around the four sides contained shops. The district surrounding the Exchange was developing as the City's financial centre; during the century many goldsmiths moved there from Cheapside. Others transferred their businesses to Fleet Street, to be near their clients in the aristocratic area along the Strand and close to Whitehall Palace. Also in response to the wealth of that district, a rival emporium was opened in the Strand in 1608 and designated the New Exchange. It failed to lure the merchants away from the City, but its shops were a success. Schellinks visited the building in 1661 and wrote: 'There are excellent shops all round on two floors, in which all kinds of fine goods can be got'. Lodewijck Huygens found there, 'all the kinds of niceties one usually buys in French haberdashery shops'.[25] Pepys was a frequent visitor in the 1660s, buying gloves, lace, haberdashery and books. Despite the shops at the New

Exchange and the removal of the goldsmiths, Cheapside remained the City's principal street, effectively its high street, described by Schellinks as 'the wide street'. It was a shopping and market street, lined with tall houses, and the best place to watch processions, including the annual lord mayor's show.[26]

While London's shops drew admiring comments from visitors, its principal buildings failed to impress. Sorbière was dismissive: 'The Publick Buildings are not very remarkable'. Gothic architecture was out of fashion and so he described London's fine fifteenth-century Guildhall as 'an inconsiderable Building and stands in a narrow Street'. The exterior of St Paul's had been embellished by Inigo Jones before the Civil War, in an up-to-date Classical style, but the cathedral attracted attention more because of its sheer size, with Sorbière describing it as 'the longest [church] that I have seen'.[27] Westminster Abbey was admired for the same reason, Lodewijck Huygens wrote that it was, 'very long and high but narrow and very dirty, and by no means comparable to the Cathedral of Utrecht'. This was faint praise and Schellinks passed no judgement, other than to note that, 'It is a very ancient building, its statues and fabric much damaged by their age.'[28] Sorbière's reaction to Whitehall Palace was mixed. He admired the Banqueting House, built by Jones for King James, which he thought looked, 'very stately, because the rest of the Palace is ill Built, and nothing but a heap of Houses, erected at divers times, and of different Models, which they made Contiguous in the best manner they could'.[29] Nor was Huygens inspired by St James's Palace, which, 'did not look impressive from the outside'. And while Howell proudly described the Tower as 'a great Ornament, by the situation of it, both to the River and the City', Huygens found it to be 'quite big but oddly enough not strong. Apart from the square tower, it has no other beautiful building; for the rest it is like a small town.' It had many functions; it was a citadel, a repository for the state's treasures and records, and the country's principal arsenal. The royal menagerie was there, and so was the mint, 'which employs a large number of people, and … consists of eight or ten workshops in a line like shops in a street'. Most notoriously, the Tower was a prison. As a royalist Howell could not resist making the comment that, 'in the raign of the long Parliament, and ever since, the Tower of London hath had more number of Prisoners, then it had in the compasse of a hundred years before'.[30]

Visitors were more impressed by London's bustling activity than its architecture. It drew in so many people that the greater numbers of deaths than births noted by Graunt did not prevent its growth, with incomers more than compensating for the high mortality rate. Most came from within England, but a significant number arrived from the continent, both economic migrants and refugees from war and persecution. In 1656 Jews were allowed to settle in England for the first time since they had been expelled in 1290. Even though this formalised a process that was already under way, the policy was not welcome in London, according to the Worcestershire gentleman Henry Townshend, whose note in his journal referred to the Whitehall Conference which debated the matter in December 1655: 'The divines meeting, and lawyers against their admittance, and all the merchants and citizens of London.' The Londoners' concerns were economic, as expressed by the lawyer Bulstrode Whitelocke, 'that such an admission of the Jews would enrich foreigners, and impoverish the natives of the land'.[31] London contained perhaps twenty Jewish households in the mid-1650s and by the end of the decade there were thirty-five. This was a small number in a city of almost 400,000 people, yet the lord mayor and corporation petitioned Charles II soon after the Restoration, requesting him to renew the expulsion of 1290.[32]

The Londoners' reaction was typical of their response to immigrants and visitors from abroad. The French traveller Jorevin de Rochford wrote that, 'Strangers in general are not liked in London, even the Irish and Scots, who are the subjects of the same king'.[33] They certainly gave Magalotti an unfavourable impression of their hospitality: 'The common people of London, giving way to their natural inclination, are proud, arrogant, and uncivil to foreigners, against whom, and especially the French, they entertain a great prejudice, and cherish a profound hatred, treating such as come among them with contempt and insult.' A few years earlier Sorbière had gained a bad impression even before he reached the city, for those travelling with him on the journey from Dover did not help him to overcome his unfamiliarity with English when they stopped at inns, so that, 'I was as little regarded as if I had been a Bale of Goods'. He subsequently mentioned that the 'Common People and Meanest Tradesmen' adopted a 'Haughtiness and Indifferency towards Strangers'. Christiaan Huygens visited London for the first time in 1661 and his reaction was that: 'The people are gloomy, the well-to-do are polite but unforthcoming, the women have nothing to say and are not anywhere near as they are in France.'[34] Yet Howell acknowledged the importance of immigrants, because of the skills which they introduced. Having mentioned the large number and variety of trades practised by London's artisans, he added, ''tis true, that mingling with Forreiners, hath much advantag'd her in this kind; but 'tis observed, and confessed by all Nations, that though the Londoners be not so apt to invent; yet when they have got the Invention, they use alwayes to improve it, and bring it to a greater perfection'.[35] The importance of innovations introduced by immigrants was widely accepted, especially their impact on the textile trades. Techniques brought in by Dutch and Flemish workers allowed a great expansion of linen and silk manufacture, and their new ways of colouring fabrics produced improvements in dyeing.

The Flemish and Dutch were concentrated largely in Southwark and in St Katherine's, just east of the Tower. Schellinks visited St Katherine's and wrote that, 'in this neighbourhood live many Dutchmen, innkeepers and others'. The Dutch church, established in 1550, was in Austin Friars. Lodewijck Huygens was told that 1,100 or 1,200 Dutch people lived in the vicinity and 500 attended communion one Sunday when he went to a service there.[36] Also in 1550, a French church was established in St Anthony's chapel in Threadneedle Street. Not all of its members were recent immigrants; 41 of the 104 elders of the French church in the 1640s and 1650s whose origins are known were born in England.[37] One Sunday in four the two congregations exchanged churches, as Pepys discovered: 'in the afternoon I thought to go to the French church; but finding the Duch congregation there and then finding the French congregation's sermon begun in the Dutch, I returned home.'[38]

Most often, Pepys, like other Londoners, attended his parish church, St Olave, Hart Street. Church services, the administration of their parish through the vestry (the main seat of local management), and its charities provided a focus for the citizens in their own neighbourhoods. Within the City, the seventy or more livery companies provided a formal structure for the regulation of its trades. Their members were freemen, those who had served an apprenticeship and so qualified to trade in the City. An apprentice enrolled when he was in his early to mid-teens and served with his master for at least seven years while learning his craft. Typically, 80 per cent or more of apprentices were from outside London and by far the majority stayed on in the city after completing their term, contributing to the flow of incomers to the metropolis from the provinces.

Within the large and growing city, trades, neighbourhoods, social groups and places of worship helped to provide a sense of identity. London consisted of a patchwork of districts, with a wealthy central area, poorer suburbs, and growing social segregation, as the aristocracy and gentry gradually withdrew from the City and settled in the burgeoning West End. Yet it all had to be administered as closely and consistently as possible, under the watchful eye of the government, to maintain an orderly and well-functioning city.

2

Congestion, Pollution & Anxiety

London's inexorable growth fuelled anxieties, that it was becoming too large and that existing problems, such as overcrowding, congestion and pollution, were worsening. These were not neglected; the city was carefully regulated and many aspects of its life were supervised, but not all regulations could be strictly enforced, and crime and social instability were long-standing causes for concern. Visitors were unaware of many of the underlying problems, although they did cast critical eyes over its streets and houses.

Its economic preponderance caused unease, because it seemed to be depriving the rest of the country of people, resources and wealth. Put succinctly, 'gentlemen drain the country of all the money that they can get, bring it to London, and spend it there'.[1] Sir William Davenant commented on this. He had succeeded Ben Jonson as Poet Laureate in 1638 and wrote a dialogue, in 1656, in which a Londoner and a Parisian praise their own city and decry the other. In it he facetiously advised Londoners to be civil to the gentry, 'who, when they have no business here to employ them, nor publick pleasures to divert them, yet even then kindly invent occasions to bring them hither, that, at your own rates, they may change their Land for your wares'.[2] And so the counties were left without leadership, as the aristocracy and gentry spent ever-longer periods of the year in the capital, which developed into the London 'season'. They appeared at court and checked on the progress of their lawsuits, and laid out money to keep abreast of the changing fashions and to maintain their dignity. London's population was said to be noticeably higher when the courts were sitting, especially in the autumn, during the Michaelmas term. Such fears had been expressed since the mid-sixteenth century and were summarised by Peter Heylyn:

> Certain it is that London … is grown at last too big for the kingdom; which whether it may be profitable for the state, or not, may be made a question. And great towns in the body of a state are like the spleen or melt in the body natural, the monstrous growth of which impoverisheth all the rest of the members, by drawing to it all the animal and vital spirits, which should give nourishment to them.[3]

Beginning with a royal proclamation in 1580, successive governments had attempted to prevent the city's growth by prohibiting new buildings that were not replacements on existing foundations. Those who contravened the regulations were penalised, by fines and by having their new structures demolished. But exemptions were made, licences were granted on payment of fees, and the scale of the problem was too great for the measures to be effective, even though the corporation supported the policy.

When the Protectorate government revived the strategy in the late 1650s, it did so to raise funds because of a shortfall in revenue. Giavarina mentioned this in a despatch to the Doge and Senate in March 1657:

> Parliament is devoting its attention to raising money in addition to the amounts already decided, as it is badly needed to carry out all the plans which they have in mind. Accordingly they have decided to impose a tax on all buildings newly erected in London and its suburbs to a distance of ten miles out, from 1620 onwards, the owners being obliged to pay one year's rent for once only. In 36 years they calculate that over 60,000 houses have been erected in and about this city, great and small.

Even if the number of new houses was an exaggeration, this would bring in a considerable sum, with the further benefit of punishing those who had ignored the earlier regulations, and would also 'restrain others by this example from doing the like, indeed they contemplate issuing even more severe prohibitions in the matter'. But he wondered if it was politically expedient to impose such a levy, given the existing level of taxation.[4] Nevertheless, the Act was passed in June and the fines were collected. According to Giavarina, this was done 'almost with violence'. The corporation itself was fined £234 for 'building contrary to the Act' and twice within seven weeks John Evelyn was summoned to appear before the commissioners implementing its terms.[5] Almost £41,000 was raised within eighteen months, yet this was less than had been anticipated and Cromwell complained to the Speaker of the Commons that, 'some supplies designed by you for the public service, that of the buildings, hath not come in as was expected'.[6]

The tax was continued after the Restoration. William Schellinks, in 1662, described how, at the annual parish beating of the bounds ceremony on Ascension Day, the minister and churchwardens, 'inspect all the wards of their parish to see whether any new houses or dwellings have been built, which should have been registered by them for the payment of tax and record these'.[7] Yet the legislation did not halt additional buildings and permitted two new developments, at Spitalfields and Moorfields.[8] And within two years of the Act, Hatton Garden was set out, on the former gardens of the Bishop of Ely's palace on the north side of Holborn. It was the property of the royalist Christopher, Lord Hatton, Comptroller of the Household to Charles I, who returned from exile in 1656. His financial problems led him to grant a lease of fourteen acres, on which a broad new street, Hatton Garden, and subsidiary streets were set out. In June, Evelyn went to see 'the foundations now laying for a long Streete, & buildings in Hatton Garden design'd for a little Towne: lately an ample Garden'.[9] That was just the kind of development, on a new site, which the earlier legislation to stop the growth of London had been designed to prevent.

Not only were such developments tolerated, but some property owners successfully claimed exemption from the levy. They included the Earl of Bedford, who was questioned concerning his estates in Covent Garden and Long Acre. He was allowed £7,000 for the building of St Paul's church and three houses, which was justified by Sir John Hobart during the debate in parliament, on the grounds that, 'Such buildings and such a church is the honour of the nation.'[10] The church had been designed by Inigo Jones and consecrated in 1638. The Covent Garden development was begun five years earlier by the earl's father, after he had paid the crown £2,000 for a building licence which permitted the building of 'howses and buildings fitt for the habitac[i]ons of Gentlemen and men of abillity'.[11] Schellinks saw it when it was completed: 'a large piazza or market place with excellent residences resting on pillars, which form a large arcade to walk through'.[12]

Covent Garden was one of the fashionable new developments to the west of the City that were attracting the aristocracy and gentry. To the north was 'a spacious street, called Long Acre, and then Pickadilly, full of fair Houses round about'. Pall Mall was laid out in 1661, parallel to Piccadilly, and later in the decade St James's Square and the adjacent streets were begun, between those two streets. At Lincoln's Inn Fields, set out in the late 1630s by William Newton, the development considerably increased the crown's annual rent. The outbreak of the Civil War in 1642 and Newton's death in 1643 halted building activity, but it resumed in 1653 and Howell described the square, the largest in London, as 'a spacious field, where many fair Houses, or rather Palaces, are taken up by the Gentry'. Newton was also responsible for developing the eastern end of Great Queen Street, which contained 'faire dwelling houses … fitt for the habitacon of able men'.[13]

New buildings in some of the existing streets were also being erected in contemporary styles. Howell drew attention to Aldersgate Street, which 'stretcheth all along North, with very handsome Edifices … [It] resembleth an Italian street more than any other in London, by reason of the spaciousness & uniformity of Building, and streightness thereof, with the convenient distance of the Houses; on both sides whereof, there are divers very fair ones'. They included Thanet House, the stylish front of which was much admired after it was re-fronted c.1641, possibly to designs by Inigo Jones. When John, Lord Tufton died in 1675 Lady Anne Clifford noted that he 'built with freestone so magnificently'. Howell also admired 'a handsome new street ... fairly built by the Company of Goldsmiths', which opened off Aldersgate Street, and he noted that in New Street, off Shoe Lane, 'there is a knot of very handsome Buildings'.[14]

But even such stylish developments did not impress all visitors. A summary of London in a letter of 1654 mentioned that, 'The nobility lodge in the suburbs, which is the best part of the city; but there is not one good house amongst them, not the king's palace itself, none of them being completely fair'.[15] The more typical city streets were also given short shrift, by Christiaan Huygens: 'the city [is] poorly built, with narrow streets having no proper paving and nothing but hovels'. In 1661 the Venetian ambassadors Angelo Correr and Michiel Morosini complained of 'the extreme narrowness and inconvenience of the houses'. By the time that Magalotti came to London, much of the City had been destroyed by the Great Fire, and so he was describing the remainder when he wrote that, 'The houses, for the most part, are of little note and of a common description, not very high, nor inhabited as at Paris, there being seldom more than one family in each.'[16] That aspect was also commented on by Sorbière, six years earlier, who noticed that in London the houses were not as tall and so did not contain as many people as those in Paris, because 'There is scarce above One Family in a House'. An exception was the area around Whitehall, which contained lodgings for those attending court for short periods.[17] Regulations from the sixteenth century onwards had forbidden the subdivision of houses into separate dwellings and prohibited householders from taking in lodgers, who were described as 'inmates'.

Davenant's dialogue for his 'Entertainment' of 1656 contained remarks about London's streets and buildings, to compare them with those in Paris. He had served in the royalist armies in the Civil War, followed by a spell with the exiled Stuart court at Paris, and so was well qualified to make the comparison. His fictional Parisian drew attention to London's winding streets, where carts and barrels of beer could obstruct the passage of noblemen's coaches: 'Sure your Ancestors contriv'd your narrow Streets in the dayes of Wheel-barrows, before those greater Engines, Carts, were invented.' And was the climate really so hot that the streets needed to be shaded by overhanging roofs? He took as an example Old Fish Street, 'where Garrets (perhaps not for Architecture, but through abundance of amity) are so made, that opposite Neighbours may shake hands without stirring from home.' And the frontages lacked uniformity because of the intermixing of buildings and their great variety: 'Here stands one that aimes to be a Palace, and, next it, another that professes to be a Hovel. Here a Giant, there a Dwarf, here slender, there broad; and all most admirably different in their faces as well as in their height and bulk.' Could any Londoner 'shew me one House like another'? The riverfront gave the same impression: 'here a Palace, there a Wood-yard, here a Garden, and there a Brew-house: Here dwells a Lord, there a Dyer'. And the houses were insubstantial, 'enclos'd with Pasteboard walls ... so slight, and so prettily gaudy, that if they could move, they would pass for Pageants'. As for the Londoners' taste in furnishings and diet, their beds seemed no bigger than coffins, the curtains were too short, the bread was too heavy, the drink too thick, 'and yet you are seldome over-curious in washing your glasses'.[18]

Davenant's chief purpose was to amuse the audience, but others, with a more serious intention, also complained about the streets. One writer attributed their narrowness to 'the covetousness of the citizens, and connivency of magistrates, who have suffered them from time to time to incroach upon the streets, and to jet the tops of their houses, so as from one side of the street to touch the other; which, as it doth facilitate a conflagration, so doth it also hinder the remedy, and besides taketh away the liberty of the air, making it unwholesome, and disfigureth the beauty and symmetry of the city'.[19] John Evelyn described the streets as 'narrow and incommodious in the very Center, and busiest places of Intercourse', and uneven, due to such an 'ill and uneasie a form of Paving under foot'. He complained, too, of the 'Congestion of mishapen and extravagant Houses' and their 'troublesome and malicious' spouts and gutters, from which the water continued to cascade after it had rained. And the city was further disfigured by 'the Deformity of so frequent Wharfes and Magazines of Wood, Coale, Boards, and other course Materials, most of them imploying the Places of the Noblest aspect or the situation of the Palaces towards the goodly River, when they might with far lesse Disgrace, be removed to the Bank-side'. He thought that a continuous quay along the riverfront was required.[20]

John and Margaret Pepys's house in Salisbury Court was a typical timber-framed artisan's house: three storeys high, probably with the upper storeys projecting above the street, and covered with a tiled roof. It had a shop on the street front, a parlour to the rear, a kitchen and a cellar, two principal bedchambers, and a chamber which contained only some bedding, a sea chest and a trunk. The lightest chamber was that at the top of the house and so it was used for cutting cloth, but it also had two bedsteads, the 'maydes bed' and other furniture. One of the principal bedchambers was well furnished, with a 'Larg hye bedsted redd serg curtaines & valençe & cups with silk fringe'; it was 'hung with stripe hangings & curtins of the sam[e]' and its contents included, 'A large ovell Table 2 Joynt stooles a turne up table & a corte cubberd, A larg Turkey carpett, 6 cheirs & an elbow cheir of the same the bedd is off'. The other principal bedchamber was 'hung with Stript hanging, with maps' and contained 'A larg standing Bedsteed' and 'a pair of virginals & a Frame'.[21] Pepys's life-long love of music may have begun from hearing and playing instruments at home.

London's streets and buildings were regulated and a policy was in place to change their construction and appearance. The orders included the requirement that jetties and projecting roofs should be at least nine feet above the street, and all roofs had to be 'of Tile, Stone, or Lead, for peril of fire'; thatched roofs had been eradicated centuries earlier.[22] The 1657 Act required that new buildings should be 'built with Brick or Stone, or both, and straight up, without butting or jetting out into the Street, Lane or place'. This continued the policy aimed at producing uniform frontages that had been initiated in 1605, and was also designed to save timber and 'for the prevention of the burning and firing of Houses'.[23]

For the same reason, the parish officers' duties included enquiring 'if any Baker or Brewer, bake or brew with Straw or any other fewel, which may indanger fyring', and also investigating the premises of 'such who use any fire-presses … for pressing, or dressing of netherstocks [stockings], Wollen Clothes, or other things … all Armorers, and other Artificers, using to work in Metals, which have or use any … places dangerous for fire'.[24] Fire-fighting equipment was kept by the wards and parishes. In 1643 an order issued by the lord mayor required that 'every parish should have hooks, ladders, squirts, buckets, and scoops, in readiness, upon any occasion'. In 1649 the officers of Cornhill ward bought three brass squirts and twenty-seven buckets, at a cost of £11 10s.[25] The first fire-engines in England were made in the 1620s and by the early 1640s they had been acquired by some of the wards, in response to a precept sent to their officers, ordering them 'to cause the Engine (if any be provided for the quenching of fire) within your ward to be imediatly without all delay prepared and fitted for use And if your ward be yet unprovided thereof then to take the speediest course you possibly may to supply the want of this Instrument soe usefull & necessary for the securing of this Citty'. Their design and effectiveness were steadily improved. In 1658 a notice in *Mercurius Politicus* recommended those made by Ahasuerus Fromantel, a clock-maker, described as 'Engins made in a new way of his own invention for quenching of fire, which have been thoroughly proved, and found to be effective … for that they are not subject to choak with Mire, and when they are clogged with Dirt, may be presently cleansed without charge, in half a quarter of an hours time, and fit to work again'.[25] They were robust and small enough to be carried upstairs. Danger came not only from the firing of buildings, but from neglecting them, leading to dilapidation. In 1647 Dorothy Field was reported for allowing her houses in an alley in St Michael, Cornhill, to fall into disrepair; some had already fallen down 'and by the fall thereof hath slaine three persons'.[26]

The officers' responsibilities also included supervising the cleanliness of the streets. Howell mentioned that they were to check if anyone, 'after rain, or at any other time, cast or lay any dung, ordure, rubbish, Sea-coal ashes, rushes, or any other thing of nuisance in the River of Thames, or the Channels of the city'. Moreover, they were 'to inquire, if any have, or use any common Privy, having issue into any common Sewer' and also to see 'if any that keep Horses in their Houses, do lay their Stable dung, or such kind of noysome filth, in any streets, or lanes of the City, and do not cause the Dung-cart to be led to the Stable door'.[27] Pigs should not be left 'to wander up and downe the streetes and lanes' and householders were responsible for keeping the street in front of their houses clean and should 'cast not out their Seacole Ashes into the streetes, but keepe them until the raker comes and cries dust'.[28]

Yet such close attention to the urban environment did not produce the favourable impression that Howell desired. A visitor wrote that in London, 'There is infinitely more dirt than in Paris.' Howell would have been mortified had he known of that comment; in his own experience, 'the dirt and crott of Paris may be smelt ten miles off, and leaves such a tenacious oily stain, that it is indelible and can never be washed off'.[30] But Hugh Peter, a puritan minister who spent some time in exile in Amsterdam in the 1630s, also complained of the state of London's streets. He wrote that in the city, 'wee see most beastly durtie streets', which fouled clothes and shoes and carried into houses, so that the merchants could not live as cleanly and neatly as did their Dutch counterparts. That would be improved if they were paved with flat, square stones, with gutters at the sides, not down the centre, and raised footways of brick in front of the houses.[31] Evelyn had travelled on the continent during the Civil War and he, too, was sharply critical of the deplorable state of the streets, which he described as 'dirty even to a Proverb'. That was partly caused by 'what is brought in by the Feet of Men and Horses', and the rubbish which was daily thrown out of the houses.[32]

The number of horse-drawn vehicles contributed to the mess in the streets and also caused congestion. Peter thought that carts should be banned and replaced by sleds, as in Amsterdam, and the number of coaches should be reduced.[33] Traffic congestion was a long-standing problem that the corporation attempted to deal with over many years. Its common council made a further attempt in 1654 with an order that limited the number of cars (two-wheeled carts, twelve feet long) to 420, of which 140 were to be used for moving goods from the wharves and the remainder for the streets. Problems were caused by negligent drivers not observing the rules, 'not onely to the pestering and great Annoyance of the Streetes and other inconveniencyes but the peril (as it hath often proved) the maimeing and sometimes slaughter of Children and Passengers'. The measure proved to be ineffective, for within four years eighty more cars had been licensed than the Act had allowed; demand for transport in the city was such that restrictions on the number of vehicles were difficult to enforce.[34]

Overcrowding was exacerbated by the hackney coaches for hire that waited for passengers. This was a relatively new development of the early seventeenth century. They competed with the watermen, whose wherries carried people along and across the river, avoiding the blockages in the streets. Schellinks described how at the principal wharves and quays, 'are stairs or jetties with steps to allow one to board boats and to disembark, and on each jetty or ferry lie many light boats to ferry people across'.[35] In 1635 the watermen's spokesman John Taylor complained that they were losing business 'by the multitudes of Hackney or hired Coaches: but they never swarmed so thick to pester the streets, as they doe now, till the yeare 1605'.[36] An order of the justices of the peace ruled that, 'noe Hackney Coachman stand in the streetes within three yeards of any man's dore, nor feede their horses in the streetes before men's dores to their great annuzance'. The fine for each offence was one shilling.[37] Hackney coaches became such a problem that a proclamation issued in 1660 banned them from waiting in the streets for a fare; they could wait only in stables and yards. But it seems that the order was disregarded, for in 1669 Magalotti wrote that, 'there are found at every corner decent coaches, well equipped, to carry passengers either into the country or about the city; of these there are reckoned to be altogether eight hundred; they are taken by time, charging so much an hour, and something extra for the first'.[38]

As well as the dirtiness and overcrowding of the streets, air pollution was a notorious problem; according to Davenant, 'London is smother'd with sulphurous fires', and Christiaan Huygens complained that, 'The stink of the smoke is unbearable and most unhealthy.'[39] The French envoy Honoré de Courtin was afflicted with a bad cough shortly after he arrived in London in 1665 and complained bitterly about the 'vapeurs du charbon de terre'.[40] Lodewijck Huygens described the effect on the city's environment when he climbed St Paul's cathedral tower in January 1652, to see the view: 'I found such a great cloud of smoke hanging over the town … that on either side of the church one could see less than a half of it.' He could not even see as far as the Tower.[41] Evelyn believed that the pall of smoke over London was 'one of the fowlest Inconvencices and reproches, that can possibly befall so noble, and otherwise, incomparable City'. He attributed the scale of the problem to profit, objecting that, 'the sordid and accursed Avarice of some few Particular Persons, should be suffered to prejudice the health and felicity of so many'. The coal fires in the houses produced 'poisonous and filthy Smoak', as did the premises of brewers, dyers, lime-burners, salt-makers and soap-boilers. Among other things, he suggested the allocation of areas downwind of the city for premises from which the smoke emissions were especially heavy and foul.[42] The king supported Evelyn's campaign and ordered the publication of his book on the subject, *Fumifugium: or The Inconveniencie of the Aer and Smoak of London Dissipated*. A Bill was drafted in January 1662, 'against the nuisance of the Smoke of Lond, to be reformed by removing severall Trades, which are the cause of it, & indanger the heal[t]h of the K: & his people &c.'.[43] But, realistically, smoke discharges could not be controlled; as the number of houses increased, so did the smoke.

Added to the air pollution, the weather occasionally made the citizens' lives difficult in the extreme. In March 1660 the spring tides caused flooding in the city's low-lying districts. Thomas Rugg, a Covent Garden barber, noted in his journal how 'the wind was very highe and caused greate tides which did exceedingly apeare heare in our Theames, so that great hurt was don to the inhabantents of Westminster, Kinge Street, in the low ware houses and poore cellors quit drowned. The Maidenhead boate was cast away and 12 persons cast away in the said boat.' The Pepyses were then living in Axe Yard, off King Street, and when Samuel went home one day he found that, 'by reason of rain and an Easterly wind, the water was so high that there was boats rowed in King-streete and all our yard was drownded, that one could not go to my house, so as no man hath seen the like almost. Most houses full of water.' There was flooding, too, at the other end of the city, 'to the loss of many 1000l to the people about Limehouse'.[44]

In very cold winters the Thames above London Bridge froze over. The gaps between the bridge piers, or starlings, were so narrow that they restricted the flow of water through them, creating relatively still water upstream. The lawyer John Greene observed the effect in January 1646: 'noe water to be seene on westminster side of the bridge, only at the bridge, but on the tower side almost noe ice'. He heard that some people had crossed the ice. In January 1652 the river froze over again. Lodewijck Huygens and his companions went to see if there was ice on it, 'as it had been freezing hard enough here for several days now and more than in many winters before'. They found that indeed it was 'almost entirely frozen over as had not been the case for many years'. When the river froze, the watermen's trade was at a standstill. The coachmen were also badly affected by an icy winter; Greene explained that, 'The streetes also were almost unpassable for coaches. There were such heapes of ice, dirt, and snow together, and the Kennells were soe hard frozen upon each side that when a coach-wheele got in it could not get out without danger of overturninge'. And so when the thaw came after six or seven weeks, it was 'very welcome both to the watermen and hackney coachmen and carmen'.[45]

The river above the bridge froze over in six winters during the second half of the century. When it froze really hard fairs were held on the ice, such as during the severe winter of 1684, the worst of the century, when the Thames could be crossed by pedestrians for seven weeks, between 2 January and 20 February. Sir Richard Newdigate of Arbury, in Warwickshire, was informed that on 5 January, 'a Coach and six horses drove over the Thames for a wager', and three days later 'whole streets of Booths are built on the Thames, and thousands of people are continually walking thereon'. A gentle thaw in the middle of the month lasted two days, 'so that all the Booths etc. had to be pulled down'. But the hard frost soon returned, and with it the fair. Towards the end of the month Evelyn noted that, 'The frost still continuing more & more severe, the Thames before London was planted with bothes in formal streetes, as in a Citty, or Continual faire, all sorts of Trades & shops furnished, & full of Commodities, even to a Printing presse, where the People & Ladys took a fansy to have their names Printed & the day & yeare set downe, when printed on the Thames'. Newdigate's informant, Thomas Dodd, explained that the 'Coaches ply as frequently as Boats did before'; there were about forty a day, going as far upstream as Lambeth and Vauxhall. On 2 February, 'was a whole Ox roasted on the Thames, and meat is roasted at the fire in many booths'. There were wine booths and music booths, and others sold 'Ale and Brandy and Gingerbread and Cakes in abundance'. A bull was baited on the ice on one occasion, and horse and coach races were held.[46]

With his concerns about air pollution, Evelyn was aware of the deleterious effects of the long cold spell: 'by reason of the excessive coldnesse of the aire, hindring the ascent of the smoke ... hardly could one see crosse the streete, & this filling the lungs with its grosse particles exceedingly obstructed the breast, so as one could scarce breath'. And with the water pipes frozen, 'the Brewers and divers other Tradesmen' could not work, 'miserable were the wants of poore people', and 'every moment was full of disastrous accidents'. As the thaw began, the booths had to be taken down, 'but there was first a Map or Landskip cut in copper representing all the manner of the Camp, & the several actions, sports and passe-times thereon in memory of this signal Frost'.[47]

Floods and severe frosts were disruptive, but were unavoidable and occasional events, and there was confidence that some other concerns, environmental and social, could be managed. In 1662 a commission was appointed with a wide-ranging brief for 'reforming the buildings, wayes, streets, & incumbrances, & regulating the Hackny-Coaches in the Citty of Lond:'.[48] And Howell's description of the many regulations and the steps taken to combat problems gives the impression of a closely governed city. Within the City's twenty-six wards, roughly one in ten householders held a post with the ward or in one of the 111 parishes each year, and 3,000 officials were elected regularly.[49] Westminster was similarly governed, being divided into twelve wards, each with a burgess, and twelve assistants. The burgesses and assistants were empowered to 'doe and deal in every thing and things as Aldermen's deputies in the City of London lawfully do or may do'.[50]

Among their many tasks, the officers had to be aware of socially undesirable elements, keeping a check for drunkards, gamblers, bawds, procurers, 'maintainers of quarrels ... Witches, Strumpets, common punks [prostitutes], and Scolds'. They were also to be alert to 'Women-Brokers, such as use to resort to mens Houses to suborn young Maydens with promise to help them to better service'. Another of their responsibilities was to report inns, taverns and similar premises that were open at 'unseasonable houres' and the 'hot houses, and sweating houses, whereunto any lewd Women resort, or others of ill repute'.[51] James Stuart was indicted at the Session of the Peace, 'for beinge a napper [cheat], and for employing lewd woemen to take up gentlemen and bring them to Adam Wallis his house to be nappt'. In Wapping, a watchman was so conscientious that he did 'in the middest of the night going his round knock and call at the doore' of a woman who was 'knowen for a woman of evill fame'. When she appeared at the window he asked who was in the house and she replied that there was no one else there, but refused to let him in to check, so he placed two watchmen to apprehend anyone who should emerge.[52] Hitherto prostitutes could be identified because they painted their faces, but that was changing, according to Evelyn, who noted in 1654: 'I now observed how the Women began to paint themselves, formerly a most ignominious thing, & used onely by prostitutes'.[53] This was perhaps a surprising development during the period of puritan ascendancy, commonly equated with austerity and plainness.

Howell believed that London's streets were safe for someone to walk in, 'all hours of the night, if he gives good words to the Watch'.[54] They were patrolled by watchmen on the lookout for undesirables who were 'without light at unseasonable hours', and they took action to curb anti-social behaviour.[55] In 1656 some revelling merchants were arrested and ordered to appear at the sessions to 'answer the complainte of the officer of Norton Fallgate for beinge taken late in the night by the watch in a rantinge manner with other company with bottles of sacke in theire handes and for affronting the officer in the execution of his office'.[56] And the streets were well lit; every household was required to hang out a lantern containing a lighted candle during the hours of darkness. According to Magalotti: 'At night, the streets are lighted till a certain hour in the morning, by large lanterns, disposed in various forms, and fixed with great regularity against the doors of houses; and whenever you wish for them, you may find boys at every step, who run before you with lighted torches.'[57] On a March night in 1661 Pepys 'took up a boy that had a lanthorn, that was picking up of rags, and got him to light me home'. They chatted as they went, about the price of rags and other things, and Pepys, with his insatiable curiosity, discovered 'what and how many ways there are for poor children to get their living honestly'.[58]

Despite regular patrols by the watch, and the street lighting, the citizens did run some risk of violent and petty crime. They could also be duped or kidnapped by people traffickers, who sold their victims into servitude, to labour in the colonies in North America and the West Indies, especially Virginia and Barbados. They would then have to work for a number of years to recover their freedom. A man lodged an allegation against another, 'for enticinge and carrienge away of his wife on shipp-board intendinge to sende her to the Barbadoes', and a similar complaint was made by Samuell Embry against Simon Harris, 'for spiriting away one Mary Embry his sister and selling her for 48s. in mony, to bee transported beyond the seas to Barbadoes'. Another woman was sold to a ship's captain for just £2. Many of those taken were children; the kidnappers were described as 'those that take up children in the streets and are commonly called by the name of Spiritts'. Margaret Caser accused a waterman of Shadwell 'of selling hir onely son Thomas Caser and also of selling one Mihill Church (who was left to her charge – being two months) unto the Boatswaine of the ship John and Katherine to convey them therein to the Barbadoes'. Katherine Danvers was bound over at the sessions to answer 'for having a girle or young mayd with her, which she profferred to sell demaunding a hundred pound for her, and afterwards would have taken fiftene shillings for her, and for suspition of being such a person that doth take up children and sell and convey them beyond sea'. Another woman was said to be 'a common taker up of children, and a setter to betray young men and maydens to be conveyed into shipps, and … she confessed to one Mr. Guy that she hath at this time fower persons aboard a ship whereof one is a child about eleven years of age, all to be transported to forrain parts as the Barbadoes and Virginia'.[59] More settlers were required after the capture of Jamaica from the Spanish in

1655 and its subsequent colonisation by people shipped from other islands, including Barbados. The government then took direct action, and soldiers 'visited various brothels and other places of entertainment where they forcibly laid hands on over 400 women of loose life, whom they compelled to sail for the Barbados islands'.[60]

Men could be seized by press gangs recruiting sailors. The Navy was engaged in wars throughout the 1650s, against royalist privateers, the United Provinces during the First Dutch War between 1652 and 1654, and from 1655 against Spain. The need for crews was so great that men were tricked or seized. Paulucci reported in March 1653 that, 'Hands are so much needed that last week 1,500 men were pressed on the Thames, with the intention of sending them on board at once.' In the following month he added that seamen were being pressed from all the ships that arrived at London.[61] Not surprisingly, this was much resented among the seafaring communities along the river and in 1654 a man was indicted for helping 'a company of tumultuous seamen who rescued from the Prestmasters several seamen who were imprest for the service of the Commonwealth at sea'.[62]

Not all such hazards, crimes and nuisances were eliminated. Environmental problems existed even in St Paul's. It had been neglected and suffered from having soldiers quartered in it, using part of the building to stable their horses. Lodewijck Huygens wrote that, 'it was as dirty as it can be in any stable … In some places women sat selling apples and fish.' Howell complained that, 'this famous Fabrick, which was accounted the greatest glory of London, is become her greatest shame'. Indeed, the building had deteriorated to such an extent that it was 'like to be buried shortly in her own ruines, and so become a heap of rubbish'. It had been divided for services: 'Among the various sects … that of the Anabaptists which at present numbers many proselytes, had a place assigned it there for preaching purposes.'[63]

The condition of St Paul's and the garrison of soldiers there were reminders of the Civil War, and a few others remained. Cheapside Cross and Charing Cross had been demolished and their sites stood empty, and the vestiges of the Lines of Communication were still visible. Londoners who saw Scottish prisoners paraded through the city in 1651, after their defeat at the battle of Worcester, or the 1,200 Dutch captives who were marched along its streets two years later, may have recalled that the same treatment had been meted out to royalists after the battle of Naseby in 1645.

In other respects the effects of the civil wars had receded. There was a revival of the court at Whitehall, where Cromwell adopted many of the trappings of royalty in the 1650s. Evelyn visited the palace in 1656 and wrote in his diary: 'I adventured to go to White-Hall, where of many yeares I had not ben, & found it very glorious & well furnish'd, as far as I could safely go.'[64] But much of the royal collection of sculpture, tapestries and paintings was disposed of in a spectacular sale that began in 1649 and continued for a few years, leaving some buildings very bare. In January 1652 Lodewijck Huygens visited the Banqueting House, 'where there was nothing in the world now except three long deal tables', and at Somerset House he found that in the chapel 'all the paintings which covered the ceiling are painted over with blue.'[65] The building had been Henrietta Maria's palace, but was used as the salerooms for the disposal of the king's collections, as a barracks and also as lodgings, for Members of Parliament and foreign ambassadors.[66] Throughout London, the royal arms had been replaced by those of the Commonwealth.

As well as the embellishments, the mood had altered. Sagredo contrasted the atmosphere in London during Charles I's reign with that in the mid-1650s:

> The exquisite Court, once the most sumptuous and joyous in the world, frequented by noble ladies and abounding in the most refined entertainment, is now changed for the perpetual marching and countermarching of troops, the ceaseless noise of drums and trumpets, and numerous companies of officers and soldiers at their various posts.[67]

The citizens found their presence irksome. The soldiers at St Paul's stopped and questioned passers-by and annoyed local residents, according to an order of 1651, which stated that, 'the inhabitants of Paul's Churchyard, are much disturbed by the souldiers and others, calling out to passengers and examining them, (though they goe, peaceably and civilly along,) and by playing at nine-pinnes at unseasonable hours.'[68]

Royalists and disenchanted Londoners whose resentment went much deeper, and did not regard the political settlement as final, came to the attention of the magistrates, because of their subversive comments, belittling the regime and the lord protector. In 1656, a labourer in Spitalfields, Morris Seiston, was accused of 'drinking a health to the confusion of His Highnesse the Lord Protector and saying that he the said Morris was more fitt to be a Protector than his said Highnesse'. In the following year Dorothy Isaack of St Clement Dane was reported 'for confederating with those that are seditious and dangerous persons in reference to His Highnes and the Common Wealth, and that have threatened his life, and with drinking a health to the Confusion of his said Highnes the Lord Protector'. Mary Hobson and Jane Neviston of St Giles-in-the-Fields got themselves into trouble in June 1658, Mary for saying that 'she hoped to see Whitehall on fire about the Lord

Protector's eares', and Jane for remarking that 'the Lord Protector was a base rascall-like fellow'.[69] Presumably they were not sorry to hear of Cromwell's death three months later, on 3 September.

Despite such rumbling discontent, for most of the 1650s Londoners enjoyed a fair measure of prosperity. This faltered only with the effects of war through the depredations of privateers, attacking shipping in the North Sea and English Channel, and causing anxiety in case they interrupted London's coal supplies. But the long-standing problem of those based at Dunkirk, in the Spanish Netherlands, was solved when the English army captured the town in 1658. Giavarina explained that London's merchants 'are pleased at the capture of Dunkirk, as now they are safe from further molestation from the corsairs of that place who did no small damage to their ships'.[70] Yet the war with Spain had been a mistake by Cromwell, according to Slingsby Bethel, who argued that the country's prosperity depended on its trade and the war was 'the cause of the losse of our Spanish Trade, during all that time, [and] Of the losse of 1500 English ships in that War'.[71]

Bethel was a London merchant and member of the City's common council, who had lived on the continent for a number of years. He was aware that London's mercantile community needed peace abroad and political stability at home. Peace was achieved with the Treaty of the Pyrenees, signed in November 1659, but by then the domestic political consensus had disintegrated, creating uncertainty that was unwelcome to Londoners.

3

London & the Restoration

Oliver's son Richard succeeded him as Lord Protector, but relinquished power within nine months, in the spring of 1659. The collapse of the protectorate regime ushered in a period of political instability. Anyone who attempted to gain power and direct events needed control of London or the acquiescence of its citizens, who were not only interested observers of developments, but also potential participants. Their active opposition to Charles I in 1641–2 had been decisive in defeating his political manoeuvres, while their failure to adequately support the opposition to the army sealed the fate of the attempted counter-revolution in 1647, when the city was occupied by the New Model Army. Those were precedents to be borne in mind by the political and military leaders, as they struggled to achieve a settlement in the wake of Richard Cromwell's resignation.

Political power in the City rested with the twenty-six aldermen, one representing each of the City's wards. They held the position for life, and the lord mayor was chosen from among them, usually by seniority. The Court of Common Council was a much larger body, with over 200 members, elected by the 8,000 or more freemen. But it could not act independently of the lord mayor and aldermen. The apprentices had no political status, but, with young journeymen and those who had dropped out of their apprenticeships, for one reason or another, they formed a substantial, although not necessarily cohesive, group consisting of at least 20,000 young men. They sometimes formed large and menacing crowds, joining thousands of others to demonstrate on issues which threatened their welfare or that of their city.

Opinions were also expressed in petitions, books, pamphlets and newsbooks. The bookseller George Thomason collected 282 publications in 1658, but 652 in 1659, and while just two newsbooks were issued for most of the decade, that increased to nine during the second half of 1659.[1] They had a large potential readership, for the male adult literacy rate in London was roughly 80 per cent and perhaps almost a half of women could read. Visitors remarked upon the number of bookshops. Samuel Sorbière wrote that, 'I am not to forget the vast Number of Booksellers Shops I have observed in London; for besides those who are set up here and there in the City, they have their particular Quarters, such as St. Paul's-Church-Yard, and Little-Britain, where there is twice as many as in the Rue Saint Jacque in Paris, and who have each of them Two or Three Ware-houses.'[2] Lodewijck Huygens, too, was impressed by Little Britain, which he described as 'a quarter of two or three streets where hardly anything but second-hand books are sold. We went into a shop there which had three or four rooms in a row all full of books, many rare ones among them.'[3]

Another source of information, ideas and opinions was sermons, which were attentively listened to. Some were published and so reached a much wider audience. Huygens attended a service at the chapel in Whitehall and noted that, 'behind the minister stood two or three men who wrote down his sermon. More than 20 others, both men and women, including a handsome, rather bejewelled young lady, were doing the same thing.' That was not because the service was a special one. He saw the same practice at services in the Rolls Chapel in Chancery Lane, when the man next to him wrote down the sermon in shorthand, and at St Paul's, Covent Garden, where: 'In the box [pew] next to ours three or four ladies were writing down the entire sermon, and more than 50 other persons throughout the whole church were doing the same.'[4] Lorenzo Magalotti also commented that English women were:

> remarkably well-informed in the dogmas of the religion they profess; and when they attend at the discourses of their ministers or preachers, they write down an abridgement of what they say, having in their letters, abbreviations, which facilitate to them and to the men also (thanks to their natural quickness and the acuteness of their genius) the power of doing this with rapidity; and this they do that they may afterward avail themselves of it in the controversies and disputes which they hold on religious matters.[5]

But such politically and religiously informed Londoners were not the reason for Richard's failure to retain power. He had not won over those who opposed the protectorate and favoured a republic, or the senior army officers. Following his resignation, the Members of Parliament were recalled who were sitting in April 1653, when Oliver had turned them out. They constituted the remnant of the Long Parliament, called in 1640, but without royalists expelled during the 1640s and those turned away in December 1648 by Colonel Thomas Pride's soldiers, because they were likely to oppose the trial of the king. The body that sat following Pride's Purge and until Oliver's coup in 1653 had quickly, and derisively, been designated the Rump

Parliament. Clement Walker in his *Anarchia anglicana, or, The history of Independency* of 1649 referred to it as, 'This fagge end, this Rump of a Parliament with corrupt Maggots in it.'[6]

Just 42 Members assembled for the new session in 1659; gradually others returned, including some expelled by Pride, and eventually more than 120 claimed their seats. The regime survived an uprising in Cheshire in August, led by Sir George Booth, but not the dissatisfaction of the army commanders. When it reacted strongly to a petition from them calling for a select senate, and voted to remove nine officers who had signed the document, the army responded by turning it out, on 13 October. According to the journal of the House: 'This Day the late principal Officers of the Army, whose Commissions were vacated, drew up Forces in and about Westminster, obstructed all Passages both by Land and Water, stopped the Speaker in his Way, and placed and continued Guards upon and about the Doors of the Parliament-House; and so interrupted the Members from coming to the House, and attending their Service there.'[7] Parliament had asked the City for the help of the trained bands, but it declined to meddle in the dispute.

A Committee of Safety was now appointed to govern, consisting of soldiers and civilians, including the lord mayor, Sir John Ireton. Prominent among the officers were Charles Fleetwood, Oliver's son-in-law, who was the commander-in-chief, and John Lambert, one of Oliver's most capable senior commanders. The committee set about devising an acceptable constitutional arrangement, which it failed to achieve. George Monck, the commander in Scotland, opposed this second expulsion of the Long Parliament and could not be persuaded to change his mind. The navy's commander, Vice-Admiral John Lawson, also disapproved of the expulsion of the Rump. Monck had funds to pay his troops and was able to keep their support, while purging those officers whom he judged to be politically unreliable. The army council in London, on the other hand, could not pay its men promptly and they were owed several weeks' pay. The officers' power rested on their soldiers' loyalty, not popular support, and that became increasingly fragile. When the officers' backing among the infantry regiments crumbled, and they could not persuade Lawson to change his stance, they had little choice but to return power to parliament, which resumed its sitting on 26 December.

Parliament had come to have differing meanings. It could be taken to refer to the Rump Parliament that had ruled, as the Commonwealth, from 1649 until 1653, to the Long Parliament that had sat until Pride's Purge in December 1648, or to an assembly chosen at a new election, which, as was generally thought, would negotiate the restoration of the monarchy.

The political groups were broadly those who favoured a constitution with a single leader but not a monarch, republicans, and royalists. This was complicated by religious divisions, between Anglicans, Presbyterians and the nonconformists.

London was quiescent during the summer of this politically bewildering year, but began to stir during the autumn. Parliament had intervened in the City's affairs in June when it had remodelled the militia, creating a commission with power to raise militia regiments. This encroached on the City's traditional right to command its own trained bands, which should not be required to serve outside London. Although the commission included the lord mayor, sheriffs, fourteen aldermen and other senior figures in the City's government, the City petitioned that it should be commanded only by 'persons of quality, freemen and inhabitants of the city'.[8] Ireton was a member of an Independent congregation and a supporter of the Rump. He took steps to maintain order during the summer, should Londoners be tempted to support Booth's uprising. The extent of his success may be judged from a comment by Thomas Rugg, a royalist sympathiser: 'in this City of London not one man that held up his hand in opposition against any of the Parlime[nt's] commands, but was as quiet as any mule'. He also noted that calls for a free parliament 'did not in the least apeare in the Citty of London att this day'.[9] That was partly because Ireton would not call a meeting of common council, some of whose Presbyterian members may have voiced such a demand. According to one of those who supplied Charles II's councillor Edward Hyde with information, there was no lack of support for the royalist cause, for 'the meaner sort – butchers, watermen, dyers, &c. – talk high, the better sort, no less discontented say little publicly'.[10]

Parliament regarded Ireton as a safe pair of hands and so voted, on 2 September, that 'as well in relation to the Safety of the Commonwealth, as of the City of London, as Affairs now stand, doth declare, and hold it fit, that John Ireton, now Lord Mayor of the City of London, do continue to execute the Office of Lord Mayor of the City of London for the Year ensuing'.[11] But a lord mayor served for only one year and this attempt to continue his term for a second year was therefore regarded as an attack on the City's privileges, enshrined in its charter and jealously guarded. The common council objected and petitioned parliament, which backed down. Ireton was succeeded by Thomas Aleyne, and parliament and the corporation showed their unity in a feast at the grocers' hall, where, according to Rugg, 'they dined altogeather very loveingly'.[12] But that could not conceal the divisions which existed, summarised by Francesco Giavarina in mid-November: 'The common council of the city of London is divided ... part being for the army and part desiring the re-establishment of the parliament. Those who govern are very uneasy on this account and the army has for this reason posted guards of infantry at the gates of London and sent some companies of horse and foot into the city.'[13]

Increasing the number of troops in London was intended to curb the disruptive activities of the apprentices and other groups. Garrisons were established in St Paul's, the Royal Exchange, Lord Petre's house in Aldersgate Street, Syon College, Baynard's Castle and Gresham College, between Bishopsgate and Great Broad Street. According to Thomas Sprat, the group of scholars that had been meeting at the college since the previous year 'were scatt'red by the miserable distractions of that Fatal year ... For then the place of their meeting was made a Quarter for soldiers.'[14] The troops billeted in St Paul's worsened the conditions in the building, according to the inveterate traveller Peter Mundy a few months later: 'Pauls Church in these tymes converted to a stable full of horse dung and excrements of men.'[15] But, according to Rugg, the presence of troops was more widely disruptive and the number of soldiers was in itself tiresome to 'the aprentiss and others that ware weary of the souldiers and theire lawes and maners and also theire company in the Citty, which was then indeffrent full of them'.[16] One of their objections was that the presence of troops deterred the gentry from going into the city and spending money in its shops, which were 'but very empty of costomers'. The metropolitan economy was faltering, which was attributed partly to the effects of the war with Spain. In April parliament had been told that, 'A rot has got amongst the merchants. They break every day, ten at a time.'[17] This had not improved by the autumn, when the apprentices were aware 'that theire trading begane daylye to decaye'. On 10 November the aldermen ordered a collection for the poor because of 'the deadness of Trade and the dearness of provisions at this season'.[18] The problem was exacerbated by the early onset of winter; just a few days later Giavarina referred to 'the present very cold weather', and the vicar of Earls Colne in Essex wrote in his journal on 15 January: 'The season very vehement cold; this hard weather hath continued from Novemb: 11 till now.'[19]

The apprentices responded to the presence of the soldiers by goading and mocking not only them but also the Committee of Safety, 'which was then called Shifftey'. Nor was the resentment confined to the apprentices, for a minister heard a bellman intoning a subversive ditty that included the lines:

Whilst you securely Sleep, I ring my Bell,
Which lately hath Rung out your Freedoms Knell.
Your Souldiers, now, your Sovereigns are become,
Your Laws and Liberties command by sound of Drum.[20]

Early in December Pepys wrote that 'many endeed have beene the affronts offered from the apprentices to the Red-coates of late'. A petition that the apprentices were known to be preparing, in favour of a free parliament, had provoked fears of a rising, 'soe that the City was strictly guarded all night'. A proclamation was issued and read around the streets forbidding such petitions.[21]

The tension did not lessen and on 5 December the apprentices defied the order and handed in their petition to the common council. Extra forces were ordered into the City, including the regiment commanded by Colonel John Hewson, a cobbler who had enlisted in the parliamentarian forces in 1642 and had risen to the rank of colonel by December 1645. He had lost an eye during the Irish campaigns in 1649–50. Pepys believed that the apprentices interpreted this influx of troops not as action to forestall an uprising, but as an attempt to prevent them presenting their petition. Rugg described in his journal the soldiers' march along the streets:

> They mett with great opposisions ... theire was many offronts offred and a great many of uncivill actions offred to them in their march into the Citty, but especially to Colonelle Hewson regiment of foote; they ware more abused then any other ... they called him blind cobler, blind Hewson, and did throw ould shewes and old slippers and turnapes topes, brick battes and stones and tiles att him and his soulders.[22]

Some soldiers were 'disarmed and kickt', according to Pepys, who added that, 'in some places the apprentices would get a football (it being a hard frost) and drive it among the souldiers on purpose, and they either durst not (or prudently would not) interrupt them; in fine, many souldiers were hurt with stones, and one I see was very neere having his braines knocked out with a brick batt flung from the top of a house at him'. Despite such harassment they reached the Royal Exchange. Mundy, who lodged at Tower Hill, described Cornhill and Leadenhall Street as 'full of armed men, horse and foot'. Some of the troops moved on to the Guildhall and the proclamation against petitions was read, 'which the boys shouted at in contempt'. Driven beyond endurance by their tormentors, some soldiers 'fired in erenst, and fouer or five of the aprentises and others, whereof one was a cobbler, were killed and other wounded', according to Rugg. Pepys put the number killed at six or seven, 'whereof I see one in Cornhill shott through the head', and Mundy thought that five or six had been killed and 'about twenty five or thirty hurt'. Rugg noted that some of the soldiers, too, were 'very dangerously wounded'. The trained bands were assembled, 'but nothing passed between the souldiers and them but sowre lookes', according to Pepys. On their march back to Whitehall, the soldiers broke down the gates at Temple Bar. This was not entirely a victory for the apprentices, because a force of at least 2,500 soldiers remained in the City.[23]

Despite Mundy's laconic comment 'after which all was quiet againe', this was a serious incident, not least because of the loss of life and the circumstances of the deaths. The coroner's inquest on six of those killed brought in a verdict of wilful murder. It also demonstrated the scale of the tensions between the volatile young men in the City and the Council of State, and the mistrust that the apprentices felt for the lord mayor, whom they believed had betrayed them. Although the City's rulers were inevitably drawn into these events, their main concern was 'the welfare of the Citty'. But the apprentices distrusted their motives and continued to be unruly. Mundy wrote that over the two weeks following the deaths of the young demonstrators, 'there have bin severall risings of the apprentices, seamen etts., but quickly pacified'.[24] In one incident the lord mayor's coach was stoned and on another occasion apprentices gathered outside his house and 'did most basely affront the Lord Mayor', so that he had to send for soldiers to disperse them. As work was short, they had time on their hands and, according to Rugg, they 'mett and ware often discorsing of these times that they had now lived to see'.[25] The apprentices' potential influence was recognised; while the signatures to the petition were being gathered, the writer of a London newsbook had predicted that, 'As the apprentices were a great means of ejecting the father, they will now prove as great an instrument for bringing in the son.'[26]

John Evelyn reflected on the current situation when he noted a sermon that he heard on 16 December: 'We had now no Government in the Nation, all in Confusion; no Magistrate either own'd or pretended, but the souldiers & they not agreed.'[27] The extent of the disagreements could not be concealed. Giavarina summarised the state of affairs with the comment that, 'the minds of the leaders in London are not in accord but utterly divided while the boatmen, butchers, porters, apprentices and others of the lower orders who can in a moment supply an inexhaustible number of combatants, are at one.'[28] He may have overestimated the cohesion of the governed, but was broadly correct in his assessment of the disagreement among their governors.

In the gloomy December days there were plots and rumours of plots. Soldiers raided an inn near Bishopsgate where some 'young men' had collected horses and a cache of arms.[29] Royalists planned to seize the Tower, which commanded much of the City and would have further alarmed the citizens. Evelyn became involved, as he confided in his journal: 'I treated privately with Coll: Morley (then Lieutenant of the Tower, & in greate trust & power) concerning delivering it to the King, and the bringing of him in, to the greate hazard of my life; but the Colonel had ben my Schole-fellow & I knew would not betray me.'[30] His judgement was sound and he was not betrayed, but the plot was and the coup, planned for the morning of 12 December, was forestalled. On the same day a rumour ran around the City that the Anabaptists were planning a massacre. Calm consideration should have produced the conclusion that their numbers and organisation made this most improbable. The rumour reflected the citizens' fear and uncertainty and the direction in which the mood was swinging, against the nonconformists, seen as connected with the republicans and elements in the army, and in favour of the royalists.

The changing attitudes in the City were reflected in the results of elections to common council on 21 December, when more than a third of the members lost their seats, to be replaced by men who were unfavourable to the republicans and nonconformists. The new council was purposeful, holding nine meetings within a fortnight, as many as were held in a year in normal circumstances. According to Rugg, the common council 'did sitt often and was very carefull to preserve the Citty from distroyinge'.[31] It acted to regain control of the trained bands, appointing officers to the six regiments. That was a City issue, aimed at control of its security. But the council also involved itself in national affairs, appointing commissioners to negotiate with the political leaders respecting the City's safety, and also to advocate the calling of a free parliament.

On 13 December Lawson and his captains had sent a letter to the lord mayor and aldermen, demanding the recall of parliament. He brought his ships into the mouth of the Thames, where they could blockade the river if necessary and so bring trade to a standstill, which was a dreadful prospect for London's merchants. The garrison at Portsmouth then declared in favour of parliament, as did regiments sent to subdue it. The army's support for the Council of State was slipping away and when the troops in the city were ordered to rendezvous in Lincoln's Inn Fields on 23 December, they did so, but then refused to obey their officers. They proclaimed their support for parliament and marched away. As they went along Chancery Lane they stopped outside the house of William Lenthall, who had been chosen Speaker of the House of Commons when the Long Parliament had assembled in 1640 and had not been displaced. He came out and addressed them, and to show their support they 'made many volleys of shot as they marched by his gates'.[32] Lenthall then went to the lord mayor to discuss the recall of parliament, which resumed its sitting three days later. But this did not meet the objections of those who favoured a new parliament.

Monck decided to act and his army began its march from Scotland on 1 January. Lambert's unpaid and dissatisfied troops had melted away and

Fleetwood lacked the resolve or control of the regiments in London to oppose Monck, who reached the city on 3 February. His intentions were not yet known. Pepys was keenly interested and watched 'all his forces march by in very good plight and stout officers', but also noted in his diary that, 'in his passage through the town he had many cry to him for a free Parliament; but little other welcome'.[33] Londoners had no reason to greet another detachment of troops marching into their city, however well disciplined. Just the day before more than a hundred apprentices had gathered at Leadenhall, planning to mount an uprising. They were set upon by soldiers, who behaved very harshly, according to Rugg: 'they were very severe to them, for that they cut many of them and striped almost naked, for they did use these more creueley for excamples sake'.[34] After Monck's soldiers had established themselves in the city, the regiments already there were ordered to march out. Some did so only after protests and brief disturbances around Somerset House and in Salisbury Court. Two soldiers were later hanged in the Strand for taking part in that mutiny.

For the time being, Monck made no decisions and was respectful of parliament. Matters were brought to a head through the reactions to a petition addressed to the lord mayor and common council from 'divers well-affected householders and freemen'. It asked that the corporation should act only on instructions from an authority with the legislative power granted by the nation and levy those taxes voted by such an authority. Parliament's approval of a tax, on 26 January, had prompted the petition, which was received and acknowledged by common council. But the word spread that it had voted 'that they would not pay any taxes until the House was filled up'. This inflamed the antagonism between the newly elected common council and the Rump. The Council of State instructed Monck to arrest eleven members of the common council and render the City defenceless, ordering that 'the Posts and Chains in the City of London be taken away, the Gates of the City unhinged, and the Portcullices thereof wedged in'. Parliament approved those actions and went further by ordering that, 'the Gates of the City of London, and the Portcullices thereof, be forthwith destroyed', and even further, with the order that, 'this present Common-Council for the City of London, elected for this Year, be discontinued; and be, and are hereby declared to be, null and void'. New elections were to be held.[35]

Although Monck must have been aware of how provocative those instructions were, he duly carried them out, marching into the City with his regiments; estimated in one account to have consisted of 4,000 foot and 1,500 horse. This must have seemed like a military occupation, according to Mundy's notes: 'The cheife streets eastward of the Exchange full of armed men, the gates guarded by souldiers, the posts for chaines in severall streets digged up and cutt downe. Generall Munk with his troopes rode over and through the Exchang severall tymes, the merchants shutt out and the Exchange full of souldiers: many aldermen committed to the Tower.' Pepys was told that Monck had 'clapped up many of the Common Council, and that the Parliament had voted that he should pull down their gates and portcullises, their posts and their chains'. He also thought that Monck had been instructed to take away the City's charter, which was not the case.[36] Nothing could have been more calculated to alienate the citizens and turn them against Monck. Indeed, John Aubrey thought that, 'The Parliament … made him odious to the Citie, purposely, by pulling downe and burning their gates.'[37]

Having parliament ride roughshod over their privileges was a shock; so, too, was the implementation of its orders by soldiers that had come in to replace those who had made themselves odious in previous skirmishes. What right had parliament to annul the elections to common council, which struck at the heart of the City's privileges? But what could be done? The trained bands would be no match for troops if fighting began, and to call them out and so provoke a confrontation would be to risk a bloodbath, which was unthinkable. Besides, according to Rugg, the lord mayor and aldermen were reluctant to deploy the trained bands throughout this period, 'for that they was fearefull of false breathren amongest themselves, in regarde the Citty was so much of contrary judgments in way of worshipp and selfe intrest, and factious'. Pepys wrote that, 'The City look mighty blank and cannot tell what in the world to do.'[38]

After enforcing the orders, Monck spent time listening to opinions and advice from 'many visitants, of the chiefe Cittizens, & of the Secluded Members & others'.[39] He was assured by the governor of the Tower that his soldiers would support whatever actions he took. On the following day, a Saturday, Monck and his senior officers wrote to the Rump, having drawn up the army in Finsbury Fields. They first complained of being ordered to remove the gates, posts and chains, 'which was something grievous to Us, and to the Officers and Souldiers under our Commands; and that because we do not remember any such thing was acted upon this City in all these Wars; and we fear that many sober people are much grieved at it, and apprehend further force to be offered to them'. They also objected to the presence in the House of some who had been accused of treason and also that Lambert and the leading republican politician Sir Henry Vane were at liberty, against the vote of the House. But their main request was for 'the speedy filling up of the House, which you have declared for'. This they stated to be their 'main desire, upon which we cannot but insist, that you would proceed to Issue forth Writts in Order to Elections', adding, crucially, that 'all the

Writts may be Issued forth by Friday next'. Parliament replied that it had begun the process of calling new elections, which was indeed the case, but setting a deadline just a few days away put an end to further prevarication and changed the situation. So did Monck's taking lodgings and quartering his forces in what his letter described as 'that great City, formerly renowned for their resolute adhering to Parliamentary Authority'.[40]

Monck then went to Guildhall to explain his actions to the lord mayor and aldermen. They were said to have offered accommodation for him and his officers and promised 'that his soldiers would lack for nothing'. The citizens' attitude to the soldiers changed abruptly; now they offered them money and drink.[41] In effect, the senior officers had declared for a free parliament, and thrown in their lot with the City and against the Rump.

The City had won that round at least, prompting lively and prolonged celebrations in the streets. Mundy wrote that there was, 'Great rejoycing in the Citty, manifested by bonfires and ringing of bells, for that General Munck adhered to them and lay this night at the Three Tuns in Guildhall Yard.'[42] Pepys was excited by 'the common joy that was everywhere to be seen!' He counted fourteen bonfires between St Dunstan's church and Temple Bar and from Strand Bridge he could see thirty-one: 'In Cheapside there was a great many bonefires, and Bow bells and all the bells in all the churches as we went home were a-ringing.' That was about ten o'clock in the evening, yet the celebrations were still going on; when Pepys and Elizabeth went along Ludgate Hill they had to walk on the side away from the bonfires 'merely for heat'.[43] Aubrey recalled that, 'Threadneedle Street was all day long, and late at night, crammed with multitudes, crying out, *A free Parliament, a free Parliament*, that the aire rang with their clamours.' Although this development had brought the possibility of restoration of the monarchy closer, that was not yet decided, nor had it been Monck's intention, according to Aubrey. He was told that the general, 'no more intended the King's restauration, when he came into England, or first came to London, than his Horse did'.[44]

During these celebrations contempt for the Rump was demonstrated in a distinctive way, described by Gilbert Burnet, later Bishop of Salisbury: 'a sudden humour ran, like a madness, through the whole City, of roasting the rumps of all sorts of creatures, to express a derision and contempt of them'.[45] Pepys saw the 'burning and roasting and drinking for rumps – there being rumps tied upon sticks and carried up and down'. The practice did not end with those celebrations. In the following month Rugg noted that, 'the Rump Parliament was so hated and jeered that butchers boyes would say, Will you buy any Parlimentt rumps and kidneys? and it was a very ordnary thing to see littl children to make a fier in the streets and burne rumps'.[46] This continued even after the Long Parliament declared itself dissolved, on 16 March, and was to become a common way in which the crown's supporters expressed contempt for their political opponents.

After the excitement that followed Monck's resolute stand had died down, 'the City of London is very quiett and well pleased with the proceedings of the Parliament and army, and the more pleased because they have the militia in theire owne hands, which heretofore in Olivers dayes they had not'. By the middle of April Monck had attended banquets at nine halls of the principal livery companies. This sense of satisfaction even extended to the sometimes turbulent young men and apprentices, who were 'well pleased att all things the Lord Generall Moncke did'.[47] And they also showed their displeasure at the actions of republicans, breaking the windows of the Member of Parliament Praise-God Barebones, a leather-seller in Fleet Street, who had provoked their ire by presenting parliament with a petition from 'the well-affected Persons, Inhabitants of the City of London and Westminster, and Places adjacent, being faithful and constant Adherers to this Parliament', who were opposed to 'the Promoters of Regal Interest'.[48]

Among the remaining uncertainties was how the city would react to the return of the Stuarts. The issue was addressed by the satirical poet Robert Wild, in a poem published on 23 April:

> But what will London do? I doubt Old Paul
> With bowing to his Sovereign will fall;
> The royal lions from the Tower shall roar,
> And though they see him not, yet shall adore;
> The conduits will be ravish'd and combine
> To turn their very water into wine.

This was not the best poetry of the period, yet was very popular. One facetious comment was that, 'I have seen them reading it in the midst of 'Change time; nay so vehement they were at it, that they lost their bargain by the candles'. A candle was lit when negotiations were begun and they had to be completed before it burned down; the implication was that traders were so distracted by the poem and its sentiments that they failed to conclude their deals in time.[49]

The Members excluded in 1648 returned to parliament on 21 February. Pepys met friends at a coffee-house on the river and wrote that, 'it was a most pleasant sight to see the City from [one] end to the other with a glory about it, so high was the light of the Bonefires and so thick round the City, and the bells rang everywhere'.[50] The following day saw another symbolic victory for the City, when parliament voted, 'That the Gates, Portcullices, and Posts, of the City of London, be made up, at the publick Charge of the State.'[51] In 1650 the inscription 'Exit Tyrannus Regum Ultimus, Anno Libertatis Angliea, Anno Domini 1648, Jan. 30th' had been written in gold letters beneath the decapitated statue of Charles I in the Royal Exchange. Now this was 'washed out by a kind of painter, who in the day time raised a ladder and with a pot and brush washed the writing quit out'. The response, according to Rugg, was: 'the marchants glad, a joyfull many people gathred togeather and against the Exchange made a bonefier', and Pepys noted in his diary that, 'people cried out "God Bless King Charles the Second"!'[52]

Some Londoners displayed their support for the restoration of the monarchy in other ways. According to Rugg, watermen began to wear the badges that they had worn during Charles I's reign, and 'the picture of King Charles the Second was often printed and sett up in houses without the least molestation, for whereas [previously] it was almost a hanging matter so to doe'.[53] Gradually, the arms of the republic were taken down and replaced by the royal arms, in churches, the livery company halls and other buildings. And people could now openly toast the king without fear.

The new parliament met for the first time on 25 April, both Lords and Commons. This was to become known as the Convention Parliament. Negotiations were opened with the king, on whose behalf Hyde had skilfully drafted a manifesto, which was dubbed the Declaration of Breda. It offered a general pardon, except for those specifically excluded by parliament. The declaration also reassured the purchasers of properties belonging to the crown, bishops, and deans and chapters, many of whom were Londoners, including nineteen of the aldermen, with the statement that: 'all things relating to such grants, sales and purchases, shall be determined in Parliament, which can best provide for the just satisfaction of all men who are concerned'. A letter was addressed to the corporation, which had sent a petition, exculpating its members from any acts that had led to the execution of Charles I. The most prominent republicans among the aldermen, Robert Tichborne and John Ireton, were imprisoned in the Tower. Ireton was later released, but Tichborne, a regicide, was not and died there in 1682.

The City was promised the renewal of its charter and traditional privileges and new favours that might improve its trade, wealth and honour. This letter was read on 1 May, the day on which parliament voted to restore the monarchy. On the following day it asked the City for a loan of £100,000, a half of which was for the king and a half to pay Monck's soldiers. That was readily agreed to and the City began to raise the money, adding a further £10,000 for the king, contributed by the livery companies, and £2,000 for his brothers, the dukes of York and Gloucester. Had such a sum been made available to pay the Rump's soldiers, to retain their loyalty, the changes of the previous months might have had a different outcome. On 8 May Charles was publicly proclaimed king by the lord mayor, dressed in a new crimson velvet gown, at a number of places in the City, including the Royal Exchange, where the windows were 'laden with spectators'. Celebrations followed:

> that night was spent with the greatest of joy that could be expressed. All the bells in the Citty range; Bow Bells could not be heard for the noise of the people; numberless of bonfiers, great gunes playing from the Tower, great store of wine give[n] by many and att evry bonefier beere, where they dranke his Majesties health, plentifull. Many of the bonefiers abided all night; many poore harts was sadly belated to their beds.[54]

Preparations now went ahead for the king's arrival in London. These included the removal from Westminster Hall of the Scottish flags captured at the battles of Dunbar and Worcester. People who had been given accommodation in the royal palaces were expelled and portraits and inscriptions set up during the Interregnum were removed or painted over 'as if they never had been'. Great bonfires were prepared, one at Southwark was 'higher than any house, made with a great deal of art and skill'; in Covent Garden a ship's mast formed the core of the bonfire 'and a barrel one the top of it'. The livery companies' halls were decorated and their footmen were given new liveries. When the great day arrived, 29 May, the king's birthday, the streets were 'richly hanged with tapstry' and packed with people, 'all bellconeys and windows full of spectators'. The fountains ran with wine, the bells rang and there was 'such shouting as the eldest man alive never heard the like'. Charles was greeted at St George's Fields by the members of the corporation, attended by the trained bands, and, according to Hyde, he 'knighted the mayor, and all the aldermen, and sheriffs, and the principal officers of the militia: an honour the city had been without near eighteen years, and therefore abundantly welcome to the husbands and their wives'. The royal procession took seven hours to pass through the City.[55]

Was this really the same city that had resolutely opposed Charles I during the political crisis in 1641–2 and sustained the parliamentarian effort during the Civil War, with men, money and arms? Were those who had objected so strongly to the forms of service insisted upon by the church in the 1630s now willing to see that church restored, without fear for their own freedom to worship? Could they be certain that there would be no royalist backlash that would affect them? Some citizens must have been alarmed by such events as the wrecking of the Baptist meeting house of William Kiffin, a merchant, in St Dunstan's-in-the-East. On the night that the king was proclaimed, a crowd 'brake downe the pulpit, seats, etts. and carried away all the bordes: part throwne into the bonfire'.[56] But the enthusiastic crowds showed that many citizens felt secure enough to welcome the king.

Not all Londoners who took part in the celebrations can have approved wholeheartedly of the restoration, but, as Hyde shrewdly put it, 'whosoever was not pleased at heart, took the more care to appear as if he was'.[57] By the day of the king's arrival the republican Edmund Ludlow had taken refuge at a friend's house in Holborn, and she 'to avoyd suspition of being disaffected (least by such a jealousy her howse should be searched, and I in danger of being seized on), causeth a fire to be made before her doore'. It was safer to conform than to ignore the celebrations.[58]

Parliament ordered that the Oaths of Supremacy and Allegiance should be taken by those holding offices and it prepared an Act of Indemnity and Oblivion, debating at length who should be exempted from its provisions. Those who had taken part in the trial of Charles I or signed his death warrant could not expect to be included. Ludlow slipped away. Others were arrested or surrendered. According to Ludlow, Colonel John Jones 'endeavoured to conceale himselfe in the citty of London, but being discovered, was seized'.[59]

Royalists who had been displaced from their positions now returned to reclaim them, while puritans were turned out of their posts. London's aldermen expelled because they were excepted by the Act of Indemnity were replaced by five former aldermen, who were now reinstated, a sixth, Sir John Langham, having been excused at his own request because of his age. Francesco Giavarina explained that the king had written to Aleyne, directing that, 'deserving persons are chosen to take the place of others deposed by the Act of Indemnity'.[60] The town clerk was also expelled. At Sutton's Hospital, four governors supplanted ten years before were reinstated on 18 May and by the end of 1661 twelve of the sixteen governors had either been restored or were newly appointed. Some men left their posts voluntarily. They included John Thurloe, appointed secretary to the Council of State in 1652, who directed the intelligence service and acted as one of Cromwell's leading advisors and confidants. He retired, having prudently concealed his papers behind a false ceiling in his chambers at Lincoln's Inn, where he died in 1668. No doubt others were even more cautious and destroyed their papers, fearful that some item or comment might incriminate them.

During the summer of 1660 numerous royalists came to London, hoping for repayment of sums spent by them during the Civil War, or appointments or sinecures to compensate them for their losses of money, property, offices and dignity. Hyde acknowledged that some had suffered badly, yet, 'They were observed to be the most importunate, who had deserved least, and were least capable to perform any notable service.'[61]

Returning clergy reclaimed their livings, perhaps supported by their erstwhile parishioners. This happened in about twenty-five London parishes and the Act of Uniformity of 1662 produced even more changes. It required all clergy to conform to the Church of England's liturgy, and 55 ministers in the City and roughly 130 in the diocese of London were displaced as a result. Townshend noted in his diary, 'Many ministers about London refused to subscribe and read the book of Common Prayer according to the new Act for Uniformity. Some, fanatics about London Bridge disturbed the Ministers in reading the Book of Common Prayer.' Those who defied the Act were harshly dealt with; the Presbyterian minister Edward Calamy was imprisoned in Newgate by the lord mayor, 'for preaching without license of the Bishop of London in his late church of St Mary, Aldermanbury'.[62] He received so many visitors that Newgate Street was said to be congested with their coaches. Well over a half of London parishes had a change of minister in little more than two years.

Pepys witnessed the reintroduction of the liturgy in 1660. He attended a service at Westminster Abbey on 1 July, when he noted tersely, 'no Common Prayer yet', but a week later at the chapel in Whitehall, 'I heard very good Musique, the first time that I remember ever to have heard the Organs and singing-men in Surplices in my life.' Towards the end of July he attended another Sunday service there, noting that 'the ceremonies did not please me, they do so overdo them', and he reacted in a similar way a few weeks later at the abbey: 'I heard them read the church-service, but very Ridiculously, that endeed I do not in my mind like it at all'.[63]

The Presbyterians had hopes for some sort of compromise with the Anglicans, but they were doomed to disappointment. By October Giavarina could report: 'The Presbyterians ... cannot bear to see the episcopal dogmas of the time of Queen Elizabeth set up again, and the doctrine of Calvin lost ... [but] they are well aware that they are in no condition to kick against the existing authority, which is gradually becoming more and more formidable.'[64] The Anglican liturgy was adopted by the parish clergy. In Pepys's parish of St Olave, Hart Street, the rector, Daniell Milles, began to introduce it on 4 October: 'In the morn to our own church, where Mr. Mills did begin to nibble at the Common Prayer by saying "Glory be to the Father," &c after he had read the two psalms. But the people have beene so little used to it that they could not tell what to answer.' But on the following Sunday Pepys's reaction was more favourable: 'This day also did Mr. Mills begin to read all the Common prayer, which I was glad of.'[65]

The royal palaces had been prepared for the king's arrival and many pieces from the royal art collection were returned. On 18 June Evelyn noted that, 'Goods that had ben pillag'd from White-hall during the Rebellion, now daily brought in & restor'd upon proclamation: as plate, Hangings, Pictures &c:'.[66] Somerset House required repair, as did its gardens, which were 'utterly spoiled and defaced, and many great dunghills made there, by the three regiments that lately have quartered there'.[67] They were restored so that the palace could be re-occupied by Henrietta Maria, but she had never been popular and, on her return to London on 2 November, Pepys wrote that, 'I observed this night very few bonfires in the City, not above three in all London for the Queenes coming; whereby I guess that (as I believed before) her coming doth please but very few'.[68]

By the time of Henrietta Maria's arrival, the mood in London had changed, from rejoicing to recrimination. The trials of the regicides and others accused of being involved in the trial and execution of Charles I had taken place in October. They were tried for treason and those convicted were executed at Charing Cross by the traditional method of hanging, drawing and quartering. After a victim was hanged, he was cut down alive and emasculated and disembowelled, with the eviscerated parts thrown on to a fire. He was then beheaded and his body was hacked into quarters. People living nearby complained of the stench of burning human flesh. Evelyn arrived too late to see the executions of four of the condemned, 'but met their quarters mangld & cutt & reaking as they were brought from the Gallows in baskets on the hurdle: o miraculous providence of God'.[69] Pepys went to see the execution of Major-General Thomas Harrison, 'he looking as cheerfully as any man could do in that condition. He was presently cut down and his head and his heart shown to the people, at which there was great shouts of joy.' But a week later Pepys's attitude had altered: 'I saw the limbs of some of our new Traytors set upon Aldersgate, which was a sad sight to see; and a bloody week this and the last have been, there being ten hanged, drawn, and Quarterd'.[70] They included John Jones. Both Rugg and Mundy made entries in their journals detailing the executions and the distribution of the heads and quarters of the victims on the gates and buildings of London, including the gatehouse on London Bridge. They were, wrote Mundy, 'set over the gates of the Citty, stuck on and fastned unto long poles set upright, to be discerned afarre offe'. He added that, 'Never the like was seene before at any tyme in the Citty of London'.[71]

The number of gruesome trophies was increased in the wake of Venner's Rising in the City in January 1661. This had its origins in the Coleman Street area, which had a reputation for political and religious radicalism stretching back to the 1630s. Meetings were held there from which developed radical political and religious convictions, held by two groups in particular, the Levellers and Fifth Monarchy Men. The congregations of the meeting-houses in the district welcomed those nonconformists who returned from New England and Holland after the outbreak of the Civil War. They included Thomas Venner, a London cooper who had emigrated to Massachusetts. He was prominent among the Fifth Monarchists, a millenarian sect whose programme was based on the establishment of a theocratic government, elected by members of the sects, with reform of the legal system and land tenure. They were particularly strong in London, where they were estimated to have 5,000 members in 1661, although the true number is impossible to establish.[72]

Venner's force, perhaps fewer than fifty men, assembled on Sunday 6 January at their meeting-house in Bell Alley off Coleman Street and began an insurrection, armed with 'musquets, pikes, and such other instruments as they thought most convenient'. Their banners proclaimed 'The Lord God and Gideon', and their slogan 'King Jesus, and the heads upon the gates' referred to the treatment of the bodies of those executed in the previous autumn. Giavarina explained that the day chosen for the uprising was Epiphany, 'usually spent in exceptional merriment with banquets and drinking. The rebels expected to find the people buried in slumber in the dead of the night and resolved to rise and surprise the guards, whom they expected to be drunk after the day's rejoicings.' They first went to St Paul's, where, according to Henry Townshend, there were 'some 5 or 6 killed, some taken and many arms'. After further skirmishes, they retreated from the streets to a wood near Highgate. There they evaded a party of the guards, after an exchange of fire.[73]

On Tuesday Pepys walked through the City and found 'the streets full of trainebands, and great stories what mischief these rogues have done'; the shops were closed 'and all things in trouble'. On the following night the insurgents emerged again, 'creating more terror than the other, because it was stated that they had set fire to different parts of London, which afterwards proved false'. They had some success against the troops sent to suppress them. Rugg wrote scornfully that when Colonel Corbett charged the insurgents at the corner of Cheapside and Wood Street, some of his men 'did a little disert him and retreated to the uper end of Cheape side, calling out for foote, which was a little staine in their redd scarves'. Only after further fighting did the rebellion collapse, when Venner and his surviving followers were defeated by the king's life-guards in Wood Street. They had inflicted about twenty casualties on the soldiers and members of the trained bands, but had lost twenty-six of their own men. Of those captured, twenty were put on trial, sixteen were convicted and thirteen executed. Venner and

Roger Hodgkins were hanged outside their meeting-house, their bodies were quartered and the quarters 'hanged up on the city gates'. The others were hanged and 'five beheaded and their heads set on London Bridge'.[74]

Harassment of nonconformists was intensified in the aftermath of the rising. In the search for arms that followed, 'many abuses was commited … in the houses of the Fift Monarchy men, Quakers, and Anabaptists, that many were very ill delt withall; for that they robed them, sorely wounded others, and dragged some to prison, and all this done without orders'.[75] Venner's meeting-house was demolished and, as Mundy noted, Quakers were arrested at their meetings in Aldersgate Street and Tower Street, and 'private meeting places [were] now shutt upp'. So many were arrested that Townshend observed that, 'The prisons in London [were] full of them.'[76]

The government, already fearful of an uprising by the nonconformists, should have been reassured by the Londoners' response to Venner's revolt. The citizens had come out on to the streets with their weapons, but not to support the insurgents, and the trained bands had responded when summoned to assist the troops. Pepys found 'everybody in arms at the doors; so I returned (though with no good courage at all, but that I might not seem to be afeared) and got my sword and pistol, which however I have no powder to charge, and went to the door'.[77] Others may have ventured into the streets because they did not want to lose face.

Its apprehensions did not deter the government from the policy of taking visible revenge on the regicides, even those already dead. On 30 January, the anniversary of Charles I's execution, the bodies of Oliver Cromwell, his son-in-law Henry Ireton, and John Bradshaw, who presided at the king's trial, were exhumed and, as Mundy explained, they:

> were drawn from Westminster on sleads to Tiburne and there hangued on the three parts of the gallowes … four or five houres untill sunset, then cut downe, the heads severed from the bodies. The three bodies, all three, were tumbled together in one pit under the gallowes … Their heads were set on a pinacle at the west end of Westminster Hall, right over the High Court of Justice where the old King was sentenced to dy.[78]

The heads of the regicides John Okey, John Barkstead and Miles Corbet were also displayed after they were executed at Tyburn in April 1662, before 'an immense crowd of people'. They had been captured in Holland. Sir Henry Vane was not a regicide, but was thought to be too skilful a politician to be allowed to live, and so he was beheaded on Tower Hill two months later. Others who were not regicides were decapitated and their heads displayed. Schellinks noted in December 1661 that, 'a weaver called John James was hanged and quartered at Tyburn for having preached against the King at a certain house in Whitechapel; his head was put up on a stake as a warning for others'. James was a Baptist preacher and Fifth Monarchist; some thirty or forty members of his congregation had been arrested with him. He was convicted of high treason by a jury that was said to have consisted of 'all pickt men, and most of them knights and gentlemen'.[79]

Most regiments of the army were disbanded in the autumn of 1660 and a poll tax was levied to raise the necessary funds. Parliament passed the Act authorising the tax in September and Evelyn paid promptly, on 6 October: 'I paied the greate Tax of Pole-mony, levied for the disbanding of the Army … I paid as Esquire 10 pounds & 1s: for every Servant in my house &c:'.[80] Pepys knew that he was liable for the same sum and set it aside, but did not volunteer payment. Not until 10 December was he called upon to pay: 'This afternoon there was a Couple of men with me, with a book in each of their hands, demanding money for polemony … which I did presently pay without any dispute.' To justify to himself his tardiness in paying he noted, 'I think I am not bound to discover myself'.[81] So many others were reluctant to pay that by 24 November only £252,167 had been received, although the tax was expected to raise £400,000. Nevertheless, enough was collected to settle the soldiers' pay arrears.

One consequence of disbandment was that several thousand men, most of them young, now required employment. Rugg noted in December 1660 that, 'for the most part of them they came up to London to endeoure a livelyhood'.[82] They joined the indigent former royalists whose hopes of recompense had far exceeded the crown's ability to satisfy them. This created a potentially explosive brew of political and religious rivalry, which was defused in the short term by a proclamation, recorded by Henry Townshend, 'for the removing of all disbanded Soldiers and all others who cannot give a good account for their abode in the Cities of London and Westminster, etc. And not to be within 20 miles of the said Cities until new orders the better to secure the court and city'.[83]

In November 1663 Pepys had a long conversation with Robert Blackborne, a naval administrator who had lost his post at the Restoration. He told Pepys that the dissenters, now commonly designated fanatics, supported the king, and that 'generally they are the most substantial sort of people, and the soberest', and added:

that of all the old army now, you cannot see a man begging about the street. But what? You shall have this Captain turned a shoemaker; the lieutenant, a Baker; this, a brewer; that, a haberdasher; this common soldier, a porter; and every man in his apron and frock, &c., as if they never had done anything else – whereas the other[s] go with their belts and swords, swearing and cursing and stealing – running into people's houses, by force oftentimes, to carry away something. And this is the difference between the temper of one and the other; and concludes (and I think with some reason) that the spirits of the old Parliament soldier[s] are so quiet and contented with God's providences, that the King is safer from any evil meant him by them, a thousand times more then from his own discontented Cavalier[s].[84]

Even an erstwhile parliamentarian such as Blackborne had to admit that the political settlement had achieved stability in London. Its citizens were satisfied with the arrangements as far as they affected their city, and the nonconformist threat, real or imagined, had not materialised. The return of the monarchy had brought changes, but much had endured through the fluctuating political fortunes since the 1640s and the uncertainty that had followed Oliver's death.

4

The Pleasures of the Town

Between the periodic political crises, Londoners could pass their spare time watching the formal occasions that were part of the annual round of civic life, or take part in a range of entertainments, sports and pastimes. The Civil War and its aftermath had curtailed some of these, although they were gradually revived. And new ones appeared in London, with the rapid rise in popularity of coffee, tea and chocolate, and places where they could be consumed, business transacted, and news and gossip exchanged.

Each year the swearing-in of the new lord mayor had been accompanied by a major show and processions, on the Thames and through the streets, but they had been halted by the outbreak of war. The pageant to celebrate the installation of John Dethick as lord mayor in 1655 was the first for fifteen years. The author of the pamphlet published to mark the event regretted 'the late extinguishing these Civic Lights, and suppressing the genius of our Metropolis, which for these planetary Pageants, and Pretorian Pomps, was as famous and renowned in foreign nations, as for their faith, wealth, and valour'. And so he welcomed the 'return of the City gallantry and manifestation of her several splendours'.[1] The suppliers of finery, food and drink benefited from the reinstatement of the event, which continued to be held annually thereafter. In 1661 the display on the Thames was revived, as part of the celebrations, and was seen by Evelyn, who noted: 'I saw the Lord Major passe in his Water Triumph to Westminster being the first solemnity of this nature after 20 yeares'.[2] William Schellinks included a full description of that year's show in his journal and was greatly impressed by the livery companies' barges and other vessels, which were:

> most elegantly decorated, gilded and painted with all kinds of devices, and with covers with their coats of arms draped over them, with banners, vanes, pennants, flags, standards etc. fluttering all round, below and above, also front and rear full of musicians competing with each other in playing their bass-viols, cornets, crumhorns, shawms, trombones etc. … Many other barges, which did not belong to

any particular Company or Guild, were also on the water, and were vying with the others in their finery.

The event drew 'an incredibly large crowd of sightseers, from the country all round as well as townspeople and strangers to London'.[3]

From 1657 to 1664 the texts for the lord mayors' celebrations were written by the playwright John Tatham, and he penned the script for the entertainment of Charles II when he dined in the City for the first time, in July 1660, entitled *London's Glory; represented by Time, Truth, and Fame*. The City was also involved in the celebrations that accompanied the king's royal entry, held on the day before his coronation on 23 April, St George's Day, 1661. Evelyn described it as 'the splendid Cavalcade of his Majestie from the Tower of Lond: to White Hall'.[4] John Ogilby designed four triumphal arches, erected in Leadenhall Street, Cornhill, Wood Street and Fleet Street.

These were expensive operations to mount, but they celebrated the City, its good government and commercial prosperity. The costs of the annual lord mayor's inauguration were customarily borne by his livery company, while he and the sheriffs paid for the dinner on his inauguration day, which Pepys was told could cost £700 or £800. In addition, during his mayoral year, he was expected to entertain those wishing to dine with him. Lorenzo Magalotti explained that, 'every day in the year, during his administration, the mayor is obliged, by virtue of his post, to keep open table, which is necessarily attended with great expense; and, on this account, the burden of the situation is always thrown upon some wealthy individual, that it may be kept up with credit and dignity'. Schellinks was at one such meal, in February 1662, which he described as 'a wonderful dinner; all the judges were there in their red, fur trimmed robes, and many other officers, altogether some eighty people'.[5] Pepys noted in October 1663 that he had enjoyed the lord mayor's hospitality at 'a very great noble dinner'. A few days later he attended the feast celebrating the inauguration of the new lord mayor, Sir Anthony Bateman, 'where ten good dishes to a messe, with plenty of wine of all sorts'. However, the occasion was somewhat marred:

> It happened that, after the Lords had half dined, came the French Embassador up to the Lords' table, where he was to have sat; but finding the table set, he would not sit down nor dine with the Lord Mayor, who was not yet come, nor have a table to himself, which was offered; but in a discontent went away again.[6]

Pepys had witnessed a breach of etiquette that could have caused a diplomatic incident; the ambassador, the Comte de Cominges, described it in his dispatch to Louis XIV as a 'piece of gross incivility'. Lord Montagu, Henry Jermyn, Earl of St Albans, and then the lord mayor himself waited on the ambassador on the following day to offer their apologies. Cominges explained that the lord mayor arrived, 'followed by ten or twelve coaches and a rather large number of people, who accompanied the procession out of curiosity'. Despite Sir Anthony's admitted lack of proficiency in French and the failings of the interpreter that he had brought with him, the matter was resolved and, as Cominges wrote, 'All went off satisfactorily on both sides.'[7]

It was entirely typical that a crowd should have gathered and followed the lord mayor as he went to the French ambassador's; Londoners also turned out in force to witness the formal arrival in London of other ambassadors and delegations. The procedure was well established; the ambassadors and their retinues having settled privately in London then made a formal entrance. They were taken by barge from Greenwich to Tower Wharf and from there they processed through the City to Whitehall Palace. Cominges described the reception of the Russian ambassador in 1662: 'all the merchants were under arms; the aldermen … went to pay him a visit and congratulate him upon his coming; the King defrays all his expenses and provides him with lodgings'.[8] The citizens watched those processions, partly to see the unusual styles and dress of the foreign visitors. Pepys joined the onlookers at the arrival of the Russian ambassador and saw 'his attendants in their habitts and fur-caps very handsome comely men, and most of them with Hawkes upon their fists to present to the King. But Lord, to see the absurd nature of Englishmen, that cannot forbear laughing and jeering at everything that looks strange.'[9]

A particularly large crowd assembled to watch the arrival of the Swedish ambassador on 30 September 1661, but in anticipation of a fight, not to admire the display. The French and Spanish embassies had been squabbling for some years about precedence, disputing which of them had the right to be the next coach behind that of the newly arrived ambassador in the procession through London. Violence had nearly erupted on the arrival of the previous Swedish ambassador three years earlier and a clash was now almost certain. Pepys was 'up by moonshine, at five o'clock', aware that the French and Spanish 'entended to fight for the precedence' and he visited both embassies, 'and there saw great preparations on both sides; but the French made the most noise and vaunted most, the other made no stir almost at all'. When the formal reception had been completed and the Swedish ambassador was safely in the royal coach at Tower Hill, the procession moved off. To ensure that their coach went next, 'The French attacked the Spaniards, using muskets, pistols and carbines'. But the

Spanish, who were heavily outnumbered, were prepared and fought back, 'making them retire, and so with stones, sticks and swords drove them off three times ... and kept them always away from their coach and from the horses, guarded by three men each, the harness being chains covered with leather, to prevent its being cut, so that they could not receive the slightest hurt'. The French had not taken similar precautions and could not defend their horses so that, 'four of the six coach horses [were] killed and the other two in a sorry state, so the coach was unable to follow the others'. According to Pepys, 'There were several men slain of the French, one or two of the Spaniards, and one Englishman by a bullett.' The French ambassador, the Comte d'Estrades, admitted that of the French force, 'five were killed and thirty-three wounded'. Charles II had stationed troops there, but they had been unable to prevent this sorry affair from being played out on the streets of his capital, when 'Many thousands of spectators came to behold this strange and desperate conflict.' They cheered on the Spanish and their coach was 'escorted by a crowd, which came out of all the shops, applauding the event with words and cries, showing great affection for Spain, even ringing the bells in some places'.[10]

How things had changed over the previous forty years or so. During James I's reign the Spanish diplomatic retinue had been the most unpopular in London; their ambassador, Count Gondomar, was detested and the target of satirical attacks, in print and on the stage. At that period Spain had been seen as the country which presented the greatest threat to England, but by the 1660s her power was on the wane and France had become the major menace. Londoners had adjusted their sympathies accordingly.

They were also fascinated by the more typical, peaceful performances of foreign entertainers, such as 'a famous Rope-daunser call'd the Turk', who impressed Evelyn:

> I saw even to astonishment the agilities he perform'd, one was his walking bare foote, & taking hold by his toes onely, of a rope almost perpendicular & without so much as touching it with his hands ... Lastly he stoode on his head, upon the very top of a very high mast, daunced on a small roope that was very slack, & finaly flew downe the perpendicular, with his head forward on his breast, his legs & armes extended: with divers other activities, to the admiration of all the Spectators.[11]

A similar entertainment drew Samuel and Elizabeth Pepys to watch 'the Italian dancing the ropes and the women that do strange tumbling tricks', at Bartholomew Fair in 1661. In the following year Samuel went to Covent Garden, 'to see an Italian puppet play that is within the rayles there, which is very pretty, the best that ever I saw, and great resort of gallants'.[12]

Such displays attracted not only 'gallants', according to the residents of Lincoln's Inn Fields, who complained in 1664 that one Thomas Newton had erected 'severall wooden houses or shedds and ... employed the said houses for puppet playes, dancing on the ropes, mountebanks, and other like uses, whereby multitudes of loose disorderlie people are daylie drawne together'.[13]

At Bartholomew Fair were many stalls selling a whole range of goods, food and drink. The entertainments included 'all kinds of conjurers and gamblers', according to Schellinks, and animal displays, such as the 'Munkys dancing on the ropes', that offended Pepys: 'such a dirty sport that I was not pleased with it'.[14] The fair was held annually, originally on three days around St Bartholomew's Day, 24 August, but by the mid-seventeenth century it continued into September. The other major fair in London was in Southwark, a few weeks later.

More frequent entertainments could be seen at Moorfields, a popular spot for Londoners to take exercise and watch the fun. On a pleasant February day in 1660 Pepys 'took a walk round the parke' and later 'walked half an hour in Moorefields, which was full of people, it being so fine a day'.[15] Schellinks described it as 'divided by some fine avenues into three large squares, the one nearest the town wall fenced in with wooden railings round its green fields and provided with comfortable seating'. In the third, or highest, square 'on summer evenings, there is always wrestling and fencing with sticks and billhooks, watched by crowds of people, who stand around in a large circle'. On one occasion Schellinks and his companions saw 'a tightrope walker perform such lusty capers that his rope snapped and he fell head over heels on to the heads of the crowd'.[16] Lodewijck Huygens's attention was drawn to the skilful archers there, and he watched 'bowmen first shooting very neatly and securely at a target in the field that was placed a stone's throw away from them and was no bigger than the palm of a hand. When we had watched this with much pleasure for about an hour, we rode on to Grub Street and saw people there in an alehouse shooting with great accuracy at two large targets'.[17]

Less edifying was an event at the Red Bull playhouse, where Schellinks witnessed fencing, 'with cleavers and swords, which the fencers borrowed from gentlemen. One was a butcher's man and the other a porter; it was dreadful to watch'.[18] Sorbière was shocked by the prize-fighting at the Bear Garden, on Bankside, where the fighters would put up prize money of £20 or £30 to tempt a challenger:

> They fight with Sword and Buckler, and Back-Sword. But I fancy there is some sort
> of Collusion between them, to make the Sport last, for they presently give over at

the first Drawing of Blood; besides, the Swords are blunt: However, they sometimes give one another terrible Hacks and Slashes, so that half a Cheek hangs down, but this is done by chance and happens not often, tho' there is always something that is fierce in this Brutish Exercise.[19]

Magalotti, too, thought that, 'by an understanding between them, they give over as soon as blood is drawn, consequently it rarely happens that they injure one another seriously'.[20] Their opinion that dangerous injuries were rare seems to be contradicted by Jorevin de Rocheford's and Pepys's experiences. At a fight that de Rocheford saw one of the combatants lost 'a slice of his head and almost all his ear' and the other sustained a 'cut on the wrist, which [was] almost cut off'. Yet the fight resumed and ended only with another severe blow on the wrist 'dividing the sinews'. Not surprisingly, his conclusion was, 'I think there is an inhumanity, a barbarity, and cruelty, in permitting men to kill each other for diversion.'[21] Pepys witnessed a bout where one of the fighters, Westwicke, 'was soundly cut several times both in the head and legs, that he was all over blood. And other deadly blows they did give and take in very good earnest, till Westwicke was in a most sad pickle.' Pepys examined one of the swords, and found it to be, 'very little, if at all, blunter on the edge then the common swords are'.[22]

In 1653 'bear baiting, bull baiting, and playing for prizes by fencers' had been banned and the Bear Garden was forcibly closed in 1656, according to Henry Townshend, who described how Colonel Thomas Pride 'caused all the Bears to be fast tied up by the noses and then valiantly brought some files of musketeers, drew up and gave fire and killed six or more bears in the place (only leaving one white innocent cub), and also all courts of the game. It is said all the mastifs are for to be shipt for Jamaica.'[23] Those sports were revived after the Restoration, with royal support, and drew Evelyn's disapproval:

I was forc'd to accompanie some friends to the Bear-garden &c: Where was Cock fighting, Beare, Dog-fighting, Beare & Bull baiting, it being a famous day for all these butcherly Sports, or rather barbarous cruelties: The Bulls did exceedingly well but the Irish Wolfe dog exceeded, which was a tall Gray-hound, a stately creature in deede, who beate a cruell Mastife: One of the Bulls tossed a Dog full into a Ladys lap, as she sate in one of the boxes at a Considerable height from the Arena; There were two poore dogs killed; & so all ended with the Ape on horse-back, & I most heartily weary, of the rude & dirty passetime, which I had not seene I think in twenty yeares before.[24]

Pepys recorded a similar reaction to cock-fighting, after a visit to a new cockpit in Shoe Lane. He had never been to a cock fight before and found it strange 'to observe the nature of those poor creatures, how they will fight till they drop down dead upon the table and strike after they are ready to give up the ghost – not offering to run away when they are weary or wounded past doing further'. This was not to his taste at all: 'I soon had enough of it'. But he was fascinated to see the variety of men who attended, from Members of Parliament to 'the poorest prentices, bakers, brewers, butchers, draymen, and what not'. Despite their apparent poverty, Pepys noted that they placed bets of £3 or £4 for one fight and, although losing their money, would wager as much again on the next contest, losing £10 or £20 at one meeting. Magalotti commented that cock-fighting was 'a common amusement of the English, who even in the public streets take a delight in seeing such battles; and their partiality towards these animals is carried to such an height, that considerable bets, are made on the victory of the one or the other'.[25] Schellinks described a cockpit that he visited as 'a circle with a table or round stage in the middle covered with mats, with the devotees sitting around it, with the seats rising up so that they can see above each other'.[26]

Playing at cards and dice was also popular, invariably accompanied by gambling. Pepys noted on one occasion that he looked into the halls of the Inner Temple and Middle Temple during the Christmas holidays, 'and there saw the dirty prentices and idle people playing'. He then went on to court, where he was interested to watch the reactions of the players as they won or lost, how they tried different tactics to change their luck, the sums involved, and, as at the cock-fight, 'how persons of the best quality do here sit down and play with people of any, though meaner; and to see how people in ordinary clothes shall come hither and play away 100, or 2 or 300 guinnys, without any kind of difficulty'. He was not tempted by this kind of 'profane, mad entertainment'.[27] Nor was Evelyn, who also watched the reactions of gamblers at court, 'observing the wiccked folly vanity & monstrous excesse of Passion amongst some loosers, & sorry I am that such a wretched Custome as play to that excesse should be countenanc'd in a Court, which ought to be an example of Virtue to the rest of the kingdome'. On another occasion he saw 'vast heapes of Gold squandered away in a vaine & profuse manner: This I looked on as an horrid vice, & unsuitable to a Christian Court'.[28] The Gaming Act of 1664 was intended to put a halt to the 'debauch of many of the younger sorte both of the Nobility and Gentry', but gambling was too deeply ingrained in the culture for such a measure to be effective.[29]

Among the other popular pastimes was football, less expensive perhaps but potentially annoying, as described by Davenant's fictional Parisian: 'I am stopt by one of your Heroick games, call'd Foot-ball; which I conceive (under your favour) not very conveniently civil in the streets; especially in such irregular and narrow Roads as Crooked Lane.'[30] Henri Misson described football as 'a useful and charming Exercise: It is a Leather Ball about as big as ones Head, fill'd with Wind: This is kick'd about from one to t'other in the Streets, by him that can get at it and that is all the Art of it.' Women played ball games as well as men, according to Magalotti, who wrote that, 'those of the lower order frequently go so far as to play at ball publicly in the streets'.[31]

James Howell summarised Londoners' recreations, including: 'some wrestling, some throwing the Barre, some the stone, some jumping, some running, some with their Dogs at Ducking ponds; some riding upon Nags, some in Coaches to take the fresh Air, some at Nine-pins, some at Stool-ball, though that stradling kind of Tomboy sport be not so handsome for Mayds.' And, among the more sedate pastimes, 'Within the City, what variety of Bowling Allies there are, some open, some covered.'[32] According to Schellinks there was a bowling alley even in the Fleet Prison, 'where a very great number of people are held for debt'. He also visited 'a recently designed bowling green on board a large barge, which lies in the river near Whitehall'. It had two rooms and outside was 'a gallery all round, and at one end is a spiral stair to the bowling green which is on the top; this is covered with green cloth when the king comes there to play'.[33]

The nobility and gentry took their outdoor recreation chiefly in The Mall and Hyde Park. Magalotti described the park as 'a large and spacious meadow, in which many carriages of ladies and gentlemen assemble in the evening, to enjoy the agreeableness of the place'. He noted how, one May evening, Duke Cosmo III 'repaired to Hyde Park, which was crowded, as usual, with carriages of ladies and gentlemen'.[34] May Day celebrations were frowned upon during the Interregnum, and maypoles were forbidden, but in 1654, according to a censorious report in the *Moderate Intelligencer*, 'great resort came to Hyde Park, many hundreds of coaches, and gallants in attire, but most shameful powdered-hair men, and painted and spotted women'.[35] Six years later Schellinks was in the park on May Day and saw how special the day was: 'all the nobility from the court, town, and country present themselves in their best finery, on horseback, but mostly in carriages, so that one can see here the most beautiful ladies' dresses, horses, carriages, pages, liveries, etc, which can be seen anywhere in London, everybody trying to outdo the other in their dress in which they appear in public'. So many carriages were at the parade that he could not count them, and they were watched by 'an enormous number of people of all kinds and conditions', whose every need was catered for: 'everything one can want is for sale as in an organised camp'.[36]

A more intimate setting for leisure and assignations was provided at Spring Garden, close to Charing Cross, which Evelyn described in May 1654 as 'the usual rendezvous for the Ladys and Gallants at this season'.[37] James had appointed a Keeper of the King's Spring Garden in 1610 and it was open to the public by the 1630s, developing a somewhat raffish character. The authorities closed it in 1654, but by 1659 it had reopened, attracting the comment: 'it is usual here to find some of the young company till midnight; and the thickets of the garden seem to be contrived to all advantages of gallantry'. The fare available was also described: 'The forbidden fruits are certain trifling tarts, neats' tongues, salacious meats, and bad Rhenish; for which the gallants pay sauce.'[38] Pepys found it expensive and the service inadequate when he went there with Elizabeth in May 1662: 'seeing that we could not have anything to eat but very dear and with long stay, we went forth again without any notice taken of us'.[39]

In 1661 a new garden was opened at Vauxhall, which Evelyn described as 'a pretty contriv'd plantation'. Schellinks visited it that August: 'on to Vauxhall to see the very large and most beautiful and interesting gardens, called the new Spring Gardens. Lots of people come there to amuse and refresh themselves, as it is a very pleasant place.'[40] In May 1667 Pepys noted a visit there, with a much more favourable reaction than after his earlier experience at the old Spring Garden:

> walked in Spring-garden; a great deal of company, and the weather and garden pleasant; that it is very pleasant and cheap going thither, for a man may go to spend what he will, or nothing, all as one – but to hear the nightingale and other birds, and here fiddles and there a harp, and here a jews trump, and here laughing, and there fine people walking, is mighty divertising.[41]

Better known as Vauxhall Gardens, this became the best-known of London's pleasure grounds.

Many Londoners frequented alehouses, taverns and coffee-houses, to enjoy company and relax, drink, smoke, exchange news and gossip. Sorbière complained that their businesses were neglected because they spent so much time in hostelries:

> there is scarce a Day passes but a Tradesman goes to the Alehouse or Tavern to smoke with some of his Friends, and therefore Publick Houses are numerous here, and Business goes on but slowly in the Shops: For a Taylor and a Shoemaker, let his Business be never so urgent, will leave his Work, and go to drink in the Evening; and as he oftentimes comes home late, or half Seas over, he has no great Inclination to go to Work, and opens not his Shop, even in Summer-time, till after Seven in the Morning.

He wrote that such behaviour made English goods expensive compared with French ones, for 'our Tradesmen are usually more Industrious'. Magalotti noticed that public-houses 'are exceedingly numerous' and praised 'the different kinds of beer, which are far better than those of any other country, as ale, cyder, and the delicious and exquisite bottled beer (bouteille-biere) and another sort of beer made with the body of a capon, which is left to grow putrid along with the malt'.[42]

Thomas Sprat found Sorbière's remarks most offensive, for condemning the whole nation as lazy, and he responded by observing that Sorbière himself had admired London's shops and the work of the shipwrights along the Thames, and that in the commercial rivalry with the Dutch, the English 'will outgo them in Industry and Stock'.[43] Yet the government was uneasy about the baleful influence of alehouses and taverns, as a focus not only for idle people, but also for crime, sin and subversion. There were probably well over one thousand alehouses in London, so many that the justices occasionally tried to reduce the number. In 1649 they were required to survey them and decide how many really were needed, so that 'the now supernumerary Ale-houses be reduced to the number to be reported needfull for each parish'.[44]

While the smaller and less salubrious alehouses sold beer and ale, wine was served at the taverns and winehouses. They were also places to dine, along with the cook-shops, or ordinaries. Pepys recorded that one day he went to the 'Rhenish winehouse', where he was served 'a morning draught and a neat's tongue'. Lodewijck Huygens wrote favourably of cook-shops, 'where one can eat as well as in an inn. We chose what we wanted from the spit and ate there.'[45] The taverns were also popular for their food and catered for a wider social clientele than the alehouses. They could get very busy. In February 1665 Pepys went to 'the Sun Taverne, and there dined with Sir W Warren and Mr. Gifford the merchant ... But Lord, to see how full the house is, no room for any company almost to come into it.'[46]

Coffee-houses were a new addition to the London social scene. They rapidly established themselves as places for men to meet, chat, do business and talk politics. The first one was opened by Pasqua Rosee in St Michael's Alley off Cornhill, perhaps as early as 1652 and certainly by 1654, and the second, the Rainbow, was opened in 1656 by James Farr, adjoining the Inner Temple's gateway. Neighbours complained about the 'evil smells' of Farr's coffee, but proprietors were not deterred by the residents' opposition in a district with many customers. The new establishments became very popular, so that by the end of the decade, according to Rugg, 'theire ware also att this time a Turkish drink to bee sould, almost in evry street, called coffee, and another kind of drink called tee, and also a drink called chocolate, which was

a very harty drink'. Thomas Garraway was selling tea by 1658 at his coffee-
house in the parish of St Bartholomew-by-the-Exchange; he probably was
the first retailer of tea in England. One day in September 1660 Pepys noted
that he went to the office, 'And afterwards did send for a Cupp of Tee (a
China drink) of which I never had drank before.'[47] Within ten years of the
opening of Rosee's, the capital contained more than eighty coffee-houses,
and the number continued to increase. Adam Ebert, a law professor from
Frankfort-on-the-Oder, visited in 1678 and in his journal commented on
the vast number of coffee, tea and chocolate houses. Before the end of the
century at least one such establishment was trying to diversify, according
to an advertisement of 1695: 'At the Marine Coffee-house in Birchin Lane is
water gruel to be sold every morning from 6 till 11 of the clock. 'Tis not yet
thoroughly known; but there comes such Company as drinks usually 4 or 5
gallons in a morning.'[48]

Miles's coffee-house in Westminster was the meeting place during the
winter of 1659–60 of the Rota Club, a group centred on James Harrington
that discussed possible republican forms of government. Harrington was a
prominent republican thinker whose major work, *The Commonwealth of
Oceanea*, in which London was known as Emporium, had been published
in 1656. The group began meeting in November 1659, when, as Aubrey
wrote, 'as to human foresight, there was no possibility of the King's returne'.
He described Harrington's arrangements:

> he had every night a meeting at the (then) Turke's head, in the New Pallace-yard,
> where was made purposely a large ovall-table, with a passage in the middle for Miles
> to deliver his Coffee. About it sate his Disciples, and the Virtuosi. The Discourses in
> this Kind were the most ingeniose, and smart, that ever I heard, or expect to heare,
> and bandied with great eagernesse: the Arguments in the Parliament howse were
> but flatt to it. Here we had (very formally) a Balloting-box, and balloted how things
> should be caried, by way of tentamens [experiment]. The room was every evening
> full as it could be cramm'd.

Harrington and his friend Henry Nevill had, through his book and their
'smart discourses and inculcations, dayly at Coffee-houses, made many
Proselytes'. But their proposals that one-third of the members of both
the upper and lower chambers retired every year, and that the ballots at
elections should be secret, were not welcomed by MPs, who, in Aubrey's
damning phrase, 'were cursed tyrants, and in love with their Power'.[49]

Pepys joined the club and was impressed by the level of debate. At one
meeting he found 'a great confluence of gentlemen ... where admirable
discourse till 9 at night'. A few evenings later he 'heard exceeding good

argument against Mr. Harrington's assertion that over-balance of propriety was the foundation of government', and at another meeting he noted that there was 'very good discourse'.[50] But those stimulating debates came to an end in February, as Aubrey wrote, 'upon the unexpected turne upon Generall Monke's comeing-in, all these aerie models vanished', not least because, 'Then 'twas not fitt, nay Treason, to have donne such'. On 20 February Pepys noted, rather sadly, that 'the club broke off very poorly, and I do not think they will meet any more'.[51]

He continued to enjoy a variety of company in the other coffee-houses that he frequented. Over a few weeks in the winter of 1663–4 he had conversations about several aspects of music, the Roman Empire, the possible effects of war with the Dutch, and the Quakers 'being charmed by a string about their wrists', listened to Sir William Petty discussing the three books which 'were the most esteemed and generally cried up for wit in the world' (Sir Thomas Browne's *Religio Medici*, Samuel Butler's *Hudibras* and Francis Osborne's *Advice to a Son*), and heard a traveller telling 'very good stories of his travels over the high hills in Asia above the Cloudes'. He also discussed topics in which he had a professional interest, such as the best way to preserve ships' masts and, with Alderman William Barker, about the trade in hemp. One evening he paid his first visit to 'the great Coffee-house' in Covent Garden, where he saw the poet John Dryden 'and all the wits of the town, and Harris the player and Mr Hoole of our college; and had I had time then, or could at other times, it will be good coming thither, for there I perceive is very witty and pleasant discourse'.[52] In 1680 Aubrey wrote approvingly of 'the modern advantage of Coffee-howses in this great Citie, before which men knew not how to be acquainted, but with their own Relations or Societies'. His circle of friends included Robert Hooke, whose favourite coffee-house was Garraway's, but between 1672 and 1680 he frequented about sixty others, and almost eighty taverns, around London, meeting friends socially and also conducting business.[53]

Hooke was both a distinguished scientist and an architect and surveyor, and a member of the scientific club which became the Royal Society. He was its Curator of Experiments from 1664 and its secretary from 1677, living in a set of rooms in Gresham College, in Old Broad Street, until his death in March 1703. The college was the foundation of Sir Thomas Gresham; the first appointments to its professorships were made in 1597. The subjects, chosen by Gresham, were divinity, astronomy, geometry, music, law, physic and rhetoric. The first steps towards the establishment of the Royal Society were taken after a lecture at the college on 28 November 1660, where the club again held its meetings after having been temporarily displaced by the soldiers. Of the dozen men who formed the nucleus of the Royal Society,

five held professorships at Gresham College. By the end of the year the
society had fifty-five members.

Proposals for a university in London had been put forward in the 1640s
and given substance in a pamphlet addressed to the lord mayor, aldermen
and common council in 1647 which advocated 'the present Founding [of]
an University in the Metropolis'. They would be responsible for 'perfecting
of the publick schooles or Gresham College and compleating of the
Membership of Professors'. The professors would 'read daily, to confer,
to dispute, to make orations; both for Strangers, Natives and Citizens;
the Professors to bee outlandish and English men'. Nothing had come of
those plans, but Gresham College and the Royal Society contributed to
London's role as a focus for scientific experiments and intellectual debate.
In addition, the College of Physicians, the Barber-Surgeons' Company and
the Society of Apothecaries had research and educational functions, while
the four Inns of Court were described as England's third university. They,
with the seven Inns of Chancery, were the centre for legal education as well
as providing members of the aristocracy and gentry with a grounding in
the common law.[54]

The Royal Society received its first charter in July 1662 and a second,
revised one in April 1663. Its first secretary was Henry Oldenburg. Born
in Bremen, he had held a number of posts in several countries on the
continent before settling in England in 1653, after arriving on a diplomatic
mission on behalf of his native city. John Milton was among his wide circle
of acquaintances and he wrote that Oldenburg had 'learnt to speak our
language more accurately and fluently than any other foreigner I have ever
known'.[55] The appointment exemplified the society's involvement in the
ferment of enquiry and experiment that was engaging scientists in many
European countries, including the Netherlands and France. The Académie
Royale des Sciences in Paris was established in 1666. A few years later
Aubrey wrote to the Oxford antiquary Anthony Wood telling him that
London's booksellers were 'blockheads' and so the Royal Society's members
'want a factor to buy new bookes and maps at Paris, which either are not to
be gott (or if sent for) 5 times the Rate there'.[56]

Despite such problems, Thomas Sprat was certain that London was the
appropriate place for debate and the dissemination of practical knowledge:

It is the head of a mighty Empire, the greatest that ever commanded the Ocean: It
is compos'd of Gentlemen, as well as Traders: It has a large intercourse with all the
Earth: It is, as the Poets describe their House of Fame, a City, where all the noises
and business in the World do meet: and therefore this honor is justly due to it, to
be the constant place of residence of that Knowledg, which is to be made up of the

Above right: 1. Portrait of
Samuel Pepys by Sir Godfrey
Kneller, possibly dating
from 1689, the year in which
Pepys lost his position as
Secretary to the Admiralty
and was also briefly
imprisoned, in the aftermath
of the Glorious Revolution.

Right: 2. Samuel Pepys
married Elizabeth St
Michel in St Margaret's,
Westminster, on 1 December
1655. Her family had come
to England in the entourage
of Henrietta Maria at the
time of her marriage to
Charles I in 1625, but her
father had been dismissed
from her service because he
was a Protestant. Elizabeth
died on 10 November 1669.
Samuel erected a monument
to her on the north side of
the chancel of St Olave's,
Hart Street, surmounted by
a marble bust attributed to
John Bushnell.

3. The outcome of the Civil Wars of 1642–6 and 1648 was a political crisis which culminated in the trial of the king in Westminster Hall in January 1649. It lasted three days and the king was sentenced to death.

4. The plan-view of part of west London was drawn by Wenceslaus Hollar, probably in the late 1650s. It shows the areas around Holborn, Drury Lane and the Strand. North of the Strand is Covent Garden, with the buildings erected around a piazza, developed in the 1630s. The much larger space of Lincoln's Inn Fields, in the north-east part of the plan-view, was set out shortly afterwards, but building was not completed until the late 1650s. At the north-west of the plan-view is St Giles-in-the-Fields, still the limit of development in this part of the city.

5. This Dutch engraving shows the execution of Charles I on 30 January 1649 outside the banqueting house of Whitehall Palace, designed by Inigo Jones for Charles's father, James I. Pepys was among the crowd and said to a friend that 'were I to preach upon him, my text should be: "The memory of the wicked shall rot"'. Following the execution, the monarchy and House of Lords were both abolished and the new regime remained in power until overturned by Oliver Cromwell in 1653.

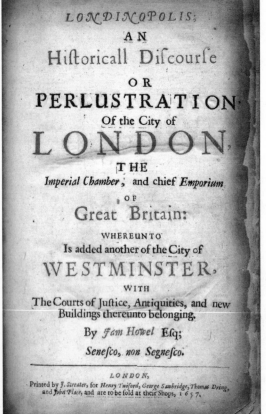

LONDINOPOLIS;

AN

Historicall Discourse

OR

PERLUSTRATION

Of the City of

LONDON,

THE

Imperial Chamber, and chief Emporium

OF

Great Britain:

WHEREUNTO

Is added another of the City of

WESTMINSTER,

WITH

The Courts of Justice, Antiquities, and new
Buildings thereunto belonging.

By Jam Howel Esq;

Senesco, non Segnesco.

LONDON,

Printed by J. Streater, for Henry Twiford, George Sawbridge, Thomas Dring,
and John Place, and are to be sold at their Shops, 1 6 5 7.

Above: 6. Hollar's depiction of the piazza in Covent Garden, drawn *c.*1640. The development was begun by Francis, Earl of Bedford in 1633 and St Paul's church, designed by Inigo Jones, became the parish church when the area was constituted as a parish in 1645. Jones was also responsible for the setting out the Italianate piazza, lined on the north and east sides with colonnaded buildings. The development was intended to attract the gentry. The coach and the dress of the passers-by are indicative of the social standing of those frequenting the neighbourhood.

Left: 7. Title page of James Howell's *Londinopolis*, published in 1657.

8. Lincoln's Inn Fields drawn by Hollar, probably during the Civil War, for troops are shown exercising: infantry in the square and a force of cavalry, with a standard, approaching from the left. The infantry may be the trained-bands, the civic militia consisting of 6,000 men. London remained loyal to parliament throughout the first Civil War and the trained-bands served with its armies. Hollar's representation of the houses is conjectural rather than accurate and perhaps reproduces a sketch done *c*.1641 as a prospectus.

9. A print of *c*.1650 showing the Holbein Gate at Whitehall, which bridged King Street and provided a connection between the two parts of Whitehall Palace. To the left stands the palace's banqueting house, designed by Inigo Jones and completed in 1622.

10. New Palace Yard, with Westminster Hall to the left and the clock house drawn by Wenceslaus Hollar, 1647. Coaches of the aristocracy and gentry stand in the yard in that part of the capital which was the focus of politics and government.

Parlament House   the Hall   the Abby

Above: 11. Westminster from the River Thames, with the Parliament House, Westminster Hall and St Peter's Abbey. Visitors to London were impressed by the scale of the great abbey building, where monarchs were crowned, celebratory services were held and prominent figures were buried, including Oliver Cromwell's son-in-law Henry Ireton, in 1652, and Cromwell himself, six years later. Charles II was crowned in the abbey on 23 April 1661 and was buried in Henry VII's chapel on 14 February 1685. Drawn by Wenceslaus Hollar.

Left: 12. Temple Bar stood at the western boundary of the City of London, with Fleet Street running eastwards from it and the Strand westwards. It was on the processional route from Westminster to the City and the the sovereign was welcomed by lord mayor and aldermen. Because of its position, the gateway was elaborately decorated. The Great Fire did not reach Temple Bar, but the structure was taken down and replaced in the early 1670s.

13. Cheapside in 1638. This effectively was London's high street; one of the wealthiest streets in the city, lined with tall and impressive houses and shops. It was also part of the ceremonial route through the capital and this illustration shows the procession of Marie de Medici, mother of the queen, Henrietta Maria, escorted by soldiers of the trained-bands.

14. London was well provided with water. The New River Head in Clerkenwell was supplied along a canal from Hertfordshire, completed in 1613, from which it was distributed by pipes and water sellers, as shown in Marcellus Laroon's *The Cryes of the City of London drawne after the life*, published in 1687.

15. Coal had replaced wood as the principal fuel for Londoners by the early seventeenth century. Much of London's supply was brought by coastal vessels from the areas around the rivers Tyne and Wear, and was sold around the streets by coal sellers, such as the one depicted by Marcellus Laroon in *The Cryes of the City of London*.

2. Gray Church

8. Dunſton in the Eaſt

9.

Lyon kay

Billings gate

BRIDGE

The Tower.

Tower Wharfe

S.Olafe

Number 5.

LONDON POST

Communicating the High Counsels of both Parliaments in *England* and *Scotland*, and all other Remarkable passages, both Civill and Martiall in his Weekly Travells through the three Kingdoms.

Printed and entred according to order.

From *Thursday February the 4. to Thursday February 11.* 1646

THe Feare we had of the scarcity of Bread, is by the mercy of God prevented, for (to adde to the number we had before) there are of late many ships come in laden with Corne in great abundance.

FRONT PAGE OF A NEWSPAPER OF 1646
The mid-seventeenth century was marked by the rise and development of the newspaper. The *London Post*—published weekly—is typical of this early journalism.
From the original in the British Museum.

Left: 18. London drew food supplies from a wide area, with grain and dairy produce brought by coastal vessels. The editor of this edition of the *London Post* chose to give front-page prominence to a reassuring report that fear of bread shortages was unwarranted because 'abundant' supplies of corn had arrived by ship.

Below: 19. Close to the Tower was St Olave, Hart Street, at its junction with Seething Lane. This was Pepys's church, as the Navy Office stood within the parish. A gallery was built against the south wall of the nave in 1660 for the use of the staff of the Navy Office, reached directly from the churchyard by a staircase. Pepys noted that the gallery was first used on 11 November: 'we sat in the foremost pew and behind us our servants; but I hope it will not be always so, it not being handsome for our servants to sit so equal with us'. The north porch was added in 1674.

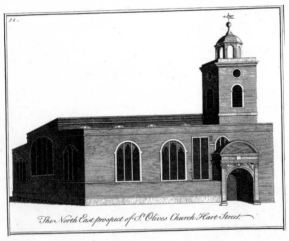

The North East prospect of S.ͭ Olives Church Hart Street.

Previous page spread left: 16. This section of Hollar's view of London from Bankside of 1647 shows a part of Southwark in the foreground, with London Bridge and the City. A fire in 1633 destroyed the buildings at the northern end of the bridge and they had not been replaced when Hollar made this drawing. The remainder of the bridge was lined with shops. The buildings along the river came right down to the waterside, with occasional quays. A vessel is shown moored at Billingsgate, which was both a quay and a market, for grain, fruit and vegetables, and increasingly for fish.
Previous page spread right: 17. Hollar's view has the crowded roofs of Southwark in the foreground, with the gables of the buildings facing the High Street that were to be destroyed in the fire of 1676. St Olave's church, dedicated to the king of Norway, who died in 1030, was rebuilt in 1740 and demolished in 1928. On the river, Hollar shows three masted seagoing ships and numerous lighters, used for transferring cargoes from the vessels to the quays, and for moving goods along the river. London was the country's largest port for overseas trade and also for coastal vessels bringing provisions and coal to the city's markets.

Above left: 20. Government attempts to prevent the further growth of London by restrictions and taxes on new buildings were largely ineffective. Despite a renewed attempt by the protectorate government, in 1658 the advertisements in *Mercurius Politicus* included one inviting would-be builders to offer for a four-acre site in Hyde Park.

Above right: 21. A house on Little Tower Hill, with a projecting and decorated upper storey, drawn by J.T. Smith in 1792. The open space around the Tower of London was divided into Great Tower Hill within the wall and Little Tower Hill outside it.

22. A new gateway to the churchyard of St Olave, Hart Street, was erected with a suitably macabre relief of skulls and bones in the archway, dated 11 April 1658.

Above left: 23. A house in Little Moorfields, with an elaborately decorated front, possibly built in the second quarter of the seventeenth century. The open space of Moorfields, to the north of the City wall west of Bishopsgate, was a popular area for recreation and sports, but it was steadily encroached upon by new buildings.

Above right: 24. Great Winchester Street was set out in 1656 on the site of Winchester House and its garden. In 1662 the demographer John Graunt wrote that the population of the parish of All Hallows on the Wall 'is increased by the conversion of the Marquess of Winchester's House, lately the Spanish Embassadour's, into a new Street'. The projecting upper storeys show that the regulations specifying that new houses should be built of brick with flat fronts were not being observed in the years before the Great Fire. The fire did not reach this street, which was drawn by J.T. Smith in 1804.

25. Furnivall's Inn, on the north side of Holborn, was an Inn of Chancery, which developed connections with Lincoln's Inn. The frontage was rebuilt in 1640, by Daniel Thomas. Like the other Inns of Chancery, Furnivall's Inn declined in the eighteenth century and in 1818 the society was dissolved and its buildings demolished.

Above: 26. Seventeenth-century houses in King Street, Westminster, shown on a print published in 1791. The street consisted chiefly of substantial houses, with each storey projecting above the one below. By the 1720s it created an unfavourable impression; Daniel Defoe described it as 'a long, dark, dirty and very inconvenient passage'.

Right: 27. A house in Leadenhall Street, which escaped the Great Fire. The notice above the door and window reads: 'Parcels Passengers Books for the year 1672'. The late seventeenth century was a period when the postal service was expanding, both within London and to the rest of the country.

28. The courtyard of a house known as Whittington's Palace on the south side of Hart Street, near the Navy Office, drawn by J.T. Smith in 1792. It attracted attention because of its carved timbers, the designs of which included beasts' heads and crouched goblins. Within the building, the ceiling decoration included carved cats' heads, drawing attention to the supposed connection with Richard Whittington. The building was demolished in 1801.

HET HUIS VAN DEN
OOST INDISCHE COMPAGNIE IN
LON DEN

THE OLD EAST INDIA HOUSE, LEADENHALL STREET (1648-1726)

From an Engraving by Pulham, in the "Crace Portfolio of London Views" at the British Museum.

Above: 29. The New Exchange was built in 1609 on the street frontage of Durham House, in the Strand. It had an arcaded ground floor for merchants and shops on the upper floors. It became a fashionable place for shopping and the customers there in the 1660s included Samuel and Elizabeth Pepys; by the early eighteenth century a half of its shops were occupied by milliners and mercers.

Left: 30. The East India Company was formed in 1600 and took a lease of Lord Craven's house in Leadenhall Street in 1648. This Dutch print shows the building's richly embellished front. Daniel Defoe described it in 1722 as 'an old, but spacious building; very convenient, though not beautiful', which was to be rebuilt 'with additional buildings for warehouses and cellars for their goods, which at present are much wanted'. It was demolished in 1726.

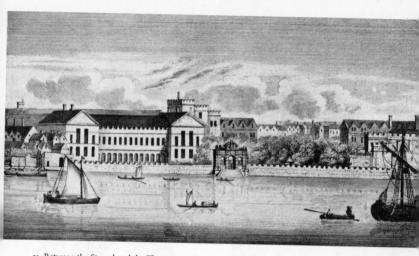

31. Between the Strand and the Thames stood aristocratic palaces, which had replaced the London houses of senior churchmen after the Reformation. Three of them are shown on Wenceslaus Hollar's drawing. They were demolished during the late seventeenth and early eighteenth centuries, when developers replaced them with streets of houses for the gentry and members of the professions.

32. In very cold winters the Thames above London Bridge froze over, sometimes so deeply that a frost fair could be held on the ice. The winter of 1684 was the harshest of the century and a street of booths was built, oxen were roasted, a printing press was set up and gentlemen were driven across the river in their coaches. But such severe winters also prevented the watermen from working and brought hardship to many Londoners.

33. The chapel at Shadwell became the parish church of St Paul when the increasingly populous riverside district was created as a new parish in 1669. The chapel was built in 1656, shortly after the completion of the chapel at Poplar, begun in 1639 but largely built in 1652–4. St Paul's was replaced by a new church erected in 1817–21.

34. A lord mayor and his lady, wearing the formal attire of the mid-seventeenth century. The lord mayor's role involved attending at court and greeting diplomatic representatives.

35. The frontispiece of *Eikon Basilike*, which was claimed to be the spiritual autobiography of Charles I. Published after the execution of the king, it proved to be immensely popular and quickly went through forty-seven editions. It provided a focus for royalists during the Interregnum.

36. Fear of the apparently irreverent behaviour of the sects grew during the 1650s, adding to the disquiet with the republican regime. But the government had acted harshly in punishing James Naylor, a Quaker, who had passed along Bristol's streets in a manner which imitated Christ's entry into Jerusalem, in 1656. *Below right*: 38 Oliver Cromwell, Lord Protector, died on 3 September 1658. John Dryden's commemorative verses celebrated his achievement in ending the wars within the British Isles and his foreign policy successes. They were 'written after the celebrating of his funeral', which took place on 23 November. Oliver's eldest son Richard succeeded him as Lord Protector.

Above: 37. Among the reminders in London of the Civil Wars was the site of the cross in Cheapside, one of the ornate crosses built by Edward I to mark the places where the body of Queen Eleanor lay overnight on the journey from Harby, Nottinghamshire, where she died in 1290, to Westminster Abbey. It was demolished on 2 May 1643; according to one account, as the cross was being pulled from its top, 'dromes beat trumpets blew & multitudes of Capes wayre throwne in ye Ayre & a greate Shoute of People with joy'.

A
POEM
UPON THE
DEATH
OF
His Late Highness,
OLIVER,
Lord Protector
OF
ENGLAND, SCOTLAND, & IRELAND.

Written by Mr. Dryden.

LONDON,
Printed for *William Wilson*; and are to be sold in
Well-Yard, near *Little St. Bartholomew's*
Hospital. 1659.

Above: 39. Those members of the House of Commons who retained their places after the purge of the House in December 1648 were derisively named the Rump Parliament. They briefly returned to power after Richard Cromwell relinquished his position in 1659, and it became the practice across London for supporters of the Stuart monarchy to burn animals' rumps as a gesture of contempt. This depiction of a burning in Fleet Street near Temple Bar is an illustration by William Hogarth for an edition of Samuel Butler's *Hudibras*. The effigy that is being carried in the foreground is probably that of Jack Presbyter, a figure of derision directed at the Presbyterians.

Below: 40. Among the royalist plots to restore the monarchy was one in December 1659 to seize the Tower, which was the country's chief arsenal and treasury, as well as having a dominating presence in the east of the city. The plot came to nothing.

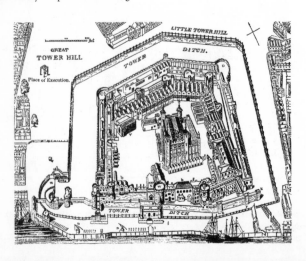

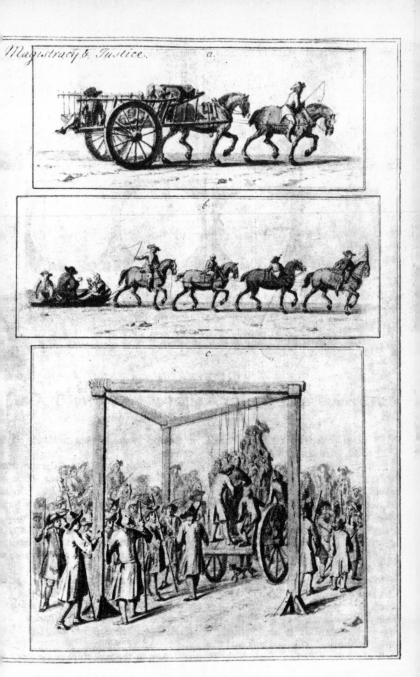

Magistracy & Justice.

41. The restoration regime took revenge on those who had been involved in the trial and execution of Charles I. Some of those who were not executed were dragged each year on a sledge to Tyburn, which was the place of execution for other miscreants.

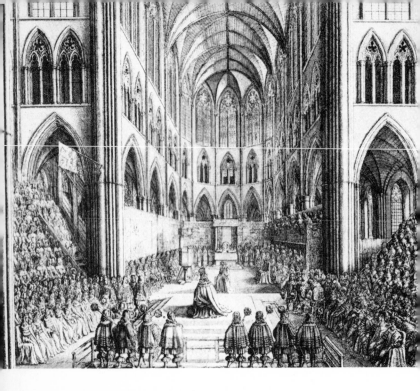

Above: 42. For the coronation of Char[les] II in Westminster Abbey, large stands were erected in the transepts and Pep[ys] took his place at about four o'clock in the morning on 'a great scaffold acros[s] the north end of the abby'. The king's procession did not arrive until about eleven. Pepys regretted that there was [so] great a noise, that I could make but li[ttle] of the Musique; and indeed, it was lo[st] to everybody'. He had been there so l[ong] that, eventually, 'I had so great a list t[o] pisse, that I went out a little while bef[ore] the King had done all his ceremonies'

Left: 43. After a period of political uncertainty in 1659 and early 1660, the Stuart monarchy was restored and Charles II entered London on 29 May. The long, winding procession is show[n] passing through an archway topped w[ith] the figure of justice. Although Charle[s] was welcomed by large crowds lining the route, the artist has shown only a handful of spectators at this point.

44. The lord mayor's annual pageant on the river was re-instated in 1661, after a break during the Civil War and Interregnum. It provided a spectacular display, with the barges of the livery companies finely decked out and accompanied by many other vessels. The event is shown here in *The Thames during the Lord Mayor's Regatta of 1683* by Jan Griffier.

45. With the restoration of the monarchy, some entertainments suppressed during the Interregnum were restored. These included the celebration of May Day and dancing around maypoles, forbidden in 1644 and 1654. In 1667 Pepys mentioned in his diary 'the Maypole in the Strand', which is shown on this print of *c.*1700.

46. St James's Palace was built by Henry VIII, but by the mid-seventeenth century was regarded as unfashionable. In this scene, Marie de Medici arrives at the palace in 1638.

47. Two views of St James's Park looking towards Whitehall, *c.1677*, from an engraving by S. Rawle published in J.T. Smith's *Antiquities of Westminster* (1804).

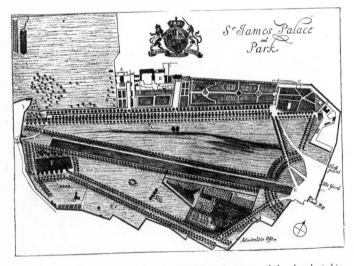

48. St James's Palace and Park by Leonard Knyff. The park was extended and replanted in the early 1660s, probably by the French landscape designer, Andre Molle, with 'The new River', and Pall Mall. Charles II introduced the French game of Pelle Melle, played on a long court, and this gave its name to both The Mall and Pall Mall. St James's Palace is shown immediately below the royal arms and the pleasure garden known as Spring Garden is the area labelled C, at the northernmost part of the plan.

Above: 49. The front of Westminster Hall facing New Palace Yard, the hall of Westminster Palace, built by William II. The hall survived the fire in 1512 that destroyed much of the palace and by the seventeenth century it housed the courts of Common Pleas, King's Bench and Chancery. It was renovated after the Restoration and the coronation banquet was held there in 1661. In 1666 it contained forty-six shops and booksellers' stalls, and Pepys shopped there for pictures, books and pamphlets, ribbons, gloves and caps.

Centre right: 50. Sedan chairs were first used on London's streets in 1623, and were described as, 'An enclosed chair or covered vehicle for one person, carried on poles by two men.' In January 1641 the Earl of Bedford hired chairs for himself and 'the ladies' from Bedford House, in the Strand, to St Clement Danes church. Pepys made a note in November 1666 that, 'Pierce had hired a chair for my wife', and four months later he wrote that Sir John Winter had 'come in his sedan from the other end of the town'. They had become common in London by the end of the seventeenth century.

Right: 51 Hackney carriages provided the taxi service in seventeenth-century London. They added to the congestion in the streets and so their number was limited and they were closely regulated, but demand for travel within the city was such that the regulations were difficult to enforce.

COFFEE HOUSE JESTS

Printed for Henry Rhodes near Bride lane in Fleet

Left: 52. Coffee-houses were viewed with suspicion in government circles, as places where the governments' critics could meet to discuss affairs and decide on their tactics. But an attempt in 1675 to suppress them failed.

Above: 53. Coffee-houses were first established in London in the mid-1650s and they quickly became places where men could meet friends, do business, exchange news and gossip, talk politics, or just pass the time, enjoying the newly introduced drinks of coffee, chocolate and tea. This broadside of 1677 shows citizens in a coffee-house, chatting, smoking and drinking, from dishes, not cups.

Below: 54. Bridewell was a royal palace, granted to the City of London in 1553 by Edward VI as a workhouse for the poor and vagrants. The buildings were restored after the Great Fire, retaining their external appearance. The journalist Ned Ward *c*.1700 commented facetiously that 'it seemed to me rather a Prince's palace than a House of Correction'. The City used Bridewell as a prison and workhouse, where prisoners were set to work beating hemp, and as a school for orphans and young criminals. The first schoolmaster was appointed in 1675.

THit Excellent, and by all Phyſitians approved, *China* Drink, called by the *Chineans, Teha*, by other Nations *Tay.alias Tee*, is ſold at the *Suitaneſs-head*, a Qopbee- houſe in *Sweetings* Rents by the Royal Exchange, *London*.

Above: 55. This advertisement in *Mercurius Politicus* in 1658 is for the new drink known as tea, which could be bought at Thomas Garraway's coffee-house. It quickly became a popular drink.

Right: 56. The theatres re-opened after the Restoration and within a few months actresses were playing women's roles on the London stage, for the first time. One of the most popular actresses in the 1660s was Nell Gwyn, who was said to have been an orange-seller in the theatre, before she became an actress. She caught the eye of the king and became one of his mistresses, popular with Londoners as an English woman from an ordinary background, in contrast to his French and aristocratic mistresses. This portrait was by Peter Lely.

Below: 57. With the restoration of the monarchy came the revival of the practice of the monarch touching those suffering from scrofula, in the belief that it would heal them. But when the plague struck the practice had to be suspended, to restrict the number of people coming close to the king. An announcement to this effect was placed in *The Intelligencer*.

This is to give notice, That His Majeſty hath declared his poſitive reſolution not to *heal* any more after the end of this preſent *April* until *Michaelmas* next : And this is publiſhed to the end that all Perſons concerned may take notice thereof, and not receive a diſappointment.

London, April 22.

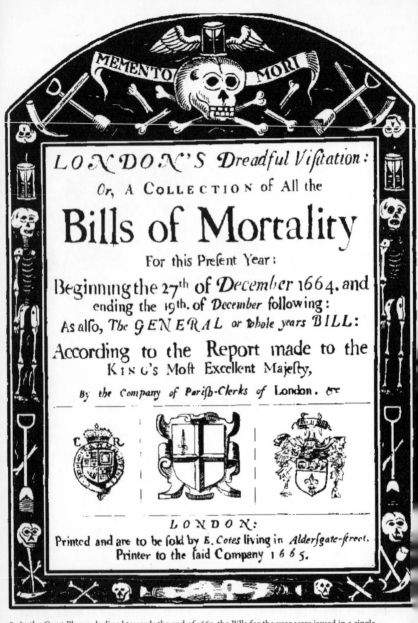

LONDON'S Dreadful Visitation:
Or, A COLLECTION of All the
Bills of Mortality
For this Present Year:

Beginning the 27th of *December* 1664. and ending the 19th. of *December* following: As also, *The* GENERAL *or whole years* BILL:

According to the Report made to the KING's Most Excellent Majesty,

By the Company of Parish-Clerks of London. &c

LONDON:

Printed and are to be sold by E. Cotes living in *Aldersgate-street*. Printer to the said Company 1 6 6 5.

58. As the Great Plague declined towards the end of 1665, the Bills for the year were issued in a single publication.

A generall Bill for this present year,

ending the 19 of *December* 1665 according to the Report made to the KINGS most Excellent Majesty.

By the Company of Parish Clerks of *London*, &c.

	Buried	Pla.		Buried	Pla.		Buried	Pla.		Buried	Pla.
St Albans Woodstreet	200	121	St Clements Eastcheap	38	20	St Margaret Moses	38	25	St Michael Cornehill	104	52
St Alhallowes Barking	514	330	St Dionis Back-church	78	27	St Margar. New Fishst.	114	66	St Michael Crookedla.	179	133
St Alhallowes Breadst	35	16	St Dunstans East	265	130	St Margaret Patrons	49	24	St Michael Queenehi.	203	122
St Alhallowes Great	455	426	St Edmunds Lumbard	70	26	St Mary Abchurch	99	54	St Michael Querne	44	18
St Alhallowes Honilu	10	5	St Ethelborough	195	106	St Mary Aldermanbury	181	109	St Michael Royall	132	116
St Alhall. Lumbardst	239	195	St Faiths	104	70	St Mary Aldermary	105	75	St Michael Woodstreet	122	62
St Alhallowes Lesse	90	62	St Fosters	144	105	St Mary le Bow	64	36	St Mildred Breadstreet	59	26
St Alhallowes Staining	185	112	St Gabriel Fen-church	69	39	St Mary Bothaw	55	30	St Mildred Poultrey	68	46
St Alhall. wes the Wall	500	356	St George Botolphlane	41	27	St Mary Colechurch	17	8	St Nicholas Acons	46	18
St Alphage	271	115	St Gregories by Pauls	376	232	St Mary Hill	94	64	St Nicholas Coleabby	125	91
St Andrew Hubbard	71	25	St Hellens	108	75	St Mary Mounthaw	56	37	St Nicholas Olaves	30	62
St Andrew Vnderstaft	274	189	St James Dukes place	262	190	St Mary Summerset	342	262	St Olaves Hart-streete	237	164
St Andrew Wardrobe	476	308	St James Garlickhithe	189	118	St Mary Stainings	50	33	St Olaves Jewry	54	32
St Anne Aldersgate	282	197	St John Baptist	138	83	St Mary Woolchurch	65	33	St Olaves Silverstreet	250	132
St Anne Blacke-Friers	652	467	St John Euangelist	9		St Mary. Woolnoth	75	37	St Pancras Soperlane	30	13
St Antholins Parish	58	33	St John Zacharie	85	54	St Martins Iremonger.	21	11	St Peters Cheape	61	35
St Austins Parish	43	21	St Katherine Coleman	299	213	St Martins Ludgate	196	128	St Peters Corne-hill.	136	76
St Barthol. Exchange	73	51	St Katherine Creechu.	335	231	St Martins Orgars	110	71	St Peters Pauls Wharfe	114	86
St Bennet Fynch	47	23	St Lawrence Iewrie	94	48	St Martins Outwitch	00	34	St Peters Poore	79	47
St Bennet Grace chur.	57	41	St Lawrence Pountney	214	140	St Martins Vintrey	417	349	St Stevens Colemanst	560	291
St Bennet Pauls Wharf	355	172	St Leonard Eastcheape	42	27	St Matthew Fridayst.	24	6	St Stevens Walbrooke	34	17
St Bennet Sherehog	11	3	St Leonard Fosterlane	335	255	St Maudlins Milkstreet	44	22	St Swithins	93	50
St Botolph Billingsgate	82	39	St Magnus Parish	103	60	St Maudlins Oldfishst.	176	121	St Thomas Apostle	162	110
Christs Church	653	467	St Margaret Lothbury	100	60	St Michael Bassishaw	253	164	Trinitie Parish	115	79
St Christophers	60	47									

Buried in the 97 Parishes within the walls — 15207 VVhereof, of the Plague — 9887

	Buried	Pla.		Buried	Pla.		Buried	Pla.
St Andrew Holborne	3958	3103	Bridewell Precinct	230	179	St Dunstans West	958	665
St Bartholmew Great	493	344	St Botolph Aldersgate	997	755	St George Southwark	1613	1260
St Bartholmew Lesse	193	139	St Botolph Algate	4926	4051	St Giles Cripplegate	8069	4838
St Bridges	2111	1427	St Botolph Bishopsgate	3464	2500	St Olaves Southwark	4793	2785

	Buried	Pla.
St Saviours Southwark	4235	3446
St Sepulchres Parish	4509	2746
St Thomas Southwark	475	371
Trinity Minories	168	122
At the Pesthouse	159	156

Buried in the 16 Parishes without the Walls — 41351 VVhereof, of the Plague — 28888

	Buried	Pla.		Buried	Pla.		Buried	Pla.
St Giles in the Fields	4457	3216	St Katherines Tower	956	601	St Magdalens Bermon.	1943	1362
Hackney Parish	232	132	Lambeth Parish	798	537	St Mary Newington	1272	1004
St James Clarkenwell	1803	1377	St Leonards Shordtich	2669	1949	St Mary Islington	696	593

	Buried	Pla.
St Mary Whitechap.	4766	3855
Redriffe Parish	304	210
Stepney Parish	8598	6583

Buried in the 12 out-Parishes, in Middlesex and Surrey 28554 VVhereof of the Plague 21420

	Buried	Pla.				
St Clement Danes	1969	1319	St Mary Savoy	303	198	
St Paul Covent Garden	408	261	St Margaret Westmin.	4710	3742	**The Total of all the Christnings —— 9967**
St Martins in the Fields	4804	2883	*thereof at the Pesthouse*		156	**The Total of all the Burials this year —— 97306**

Buried in the 5 Parishes in the City and Liberties of Westminster — 11194 VVhereof of the Plague — 8403

Whereof, of the Plague —— 68596

Diseases and Casualties this year.

Disease	Count	Disease	Count	Disease	Count
Abortive and Stillborne	617	Executed	21	Palsie	30
Aged	1545	Flox and Smal Pox	655	Plague	68596
Ague and Feaver	5257	Found dead in streets, fields, &c.	20	Planner	6
Appoplex and Suddenly	116	French Pox	86	Plurisie	15
Bedrid	10	Frighted	23	Poysoned	1
Blasted	5	Gout and Sciatica	27	Quinsie	35
Bleeding	16	Grief	46	Rickets	557
Bloudy Flux, Scowring & Flux	185	Griping in the Guts	1288	Rising of the Lights	397
Burnt and Scalded	8	Hang'd & made away themselves	7	Rupture	34
Calenture	3	Headmouldshot & Mouldfallen	14	Scurvy	105
Cancer, Gangrene and Fistula	56	Jaundies	110	Shingles and Swine pox	2
Canker, and Thrush	111	Impostume	227	Sores, Ulcers, broken and bruised Limbes	82
Childbed	625	Kild by several accidents	46	
Chrisomes and Infants	1258	Kings Evill	86	Spleen	14
Cold and Cough	68	Leprosie	2	Spotted Feaver and Purples	1929
Collick and Winde	134	Lethargy	14	Stopping of the Stomach	332
Consumption and Tissick	4808	Livergrowne	20	Stone and Strangury	98
Convulsion and Mother	2036	Meagrom and Headach	12	Surfet	1251
Distracted	5	Measles	7	Teeth and Worms	2614
Dropsie and Timpany	1478	Murthered, and Shot	9	Vomiting	51
Drowned	50	Overlaid and Starved	45	VVenn	1

	Males	5114			Males	48569		
Christned	Females	4853		Buried	Females	48737	Of the Plague	68596
	In all	9967			In all	97306		

Increased in the Burials in the 130 Parishes and at the Pest-house this year —— 79009

Increased of the Plague in the 130 Parishes and at the Pest-house this year —— 68590

---

59. The figures for the year to 19 December 1665 showed that the number of burials was almost ten times the number of babies christened. The number of plague deaths was put at 68,596, although that was too low, because of inaccurate recording and deception, to conceal some deaths from the disease.

Above left: 60. The costume developed in France and Italy for doctors treating plague victims completely covered the skin, with a long a waxen robe, gloves, boots, and a hood with a mask resembling a bird's beak that was filled with herbs to repel the tainted air. This model is in the Museum de Stratemakerstoren in Nijmegen. London's doctors were criticised for leaving the city during the epidemic.

Above right: 61. In this painting by Florence Reason, entitled *Compassion*, a father who is quarantined with his wife in their house during the Great Plague, passes his daughter to a man who will convey her to safety. It is based upon an incident told to Pepys, that 'a very able citizen', a saddler in Gracechurch Street, all of whose children had died, 'did desire only to save the life of this little child; and so prevailed to have it received stark-naked into the arms of a friend', who took her to Greenwich. She is naked because clothing was thought to harbour the venomous atoms that transmitted plague.

62. The south doorway of St Olave, Hart Street, Pepys's church, shows that, because of the number of burials, the level of the churchyard became much higher than the floor level of the porch and church. The average number of deaths in the parish per year during 1655–64 was 48, but during 1665, the year of the Great Plague, 237 were recorded.

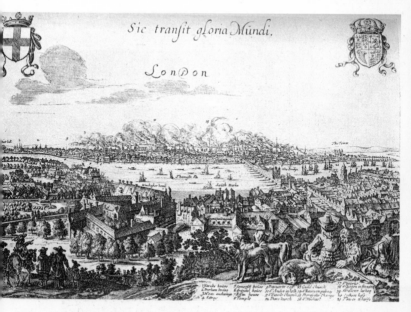

63. & 64. Two German prints depicting the Great Fire, which began in the early hours of 2 September 1666 and continued to burn for four days. The viewpoint is to the south of St Mary Overy's church in Southwark. The prints correctly show the flames and smoke being driven westwards and that the fire had not reached the Tower to the east or beyond the Temple to the west. But of course not all of the area shown would have been in flames at once.

65. The Great Fire, by Lieven Verschuur (1630–86), looking west towards the bridge, with St Paul's beyond. The river is crowded with boats, as the citizens attempted to save those goods which they could carry.

66. The fire attracted attention across Europe. This contemporary German print conveys the scale of the disaster by showing the area between the Tower and the Temple in flames.

Opposite page top: 67. This engraving from a painting by Jan Griffier (*c*.1645–1718) shows the fire burning around Ludgate, with St Paul's in the background, to the right of the gate. The buildings are already ruined, although the figures coming away from the gate are carrying loads containing their goods on their backs. Griffier worked in London from *c*.1672 until 1695.
Opposite page bottom: 68. This illustration of a fire at Tiverton in 1612 shows the practice of fire-fighting, with buckets of water carried up ladders to men trying to douse flames in the roof and on the upper storey, while others are using fire-hooks to pull the roof clear of the building.

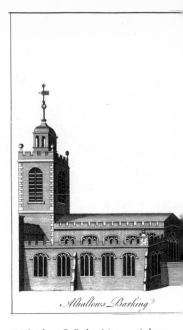

Athallows Barking

Above left: 69. A wall painting in the Royal Exchange by the artist Stanhope R. Forbes (1857–1947) shows Londoners fleeing from the Great Fire into boats on the Thames. It is one of a series by various artists, executed *c*.1900, for the ambulatory of the Royal Exchange, illustrating the history of London.

Above right: 70. The Great Fire destroyed eighty-seven churches. All Hallows, Barking narrowly escaped, as Pepys noted, the flames 'only burned the Dyall of Barkeing Church, and part of the porch'. Pepys climbed its tower on the fourth day of the fire and was appalled by what he saw, and with the fires still burning, 'I became afeared to stay there long; and therefore down again as fast as I could'. The church had been damaged by an explosion in a house across the street in 1650 and its tower was rebuilt in 1659.

71. Philippe Jacques Loutherbourg's painting shows the Great Fire through an arch of London Bridge, with St Paul's in the background. The boats in the foreground are loaded with fleeing families and their possessions. Loutherbourg came to England in 1771 and died in 1812; he was buried at St Nicholas's church, Chiswick.

Reports, and Intelligence of all Countreys. To this I will adde ... the Noble, and
Inquisitive Genius of our Merchants.[57]

Distinguished visitors to London included attendance at the society's
meetings in their itinerary. Cosmo III of Tuscany did so in 1669, and
Magalotti, his secretary, explained in his account that the society:

meets every Thursday after dinner, to take cognizance of matters of natural
philosophy, and for the study and examination of chemical, mechanical, and
mathematical subjects. This Royal Academy took its origin from some philosophers
of London, and was restored in the reign of King Charles II; who (besides his own
inclination) in order to encourage the genius of men of quality (who, at the time that
there was no court in this kingdom, applied themselves diligently to such studies)
established and confirmed it; making himself in fact its founder, by granting it the
most ample privileges.[58]

Sprat emphasised that the society was open to all men, regardless of religion,
nationality and background, citing the example of John Graunt. Aubrey
described Graunt as, 'by Trade, Haberdasher of small-wares, but was free
of the Drapers-Company'. This was no bar to the fellowship, according to
the king: 'His Majesty gave this particular charge to His Society, that if they
found any more such Tradesmen, they should be sure to admit them all
without any more ado'.[59] Pepys, a tailor's son, was elected a fellow in 1665
and its president in 1684.

The metropolis was also a centre of music, although closure of the
theatres in 1642 and the removal of music from church services greatly
reduced the opportunities available for musicians. So did the absence and
then the disintegration of the court. But under the Protectorate regime
music was again required for state occasions. The masque *Cupid and Death*
was performed before the Portuguese ambassador in 1653, with the libretto
by James Shirley and music by Christopher Gibbons and Matthew Locke. A
banquet for the French ambassador Antoine de Bordeaux-Neufville in 1655
was accompanied by splendid vocal and instrumental music.

Recitals were given in the better-off houses, which were open to friends.
Lodewijck Huygens dropped in on one such performance: 'When we
entered they were performing a concerto for organ, which [Christopher]
Gibbons played, bassviol and two violins, one of which was played by the
master of the house, who performed tolerably well. After that they played
another concerto for harpsichord, lute, theorbo, bassviol and violin.'[60]
Domestic music-making became very popular. Roger North later explained
that, 'Musick held up her head, not at Court nor (in the cant of those times)

profane Theaters, but in private society, for many chose rather to fidle at home, than to goe out, and be knockt on the head abroad'.[61] The demand for music was reflected in the popularity of John Playford's publications, beginning with *A Musicall Banquet* and *The (English) Dancing Master*, both of which were issued in 1651, and followed by several others during the 1650s and after the Restoration, some of them going through a number of editions.

In 1657 the Privy Council established a Committee for the Advancement of Musicke, and some musicians petitioned, unsuccessfully, 'That there be a Corporacion or Colledge of Musitians erected in London'. They suggested that its members' functions should be, 'to read and practise publicly all sorts of music, and to suppress the singing of obscene scandalous and defamatory songs and ballads, and to reform the abuses in making of all sorts of instruments of music'.[62] They may have been referring to the music that could be enjoyed at taverns and alehouses, implied in the indictment of Christopher Waters, in 1657. He stood accused of living, 'loosely and idlely, going up and downe from Alehouse to Alehouse, and from Tavern to Tavern to play upon organs and virginalls which are prepared in sundry such houses to delight persons that live loosely and ungodlily to the great dishonour of God'.[63] The Mitre tavern in Fleet Street had a room described by Pepys as the music-room; one winter's day in 1660 he and a friend sat in the room above to listen to the performers, 'where we heard … very plainly, through the ceiling'.[64]

The theatres remained closed during the 1650s, but the ban was challenged by occasional productions, such as Thomas Killigrew's staging of his play *Caracilla* at the Vere Street Theatre in 1653. That was closed down by soldiers, as were attempts to stage plays at the Red Bull theatre over the following two years, but in 1656 Sir William Davenant mounted two productions. In February he and his partner William Cutler invited a number of people to invest in a project to build a theatre 'neare the Charterhowse' for performing 'representations'.[65] The investors provided £275 each and were to receive a one-sixteenth share of the profits, although in 1661 four of them complained that they had been paid nothing. Evidently the theatre was begun but not completed, and so the performances were held in Rutland House in Charterhouse Square. In May Davenant staged *The First Days Entertainment at Rutland-House*, described as a 'Morall Representation' and consisting of dialogues on various historical topics, with music by Henry Cooke, Henry Lawes, Charles Coleman and George Hudson. A few months later Rutland House was the setting for performances of Davenant's *The Siege of Rhodes*, which he described as 'a representation by the Art of perspective in Scenes, And the Story sung in Recitative Musick'. The action centred on the Ottoman defeat of the Knights of St John in 1522; the same composers, with Matthew Locke, supplied the music and the dances were choreographed by Luke Channell, who later became dancing master to the Duke of York's theatre company.[66]

Davenant transferred *The Siege of Rhodes* to the Cockpit Theatre in Drury Lane, which had been wrecked by soldiers in 1649 but restored by William Beeston two years later. In 1658–9 Davenant staged two more operas, *The Cruelty of the Spaniards in Peru* and *The History of Sir Francis Drake*. Davenant's productions were the beginnings of English opera, although not appreciated by everyone. In May 1659 Evelyn was taken by his brother to see an opera, probably *The History of Sir Francis Drake*, and slightingly described it in his diary as 'a new Opera after the Italian way in Recitative Music & Sceanes, much inferior to the Italian composure & magnificence'.[67]

These stirrings were halted by the restored Long Parliament early in 1660. Thomas Lilleston was indicted on the charge that he acted 'a publique stage-play ... in the Cock-Pitt in Drury Lane', and an order was issued 'forbidding Stage-Players to Act'. Davenant remained optimistic, nevertheless, and in March took a lease of 'the new Tennis Court in Lincolnes Inn fields to be ... converted into a Theatre'.[68] His judgement proved to be sound and the restoration of the monarchy was followed by the reopening of London's theatres. In July 1660 Charles II granted to Killigrew and Davenant the right to erect two playhouses, and suppress all others, effectively giving them a monopoly of theatre productions.

They established separate companies, Davenant at the Lincoln's Inn Fields Theatre, converted from the tennis court, where in November he established a company under the patronage of James, Duke of York, known as the Duke's Men. The building was adapted as an Italianate theatre, with the first proscenium arch behind an apron stage in England. The auditorium had a 'broad space' for the audience at ground level and an upper level of boxes for the ladies and gentlemen. Davenant also introduced completely movable scenery, which eventually was to replace painted backgrounds in the London theatres. This was commented on by Magalotti: 'The scenery is entirely interchangeable, with various transformations and lovely perspectives.' Sorbière also commented on the scenery: 'the Stage is very handsome, being covered with Green Cloth, and the Scenes often change, and you are regaled with new Perspective'.[69]

Davenant opened his new theatre on 28 June 1661 with a performance of the first part of *The Siege of Rhodes*. Later that year Thomas Betterton took the title role in *Hamlet* and Davenant also staged a production of *Romeo and Juliet*. Magalotti described the theatre as:

nearly of a circular form, surrounded, in the inside, by boxes separated from each other, and divided into several rows of seats, for the greater accommodation of the ladies and gentlemen, who, in conformity with the freedom of the country, sit together indiscriminately; a large space being left on the ground-floor for the rest of the audience.

According to Sorbière, 'the best Places are in the Pit, where Men and Women promiscuously sit, every Body with their Company'.[70]

Killigrew attracted the king's patronage, with a grant in July 1660 permitting him 'to erect one Company of players which shall be our owne Company'.[71] The King's Company initially used the Vere Street Theatre, opened on 8 November with a production of *Henry IV Part I*. This was effectively the first theatre royal. Later that month Pepys described it as 'the finest play-house, I believe, that ever was in England'. The earliest recorded instance of actresses on an English stage was in a performance of *Othello* in this theatre a month later, on 8 December, probably with Margaret Hughes as Desdemona. Not for another few weeks did Pepys see an actress, until he attended a performance of John Fletcher and Philip Massinger's play *The Beggar's Bush* at Vere Street, on 3 January, when he wrote that this was 'the first time that ever I saw Women come upon the stage'.[72] But the building was unsatisfactory, especially as it lacked provision for scenery, and Davenant was mounting attractive productions with scenery at Lincoln's Inn Fields.

Plans for a new theatre, off Drury Lane, began in December 1661 and a lease was obtained from the Earl of Bedford, which specified that a theatre should be built by Christmas 1662, costing at least £1,500. In fact, the cost was £2,500 and the new Theatre Royal was not opened until 7 May 1663. Because the plot of ground was small, so was the theatre, probably holding between 700 and 1,000 patrons. There was provision for scenery, but the building's size was restrictive and in 1666 the stage was widened. Nor was the approach agreeable, through a narrow passage. Thomas Rugg described it as being 'in the back side of Bridges street in Covent Garden'.[73]

Among the shareholders was Sir Robert Howard, John Dryden's brother-in-law, and Dryden wrote a number of plays for the company. Nell Gwyn was said to have been an orange seller at the theatre, in 1663, but she soon became an actress and in the mid-1660s developed a stage partnership in comedies with the actor Charles Hart, which gave the theatre a distinctive identity.

The theatres attracted a broad social range of patrons, from the royal brothers, courtiers, gentry, professional men and civil servants such as Pepys and his friends, to the citizens. Schellinks saw eleven plays between 9 December 1661 and 4 April 1662, during his visit to London. Pepys was a regular and enthusiastic patron, going to the theatre no less than seventy-three times in the first eight months of 1668. From the reopening of the theatres in 1660 until the close of the diary period in May 1669, he saw or mentioned more than 140 plays, some in more than one production. They were broadly divided into the 'old' plays, from before the closing of the theatres in 1642, and the new ones. Shakespeare, Beaumont, Fletcher, Jonson and Dryden were the playwrights whose works he saw most often. Some of the 'new' plays were rude, and Pepys did not always approve. When he saw Dryden's comedy *An Evening's Love, or The Mock Astrologer*, he wrote: 'I … do not like it, being very smutty'.[74] Evelyn was far more censorious, complaining that in London, 'there are more wretched and obscene plays permitted than in all the world besides'.[75]

As a regular theatre-goer, Pepys was sensitive to changes in the composition of the audience. On 27 December 1662 he was at a performance of *The Siege of Rhodes* at the Lincoln's Inn Fields theatre, and wrote: 'not so well pleased with the company at the house today, which was full of citizens, there hardly being a gentleman or woman in the house'. Just a few days later he made a similar comment: 'The house was full of Citizens and so the less pleasant.' When he was at Lincoln's Inn Fields on 1 January 1668, he recalled the time when he could afford only the cheaper places, 1s and then 1s 6d, for the upper and middle galleries and he noted that, 'Here a mighty company of citizens, prentices and others … I do not remember that I saw so many by half of the ordinary prentices and mean people in the pit, at 2s-6d apiece, as now'. The highest price was 4s, for a seat in a box.[76] The performances at which Pepys noted the unusual number of citizens were during holidays, which may explain why so many were there, but thirty years later Misson wrote that in the two theatres, 'The galleries, whereof there are only two Rows, are fill'd with none but ordinary People, particularly the Upper one'.[77]

Some people avoided payment altogether, by crowding in to the auditorium, especially to see the last two acts of a play. This prompted a royal order, in 1663:

> Whereas Wee are informed that diverse persons doe rudely presse & with evill Language & blowes force theire wayes into the two Theatres … without payinge the prices Established … wee doe hereby straytly … Comand that noe person of what quality soever presume rudely or by force to come into either of the two Theatres till the playes are quite finished without paying the prices Established for the respective places … Nothwithstanding theire pretended priveledg by Custome of forceing theire entrance at the fourth or fifth Acts without payment.[78]

This and other reports give the impression that the Restoration theatres were rowdy and perhaps intimidating places, but Pepys regularly took Elizabeth along and she sometimes went without him, with her maid and perhaps with friends. It may be that disorderly behaviour which disrupted a performance was the exception rather than the rule, but of course more likely to be reported.

Music also revived after the Restoration. The king re-established the King's Musick in June 1660, the Chapel Royal was re-created and each theatre allocated a band of twelve musicians. Both Sorbière and Magalotti were impressed by the performances that preceded a play. According to Sorbière, 'The Musick with which you are entertained diverts your time till the Play begins, and People chuse to go in betimes to hear it.' Magalotti's comment was similar: 'Before the comedy begins, that the audience may not be tired with waiting, the most delightful symphonies are played; on which account many persons come early to enjoy this agreeable amusement.'[79]

The revival of music in the theatre did not reduce domestic music-making, which was one of Pepys's great pleasures. The musical-instrument makers that he frequented included a harpsichord-maker in Bishopsgate Street and, in Aldgate Street, 'one Hayward that makes viginalls'. In 1668 he ordered from Hayward 'a little Espinettes [spinet]', as smaller, and so more convenient, than a harpsichord. Woodwind instruments could be bought without pre-ordering; Pepys acquired his flageolets from a Mr Drumbleby, from whom, in 1668, he also bought a recorder, 'which I do intend to learn to play on, the sound of it being of all sounds in the world most pleasing to me'.[80] He drew attention to the popularity of domestic music when he noted, while watching boats being loaded during the Great Fire, that 'hardly one lighter or boat in three that had the goods of a house in, but there was a pair of virginalls in it'.[81]

A range of pastimes and pleasures was available to Londoners, both during the Interregnum and after the Restoration. Coffee-houses added to the places where people could socialise, while domestic concerts and the beginnings of English opera made the 1650s a period of innovation in music. The reopening of the theatres added to the entertainment available, for a wide social range. And so Londoners and those members of the gentry who chose to spend part of the year in the capital could enjoy various popular, cultural and intellectual activities. But their social life would be disrupted by an outbreak of plague.

5

Population & Plague

Londoners were not without their anxieties, despite the city's prospering economy and lively social life. The risk of accident or disease, the possibility of losing children or spouse, were ever-present worries, while plague was a potential and major danger, especially when it was ravaging countries on the near continent. The older citizens could remember the great plague epidemic of 1625 and the outbreak in 1636, and would have been aware that the relatively few deaths from that most feared of diseases in recent years offered no sure guide to the future.

John Graunt addressed some of those concerns in his analysis of the causes of deaths in London during the middle of the century. He showed that the biggest single killer, as categorised in the Bills of Mortality, was 'consumption and cough', which accounted for 19 per cent of deaths, followed by strokes and 'sudden' deaths (10 per cent) and old age (almost 7 per cent). Graunt estimated that a little over a third of deaths were of children under six years old. This was not precise, as the age of death was not given; he reached his conclusion by combining figures for causes of death that commonly related to children. He could be more certain of his figures for those conditions of which 'many persons live in great fear and apprehension'. The largest numbers in that category were attributed to apoplexy, jaundice, bladder and kidney stones, and lethargy (possibly depression or a symptom of another underlying cause), but all of those which he included under that heading accounted for only one quarter of one per cent. There were even fewer deaths from accidents, violence and suicide. The largest number in this group was caused by mishaps, such as 'falls from Scaffolds, or by Carts running over them', and drowning, which together caused an average of ninety-two deaths per year, while eleven people 'hanged themselves'.[1]

Graunt was also at pains to demonstrate that there were comparatively few murders in such a large city, whereas in Paris 'few nights scape without their Tragedy'. This he attributed partly to the conscientiousness of the watchmen and the nature of the office, because of 'the Government and

Guard of the City by the Citizens themselves, and that alternately. No man setling into a Trade for that employment.' He also believed that it was due to the 'natural and customary abhorrence of that inhuman Crime, and all Bloodshed, by most English men'. When a body was discovered, 'every common unconcerned person' was at pains to track down the murderers, who were then indicted.[2]

In March 1651 William and Mary Ardington assaulted Thomas Tisdale at Gray's Inn and she, 'with a knife cut the neck and throat of the said Thomas Tisdale esq., so that he then and there died instantly'. Another murder occurred in 1655, in St Martin's-in-the-Fields, when Daniell Connell, 'assaulted Anne Allen and did kill and slay her by shooting her with a pistol, charged with gunpowder and a leaden bullet, thereby giving her a mortal bullet-wound in her right breast, of which she died'. A few months later Sir Thomas Wortley was shot dead in the same parish.[3] Quarrels in the streets could lead to violence and death. In November 1660 Pepys wrote that, 'in King-streete, there being a great stop of coaches, there was a falling-out between a drayman and my Lord Chesterfield's coachman, and one of his footmen killed'.[4] Nor was it safe on the Thames. According to Schellinks: 'It was very unsafe to travel by night on the river because of the river pirates, who attack the boats going up and down river and beat up the passengers, demanding their money; the Lord Mayor's waterman was sitting with some other in gaol for such an offence.'[5]

Despite such incidents and fears, between 1647 and 1658 only 57 murders were recorded in the Bills of Mortality, fewer than five per year. The number then rose sharply, with 70 in 1659 and 20 in 1660. Those were unusually disorderly years because of the political turmoil, and the deaths during the clashes between the citizens and soldiers were categorised as unlawful. London was not an especially dangerous city. Graunt pointed out that there were more executions than murders because several types of crime attracted the death penalty. Even so, the number of executions averaged only 21 per year between 1647 and 1658.

Visitors were interested in English justice and commented on public executions. Smithfield was the preferred place for deaths by burning in London, a form of execution imposed for heresy, arson, poisoning, witchcraft, sodomy and bestiality, and for women guilty of high treason or murdering their husbands. The last person burned in England for religious beliefs was executed in 1612, but burning of prisoners condemned for other crimes continued to be carried out. In 1662 Schellinks was there to see, 'a young woman, who had stabbed her husband to death with a tobacco pipe, being burned alive at the stake … She was put with her feet into a sawn-through tar barrel and made fast behind to the stake with an iron chain under her arms and round her breast.' Faggots were piled around her and one placed on her head, but it was normal practice to attach a gunpowder charge to the victim, to ensure a quick death. On this occasion, 'Nobody could see whether she had any gunpowder around her, neither was she strangled nor otherwise.' In the following year he went to Southwark one day when executions were scheduled and found there 'a great crowd of people'.[6]

An execution that attracted widespread, indeed international, attention was that of Don Pantaleon Sa, the Portuguese ambassador's brother, in July 1654. One evening in the previous November, while walking in the New Exchange in the Strand, he was 'accidentally jostled there by an English gentleman'. His response was violent: 'the Portuguese in a great rage, drew his sword' and a skirmish ensued, during which his intended victim was rescued by another man. On the following day he returned seeking revenge, with as many as fifty well-armed companions. They spotted someone in the gallery of the building, whom they mistakenly identified as one of those they had fought the previous evening. This man, Colonel Mayo, they attacked, 'who, very gallantly defending himself, received seven dangerous wounds, and lies in a mortal condition. They fell also upon one Mr. Greenway, of Lincoln's Inn … and pistoled him in the head, whereof he died immediately.' This was so alarming that, 'The affrighted tradesmen all took refuge in their shops and the Portuguese remained masters of the whole of Britain's Bourse, until the news reached the horse guards.'[7]

The Portuguese then sought sanctuary in their embassy, but eventually Don Pantaleon and four companions, with an English boy who was his servant, were arrested. They were charged with the murder of Greenway and Mayo, who had died of his wounds. Don Pantaleon claimed diplomatic immunity, as a member of the ambassador's household, but the judge, Henry Rolle, rejected this and informed him that if he did not enter a plea he would be pressed to death with weights. He then pleaded not guilty, but the jury brought in a guilty verdict. Don Pantaleon and his servant were executed; two other members of his entourage had their sentence commuted to imprisonment. The case attracted much attention because of the ruling that being a member of an envoy's household or one of his relatives did not confer legal immunity.

A rumour of another case involving a member of an ambassador's household was recorded by Henry Townshend. A servant of the Russian ambassador went into a mercer's shop and looked over the silk and other materials, then took a piece of silk, concealed it under his gown and left. The mercer suspected what he had done and followed him to his lodgings. Having identified the culprit:

the mercer went to the ambassador to demand money for the silk his servant bought of him, he answered he knew nothing of it nor given any such command. But he would call all his servants in and then he should see which it was, so all being called this servant came in with the rest, and the mercer said he was the man. The ambassador demanded of his servant whether he took such a piece of silk, stood little amazed, and could not well deny. So he was bid to fetch it, which done, the ambassador invited the mercer to dinner to come some five days after, and then he should have full reparation, which he did. And at the second course there was presented his servant's head in a charger. And then the ambassador told that this was the law in their country and bade him take it for satisfaction with his goods again. Great and strange justice.

This ending to the affair, an execution carried out in private by the ambassador's direction, may not have been an isolated case, for during the visit of the Moroccan ambassador in 1682 it was reported that, 'A servant having offended him he threatened to cut off his head, but some English gentlemen interposing he was reconciled to him.'[8]

The bodies of some of those executed were claimed by the Barber-Surgeons Company, for dissection. In February 1663 Pepys was invited to a lecture at their hall, 'upon the Kidnys, Ureters, and yard [penis]'. Afterwards he was shown the body that had been the exhibit for the lecture, which was that of 'a lusty fellow, a seaman that was hanged for a robbery'.[9] Medical research was progressing in a number of fields, the city contained many apothecaries' shops and the lay public was able to prepare treatments after the publication, in 1649, of an English edition of the College of Physicians' *Pharmacopoeia Londinensis*. This had hitherto been available only in Latin and the new edition contained many additional prescriptions. It was issued by Nicholas Culpeper, and in 1652 he followed this with *The English Physitian*, which came to be better known as *Culpeper's Complete Herbal*. Culpeper's works made treatments and remedies available for many conditions and diseases, including plague.

Graunt described plague as 'that greatest Disease or Casualty of all', and it generated more fear than any other, not only because of the number of deaths which it caused, but also as a reaction to its very nature.[10] Those unlucky enough to contract bubonic plague complained of headaches, which were quickly followed by a fever and vomiting. Extremely painful blotches or carbuncles developed, caused by haemorrhaging beneath the skin, and the lymph nodes in the groin and armpits and on the neck began to swell, forming buboes. The pain was so excruciating that some victims became uncontrollable and delirious, screaming and running madly around the streets. When someone developed a 'Botch, or Purple, or Swelling in any part of his body', or even 'falleth otherwise dangerously sick, without apparent cause of some other disease', then plague was suspected and the case had to be reported within two hours.[11]

This was part of the regulations developed to control the disease, by identifying its presence as early as possible. Indeed, that was the purpose of the Bills of Mortality, distinguishing plague deaths from others, so that the existence and spread of the disease could be monitored and regulations implemented. Yet there was no agreement on whether plague was caused by stagnant and foul-smelling air, which harboured the venomous atoms believed to carry the disease, or was contagious, spreading from person to person. Many thought that the disease was spread by the atoms attaching themselves to rough surfaces and objects, such as textiles and bread. It seemed to thrive in districts with overcrowded and dirty living conditions, and contemporaries regarded it as a disease that afflicted and tormented the poor. But they were tied to their place of work and did not have the means to move away, to a less infected area or out of the city altogether, while the better-off could do so, and so suffered lower levels of mortality.

The plague orders included measures covering both possibilities, attempting to ensure cleanliness in the streets and households by the frequent removal of garbage and manure, and the isolation of victims as soon as the disease was suspected. They were to be taken to the pest-houses, or plague hospitals. But London did not invest in the large pest-houses erected by some continental cities, and so as an epidemic developed they were inadequate to take the numbers infected and household quarantine was imposed.

Household quarantine had become a major, yet controversial, element in the policies adopted to prevent the spread of the disease. If plague was confirmed, the victims were confined to their houses, together with everyone else who was there at the time, even those who had just dropped in for a visit. The houses were then marked with a cross and the chilling inscription 'Lord have mercy upon us' and kept closed for at least twenty-eight days, which was favoured in London, although the full forty-day quarantine was preferred by the government. And this could be extended, if, for example, someone who had contact with those in a closed house during the period was diagnosed with plague; the full term would have to be served, starting from the date of the new contact. Not surprisingly, the policy required strict enforcement to ensure that those confined within the houses stayed there, including armed warders to guard them. When a house was to be closed on suspicion of an occupant being infected, it had to be done quickly, so that those inside would not run away and spread the infection, defeating the purpose of the policy. And so householders had little or no time to prepare for their incarceration and may have had only a small stock of food, and of course would immediately be thrown out of work. The parish officers had to arrange for a steady supply of provisions, or those inside would break out rather than patiently starve. Families that could afford to pay for their own upkeep did so, but others had to depend on food supplied by the parish authorities.

During the seventeenth century, prevention had become the preferred policy, excluding the disease by controlling shipping. Plague was a disease of the trade routes, with the eastern Mediterranean the region from which it was dispersed over the continent. Epidemics in London followed outbreaks of plague in Amsterdam and the other port cities in northern Europe with which it had trading connections. In the mid-seventeenth century this pattern was broken, with the enforcement of the quarantining of incoming vessels, which seemed to have protected London successfully. Many cities in northern and western Europe suffered outbreaks of plague from the late 1620s until the mid-1650s, yet London escaped relatively lightly. It endured an epidemic in 1636 and minor outbreaks during the 1640s, but very few plague deaths were recorded in the 1650s. By the early 1660s it had been free from a major epidemic for almost forty years and when the disease appeared at Amsterdam and Hamburg in 1663 the Privy Council acted promptly and again put the quarantining of shipping in place. Vessels, their crews and passengers were held at Canvey Island for forty days and their cargoes opened and aired. There were only nine plague deaths in London in 1663 and just five in 1664, and the risk of infection from Holland apparently declined, as diplomatic relations worsened and both countries kept their merchant shipping in port, in preparation for war, which was declared in February 1665.

But in the autumn of 1664 plague deaths were reported in London. There was no need to panic, a few cases of plague did not make an epidemic, almost every year there were a few deaths from the disease, no epidemic had ever erupted during the winter, and that winter was a cold one. William Boghurst, who lived in St Giles-in-the-Fields, wrote in his account of the Great Plague that the most common disease in his parish in 1664 was smallpox, with about forty families affected, although he did admit that, 'The plague hath put itself forth in St. Giles's, St. Clement's, St. Paul's, Covent Garden, and St. Martin's this 3 or 4 yeares, as I have been certainly informed by the people themselves that had it in their houses in those Parishes.' As an apothecary who was prepared to go into the houses of the sick to administer medicines, he was well placed to know, and his account is more dependable than the figures in the Bills, because plague deaths often were concealed. He also wrote that, 'the Plague began first at the West end of the City, as at St. Giles's and St. Martin's, Westminster'.[12]

It appeared again in the spring of 1665 which, at that time of the year, was a more worrying development, as the disease commonly was at its most virulent from then until the late autumn. On 26 April the Privy Council noted that, 'the Plague is broken out, or vehemently suspected to bee, in some houses within the parish of St Giles in the fields, and other out parishes'. It reacted sharply to an incident which reflected the citizens' hostility to household quarantine: 'That the house, the Signe of the Ship in the New buildings, in St Giles in the fields, was shutt up as suspected to bee Infected with the Plague, & a Crosse and paper fixed, on the doore; And That the said Cross & paper were taken off, & the doore opened, in a rioutous manner, & the people of the house permitted, to goe abroad into the street promiscuously, with others.' The council ordered the Lord Chief Justice and the Justices of the Peace to discover, 'the offendors in the said Ryott, And inflict ... the severest punishments, the Rigor of the Law, will allow, against offendors in accons of soe dangerous a Consequence; And soe much to the contempt of his Ma[jes]ties orders as theese'.[13]

Despite the close attention of the government and the justices in the outbreak's early stages, the disease spread, although not rapidly at first. In May Thomas Rugg noted in his journal that, 'The playes [are] thronged with people of all sorts and sizes.'[14] When Samuel Herne wrote from London to his tutor in Cambridge, in the middle of July, he claimed that 'nobody that is in London feares to goe anywhere but in st giles's'. But he also mentioned that he 'went by many houses in London that were shut up; all over the city almost'. By that time the court had moved away and many others were leaving: 'the citizens begin to shut up apace; nothing hinders them from it but fear of the houses breaking open'.[15] As early as the middle of June Pepys had noted that, 'The town grows very sickly and people to be afeared of it', and on the 21st he was in Cripplegate, 'where I find all the town almost going out of town, the coaches and wagons being all full of people going into the country'.[16] During July, 1,800 families left London, according to Rugg, and when Pepys took a coach across the city from Whitehall to Seething Lane, on 22 July, he passed 'but two coaches and but two carts ... and the streets mighty thin of people'.[17]

He had begun to be concerned several weeks before. On 7 June, 'much against my Will, I did in Drury-lane see two or three houses marked with a red cross upon the doors, and "Lord have mercy upon us" writ there – which was a sad sight to me, being the first of that kind that to my remembrance I ever saw'. Hitherto the plague had been reported in the outer parishes, close to St Giles. However, just three days later he noted in his diary that after a busy afternoon at the office, 'In the evening home to supper, and there to my great trouble hear that the plague is come into the City ... but where should it begin but in my good friend and neighbour's Dr. Burnett in Fanchurch-street – which in both points troubles me mightily.' And just a week after hearing that disconcerting news he may have had a closer encounter with the dreaded disease, when travelling in a hackney coach along Holborn: 'the coachman I found to drive easily and easily; at last stood still, and came down hardly able to stand; and told me that he was suddenly stroke very sick and almost blind, he could not see. So I light and went into another coach, with a sad heart for the poor man and trouble for myself, least he should have been stroke with the plague.'[18]

The sense of an unfolding catastrophe did not have to come from such impressions, for the Bills provided numerical evidence, as they were designed to do. They showed that by the first week in July plague deaths were recorded in 40 parishes and in the following week they were more than a half of the total deaths, for the first time. In the first week in August 86 parishes recorded plague deaths and during the week of 12–19 September the figure was 126; virtually the entire city. That was the worst week of the epidemic, with 8,297 deaths from all causes, 7,165 of them attributed to plague.[19] The numbers of plague deaths were treated with a degree of scepticism. Because of the rigours that the policy of household quarantine imposed on individuals, households and the parish administrations, there was a strong incentive to conceal the true cause of death. The searchers who diagnosed the cause were typically elderly women who had experience of the symptoms from earlier outbreaks. The task was not carried out by members of the medical profession, many of whom had left London. Searchers were liable to come under pressure to record a death as being caused by another disease, such as 'spotted fever', so that the house would not be closed, and the parish not compelled to provide guards and provisions. Or perhaps the parish clerk made a false return when he submitted his figures. The clerk in Pepys's own parish of St Olave, Hart Street admitted to such a practice when, 'upon my asking how the plague goes, he told me it encreases much, and much in our parish: "For", says he, "there died nine this week, though I have returned but six" – which is a very ill practice, and makes me think it so in other places, and therefore the plague much greater then people take it to be.' The deaths of sextons and clerks also 'hindered the exact account every week', as the Earl of Clarendon recognised.[20]

The Venetian ambassador was moved by the impact of the disaster, but at the same time was sceptical of the figures in the Bills. Towards the end of July he wrote to Venice that:

The plague is spreading with such rapidity in London that it moves to pity. In some parishes so many are dying that they take carts through the streets crying 'Bring out your dead, bring out your dead' and when the carts are full they take the bodies to be buried in a ditch a short distance from London. Of all ailments 1761 have died this week in the city and suburbs of London, of whom all, except 200 or 250 may reasonably be considered to have died of the plague, although the bulletins only confess to 1089.

For the first week in August the Bill reported 4,030 deaths, of which 2,817 were from plague. But he thought that the true number of plague deaths was, 'according to the reasonable opinion of intelligent persons at least 3700'.[21]

John Evelyn noted round numbers in his diary. When the disease was at its peak, in September, he wrote that, 'there perishing now neere ten-thousand poore Creatures weekely: however I went all along the Citty & suburbs from Kent streete to St. James's, a dismal passage & dangerous, tosee so many Cofines exposed in the streetes & the streete thin of people, the shops shut up, & all in mournefull silence, as not knowing whose turne might be next'.[22] Pepys had remained at his desk in London, although sending Elizabeth and her maid to Woolwich for safety. He was told of the deaths of people known to him, such as 'poor Will that used to sell us ale at the Hall-door' at Westminster, and he drafted his will, because 'a man cannot depend upon living two days to an end'. In the middle of August he commented, 'how sad a sight it is to see the streets empty of people, and very few upon the Change [Exchange] – jealous of every door that one sees shut up, lest it should be the plague – and about us, two shops in three, if not more, generally shut up'. A fortnight later the sense of depopulation struck him once more: 'how few people I see, and those walking like people that had taken leave of the world'.[23]

The dislocation and privations that the epidemic brought in its train were apparent to the authorities before the end of July, when the Archbishop of Canterbury, Gilbert Sheldon, sent out an appeal for charitable collections to provide help for the citizens:

to be imployed for the succour of the miserably distressed in and about this greate Citye in the wellfare whereof the wellbeing of all the Nation is allmost wholly involved And whose Calamity is farr more to be pityed than any elswhere, Not only by the raging of the Infection but even for the very want of Necessaries for life, Many perishing that way which otherwise might have escaped the danger, And many thousands of poore Artisans being ready to starve for Lacke of Meanes to be imployed in their Callings All Trading being become dangerous and layd aside by reason of the spreading of the Contagion.[24]

Most citizens remained in London, trying to limit the risk by avoiding others as far as possible, walking in the centre of the street to evade the poisonous fumes coming out of houses, not entering a shop if another customer was there, and not handling money unless it had been dipped in vinegar. Some physicians, clergymen and justices left and were roundly criticised for doing so, but others stayed at their posts. They included Sheldon and the Bishop of London, Humphrey Henchman, Monck, now Duke of Albermarle, and the Earl of Craven. So, too, did Sir John Lawrence, the lord mayor, who, 'being very fearful about the plague has caused a cabinet to be made, entirely of glass, in which he gives audience and determines the affairs of the city'.[25]

But those who remained to direct affairs were unable to enforce all of the plague orders. In particular, the system of household quarantine collapsed in those parishes which simply could not cope with the scale of the disaster. John Tillison, Clerk of Works at St Paul's, wrote on 15 August that in St Giles, Cripplegate, 'all have liberty least their sick and poor should be famished within doors; the parish not being able to relieve their necessities'.[26] The collection of the special rate to provide funds for those incarcerated was so difficult that it did not produce enough money for the parish to be able to maintain them. Not only were the collectors afraid of going into those neighbourhoods where the disease was prevalent, but many of the better-off, who paid much of the rate, had gone away. This became a general problem, especially in the populous parishes around the fringes of the City, where the mortality rate was very high. Pepys admitted that when he was at the Exchange in the middle of September, 'I did endeavour all I could to talk with as few as I could, there being now no observation of shutting up of houses infected'. Thomas Vincent, a nonconformist minister ejected from his parish in 1662, stayed in the city and he wrote that the 'shutting up of visited-houses (there being so many) is at an end, and most of the well are mingled among the sick, which otherwise would have got no help'. The upshot was that, 'we could hardly go forth, but we should meet many coffins, and see diseased persons with sores and limping in the streets'.[27] In the middle of August John Sturgeon described how the sick could be encountered in the streets: 'Heare you may mett on pale ghost muffled up under the throat, another dragging his legs after him by reason of the tumor of his groyne, another bespotted with the tokens of instant death'.[28]

Nor was it possible to enforce the order that burials should be carried out during the hours of darkness. The summer nights were too short and the number of corpses too many for this to be practical. In early August Pepys made a note in his diary that, 'The people die so, that now it seems they are fain to carry the dead to be buried by daylight, the nights not sufficing to do it in'.[29] Stephen Bing, a Minor Canon of St Paul's, wrote that in the middle of September, 'The custom was, in the beginning, to bury the dead in the night only; now, both night and day will hardly be time enough to do it. For the last week, mortality did too apparently evidence that, that the dead was piled in heaps above ground for some hours together, before either time could be gained or place to bury them in.'[30] Burial in single graves had been abandoned and corpses were deposited in pits; Sturgeon wrote dramatically that, 'Carts are the beeres, wide pits are the graves.'[31] In St Giles-in-the-Fields the sexton, John Geere, supervised the excavation of five large pits in the churchyard, and in them were placed almost 1,400 corpses. Clarendon was exasperated by the failure to maintain the regulations on burials, and especially allowing mourners to attend, because bringing people together in a group at a plague burial, 'must infecte the whole kingdome, and ought to be restrayned by the Magistrates, by all force & rigour'.[32]

Among those who stayed in the city was John Pack, in Thames Street, who was advised by his business partner Edward Wood to: 'Lock upp the Dores, & shun the danger what you can & to goe abroad as litle as may be.' They dealt in sugar, oats, barley, spices and fruit, and although Wood thought that 'every man is bound to use the meanes for his preservation in this sad visitation', he did not entirely close down their business, recommending that Pack should buy coal when the price was low.[33] Henry Oldenburg, in Pall Mall, followed a similar pattern to that recommended by Wood: 'I strive to banish both fear and overconfidence, leading a regular life and avoiding infected places as much as I can.'[34] By contrast, John Allin, who lived in Horsleydown, was thoroughly alarmed by early August, when he wrote: 'I am troubled at the approach of the sicknesse nearer every weeke, and at a new burying place wch they have made neere us, and with some piece of indiscretion used in not shutting up, but rather makeing great funerals for such as dye of the distemper.' He was also unsettled by 'the doelfull and almost universall and continuall ringing and tolling of bells', and the death of someone who he described as 'the best friend I have in the world'. Despite such anxieties, he stayed through the whole year. Stephen Bing, too, was troubled by the bells, which 'never cease to put us in mind of our mortality'.[35]

William Taswell went to London at the height of the epidemic, where, 'death stared me in the face; but it pleased God to extricate me from the danger which threatened me'. He visited a house belonging to Mrs Harrison, 'who was the only survivor of her whole family (seven children)'. At his father's house, 'a good old faithful servant named Johanna ... was seized with the plague and recovered, only one man-servant with her in the house dying'.[36]

Thomas Vincent had even closer brushes with the plague, having seen, 'some in their phrenzy, rising out of their beds, and leaping about their rooms; others crying and roaring at their windows; some coming forth almost naked, and running into the streets'. He described two cases in particular:

> one of a woman coming alone, and weeping, by the door where I lived (which was in the midst of infection) with a little coffin under her arm, carrying it to the new church-yard: I did judge that it was the mother of the child, and that all the family besides was dead, and she was forced to carry the coffin up, and bury with her own hands, this her last dead child. Another, was of a man at the corner of the Artillery wall, that, as I judge, through the dizziness of his head with the disease, which seized upon him there, had dashed his face against the wall, and when I cam by, he lay hanging with his bloody face over the rails, and bleeding upon the ground; and as I came back, he was removed under a tree in Moorfields, and lay upon his back; I went and spake to him; he could make me no answer, but rattled in the throat, and, as I was informed, within half an hour died in the place.[37]

For over a month scarcely a day passed without Vincent hearing of the death of someone he knew, and of the sixteen or more people he was used to seeing in his house, within a short time only four, five or six of them were still alive. Eight people lived in the house: three men, three youths, an old woman and a maid. They were free of the disease until late September, but then, one Monday:

> our maid was smitten, it began with a shivering and trembling in her flesh, and quickly seized on her spirits … on Thursday she died full of tokens: on Friday one of the youths had a swelling in his groin; and on the Lord's day died with the marks of the distemper upon him: on the same day another youth did sicken, and on the Wednesday following he died: on the Thursday night his master fell sick of the disease, and within a day or two was full of spots, but strangely beyond his own, and others expectations, recovered.[38]

Others survived the disease. In early September Simon Patrick, rector of St Paul's, Covent Garden, saw 'about 30 People in the Strand, with white Sticks in their Hands, & the Dr of the Pest House walking in his gowne before them. The first Woman rid on a Horse, & had a Paper Flag on top of her Stick, with Laus Deo written on it. They were going to the Iustices, being poore People sent thither, & recovered by him of the Plague. He seemed to take no small Content in his stately March before them.' A range of nostrums was available; Patrick had been sent 'plague water' to drink as a preventative, and 'Dr Michael Thwayle directed to make, & drink presently of London Treacle & Lady Allen's Water. I bought both presently, but forgot to mix them. Only now and then I take a little Treacle.'[39] Boghurst recommended someone who was to visit a plague victim to, 'first drink half a pint of sack or hold a clove or peece of a Nutmeg in your mouth, or Zeodary, Elicompane, and fear not to goe to him and doe your business'. Sack was a dry wine and a popular drink at the time, and zeodary and elecampane are herbs.[40] The London Treacle mentioned by Patrick was a favoured concoction, in which a blend of herbs was mixed in a solution of three parts Malaga wine and one part honey, with a dram of opium. Smoking or chewing tobacco was also believed to keep the disease at bay, as was syphilis, although that was in itself likely to prove fatal.

Pepys summarised his experiences during the plague in a letter to Lady Elizabeth Carteret, written on 4 September:

> The absence of the Court and emptiness of the city takes away all occasion of news, save only such melancholy stories as would rather sadden than find your Ladyship any divertisement in the hearing; I having stayed in the city till above 7400 died in one week, and of them above 6000 of the plague, and little noise heard day nor night but tolling of bells; till I could walk Lumber-street [Lombard Street] and not meet twenty persons from one end to the other, and not fifty upon the Exchange; till whole families (ten or twelve together) have been swept away; till my very physician, Dr. Burnet, who undertook to secure me against any infection (having survived the month of his own being shut up) died himself of the plague; till the nights (though much lengthened) are grown too short to conceal the burials of those that died the day before, people being thereby constrained to borrow daylight for that service; lastly, till I could find neither meat nor drink safe, the butcheries being everywhere visited, my brewer's house shut up, and my baker with his whole family dead of the plague.[41]

This must have been gloomy reading for the recipient, but, in the privacy of the diary, his summary at the end of that month included the statement: 'I do end this month with the greatest content, and may say that these last three months, for joy, health and profit, have been much the greatest that ever I received in all my life in any twelve months almost in my life – having nothing upon me but the consideration of the sickliness of the season during this great plague to mortify mee.' His cheery mood continued, and at the end of October he confided to his diary that, 'we end the month merrily', adding that this was the more so as the number of deaths had begun to fall. At the end of the year he noted: 'I have never lived so merrily (beside that I have got so much) as I have done this plague-time'. The financial gain he referred to was an increase in his wealth from £1,300 to £4,400 during the year, even though the epidemic had put him to 'great charges', by having to keep his family at Woolwich, himself and his clerks at Greenwich for part of the time, and a maid at London. But by the end of December, 'the plague is abated almost to nothing'. It commonly caused few deaths during the winter months, and 'to our great joy, the town fills apace, and shops begin to be open again'.[42]

Clearly, individuals reacted differently, according to their experiences, the number of deaths among family, neighbours, friends and business partners, and their disposition. There was no avoiding the disease, for conversations naturally included reports of those dead or taken ill, and Pepys's diary is scattered with the names of victims known to him. But he had a positive outlook and was not dismayed by the circumstances, and he continued to be focused on his career, reflected in his financial improvement. Nor was he alone in being optimistic as the Great Plague came to an end; indeed people soon returned to their normal patterns of life, as Thomas Sprat observed:

> Upon our return after the abating of the Plague, what else could we expect, but to see the streets unfrequented, the River forsaken, the fields deform'd with the Graves of the Dead, and the Terrors of Death still abiding on the faces of the living? But instead of such dismal sights, there appear'd almost the same throngs in all publick places, the same noise of business, the same freedom of convers, and with the return of the King, the same cheerfulness returning on the minds of the people as before.[43]

The Bill for the period 27 December 1664 to 19 December 1665 recorded 97,306 deaths, 68,956 attributed to plague, although because of false returns the number of plague deaths was under-stated. Some nonconformist groups were not included, and there may have been other omissions and incomplete recording, and so the total, too, may have been somewhat higher. It represented roughly one-fifth of the population and the number of deaths was 5.7 times the annual average for 1660–4. In the central City parishes the increase was lower than in those around its edge, with Holy Trinity, Minories suffering worse than any other parish in London, recording thirteen times more burials than in a typical year.

With the smaller population, the number of burials in 1666 was considerably below the average for the first half of the decade, but the figure began to increase thereafter, and the average number for 1668–72 was almost 7 per cent higher than for 1660–4. Graunt had concluded that the population recovered to its former level within two years of the major epidemics in 1603 and 1625, in both of which the proportion of the population that died was similar to that in 1665. The Great Plague therefore fitted the anticipated pattern and had only a short-term effect on London's size and growth; the city's economy may have been affected during the epidemic, but it revived thereafter. The deaths during the epidemic created openings, and incomers were drawn to the capital to replace those who had died. They were not deterred by the threat of plague, even though it continued, at a much lower level, through the spring and summer of 1666.

In the aftermath of the epidemic, the government reviewed its policies. Household quarantine had been implemented but had failed and was condemned as contributing to the deaths. The author of a pamphlet entitled *The Shutting up of Infected Houses as it is practised in England Soberly Debated* commented how dreadful it was for someone, 'to be shut up from all comfort and society, from free and wholesome air, from the care of the Physician, and the Divine, from the oversight of Friends and Relations, and sometimes even from the very necessities, and conveniences of Nature'. Close confinement created the conditions that were thought to be conducive to the disease, and so, 'shutting up would breed a Plague if there were none: Infection may have killed its thousands, but shutting up hath killed its ten thousands'.[44]

Fumigation of houses by lighting fires, and even discharging guns, was employed, to circulate the air and prevent it stagnating, and the strategy, used in previous outbreaks, of lighting fires in the streets was briefly tried. But the effort was half-hearted and was not renewed after the fires were quenched by rain. Clarendon himself concluded that 'the ayre is not infected'.[45] The Earl of Craven had supervised the efforts to contain the outbreak and in his report recommended that the early movement of suspected cases to a pest-house remained the best means of dealing with an epidemic. But Londoners still did not regard investment in pest-houses as worthwhile, perhaps because of the popular view that an epidemic would not return within the next twenty years and so they had a breathing space before they would be required. The parish officials at St Giles-in-the-Fields built a pest-house during 1665, at a cost of £315, but sold it in 1666, for just £70.[46] With no practical alternative to household quarantine, the existing policy was strengthened by an Act of Parliament in 1666. Clarendon had asked in September 1665 for, 'some good materialls for an Acte of Parliament to meete with those mischieves which fall out in the tyme of a greate contagion'. He blamed not the policies in force, but the failure to implement them.[47]

The plague policies were not put to the test again, for future epidemics did not reach England and the last death attributed to plague in the London area occurred at Rotherhithe in 1679. Of course, this was not known at the time and Aubrey's speculation that 'there is a periodical Plague at London every five and twenty Year' was noticed by Henri Misson, in 1695, who responded with the comment that, 'If it be so, the City of London about this Time is in Danger of a very dreadful Distemper; and we should all look about us.'[48]

Quarantining of shipping was implemented during the plague outbreaks in eastern Europe and the Baltic in 1709–12 and in Provence in the early 1720s. During the eighteenth and nineteenth centuries there was an intermittent and indecisive debate between the contagionists and anti-contagionists, until the 1890s, with the isolation of the plague bacillus, *Yersinia pestis*, and the following decade, when the means of transmission by rats' fleas that are parasites of the black rat was discovered. When the rats die, the infective fleas search for human hosts. That explained the pattern of deaths in 1665 and the symptoms described by contemporaries matched those displayed by victims of *Yersinia pestis* in plague outbreaks during the twentieth century. Plague was not endemic in seventeenth-century London and required a new transmission of the bacillus to initiate an epidemic, and so control of shipping and, more widely across Europe, strict limitation of movement during epidemics eventually proved to be effective. Those measures were the 'salutary precautions to which Europe is indebted for her safety' that Edward Gibbon referred to in *The Decline and Fall of the Roman Empire*, written in the 1780s.[49]

By the first half of the 1680s the number of burials in London was 28 per cent higher than twenty years before. The figures probably are a true reflection of the city's growth. But deaths still exceeded births, by as much as 50 per cent in the mid-1680s, and the city continued to rely on an inflow of people from the country and, to a lesser extent, from abroad. Young people were drawn there despite the death rate, to enrol as apprentices or, increasingly, take employment in domestic service. Misson was blunt in his assessment of apprentices' conditions: 'An Apprentice is a Sort of a Slave; he wears neither Hat nor Cap in his Master's Prescence; he can't marry, nor have any Dealings on his own Account. All he earns is his Master's.' Yet that did not deter a steady flow of new recruits to enlist with the city's tradesmen. Nor were they put off by the number of poor reduced to begging; Misson wrote that, 'London, every Body knows, is a City extreamly rich ... and yet the Town is crouded with Beggars.'[50]

Sir William Petty adopted Graunt's methods of analysing the Bills of Mortality and during the 1680s published a number of pamphlets, demonstrating London's continuing growth and its size, comparing it with other cities. He demonstrated that it was larger than Paris, indeed had 'become equal to Paris and Rome put together'. Other aspects were examined, such the state of the hospitals: 'at London the Hospitals are better and more desirable than those of Paris'. This conclusion was based on the numbers of deaths as a proportion of patients admitted, although in truth the difference was marginal. Petty deduced that, 'either the Physicians and Chirurgeons of London are better than those of Paris, or that the Air of London is more wholesome'. As the changes to improve air quality which John Evelyn had advocated had not been adopted, this remark flew in the face of existing opinion. Clearly, Petty was not impartial when drawing conclusions from the data and was an enthusiastic advocate for London and its advantages.[51]

As Petty was writing, the policy of the French government towards its Calvinist communities was changing, and that was to have an impact on the demography of London. Calvinists were permitted freedom of worship by Henri IV's Edict of Nantes, issued in 1598, but they were increasingly subject to harassment, especially after 1681, when dragoons were quartered on their communities during the so-called *dragonnades*. Then, in 1685, Louis XIV revoked the edict. London's French Protestant community had opened a second church after the Restoration, at the Savoy, and was steadily augmented by a trickle of emigrants, which became a flood during the late 1680s and 1690s. By 1700 there were 23,000 Huguenot refugees in London and the number of congregations had increased, from two to twenty-three by the end of the century.[52] This was an unusually concentrated phase of immigration from abroad that increased London's population and was to produce economic and cultural benefits, from the immigrants' skills and industriousness.

As with other incomers, the Huguenots were attracted by the economic opportunities that London offered and were not deterred by its death rate, pollution, crime, or the occasional bloody skirmish in the streets. Petty's analyses showed it to be an expanding city, capable of overcoming disasters. Not only had the number of inhabitants quickly reached and then exceeded its former level after being sharply reduced by the Great Plague, but Londoners had also faced the challenges posed by a major conflagration.

6

Fabric & Fire

As London grew, so did the risk of fire, with more people requiring cooked food and warmth in an increasing number of houses, and fires were needed in workshops with ovens, furnaces and vats. Stocks of timber and coal were kept, on the premises and at the quays. And the narrow streets and congestion of the buildings were problems when a fire broke out, making it difficult to isolate and extinguish the flames before they could spread. A swift and decisive response was required, to clear combustible matter away from the area and demolish structures in the path of the flames, if necessary.

On one occasion when Pepys saw a house on fire, near Covent Garden, he noted, 'all the streets full of people to quench it'.[1] If such a reaction occurred in similar emergencies, then the chance of preventing a fire from spreading was good. The regulations regarding building materials, hazardous premises and dangerous practices, combined with the citizens' awareness of the risks, helped to reduce the danger of a major outbreak. So did the availability of fire-engines, hand-held squirts, buckets, ladders and fire-hooks, which were acquired and maintained by the parishes and livery companies. In 1660 the vestry of St Giles, Cripplegate, ordered that 'an Engine house be built, fronting next the Street'.[2] This was duly erected, and the parish's engine and buckets were taken occasionally to fires elsewhere, including one in Noble Street in 1661 and another in Cheapside four years later. The officers checked for dangers, walking around their ward and ordering offenders to remove hazardous arrangements, or risk a fine. Those in Cornhill ward reported householders for throwing out cinders, using a hot press, drying boards and storing chip in a room with fires, and having dangerous chimneys. They were assiduous enough to investigate back premises, reporting a stove at the rear of houses in Threadneedle Street, unacceptable 'for its great annoyance and danger of fire', and a dancing master in Freeman Yard, 'for making and setting up there a Chimney upon a deale floare being very dangerouse to the neighbourhood for fire'.[3]

James Howell was confident of the effectiveness of the arrangements in London for fighting fires. He wrote that magazines of corn were maintained to prevent famine, and 'There is no place also better armed against the fury of the fire'. Yet he regretted that the regulations for building with brick had not been better observed, which would have made the city 'lesse subject to casual fyrings'. His account mentioned that in 1633 there had been, 'a most raging dismal fire upon the North side of London bridge, which by computation consum'd above the third part of the Buildings thereof'. The sites of those that had not been rebuilt served as a visible reminder of the danger of a conflagration. More recently, in 1655 three dangerous fires within a few weeks drew attention to the hazards. The first broke out in Fleet Street and destroyed twenty houses. Six weeks later a blaze in Threadneedle Street gutted thirty houses, 'with a quantity of goods of great value, while some persons were also buried in the flames'. This was so serious that it 'rag'd as far as Saint Bennets Church Walls, and there the fury was stopped, otherwise it might have destroyed all this City'. The third, at a brewer's premises in Southwark, was 'hardly less than the other two, destroying over 20 houses, great and small, and some lives being lost'.[4] However strict the regulations and the citizens' watchfulness, such accidents occurred nonetheless, and caused concern. During a fire in Botolph Lane that April, Evelyn was, 'disturbed by an alarme of Fire, which about this time were very frequent in the Cittie'.[5]

Some lives were lost in fires. Only those close to the point where the fire started would have been taken by surprise; others nearby should have been alerted to the danger in time to save themselves, if not their goods, and warn others. Yet a blaze in Lothbury in December 1662 destroyed the house of a merchant and, according to Pepys, killed the 'whole family; not one thing, dog nor cat escapeing, nor any of the neighbours almost hearing of it till the house was quite down and burnt'.[6] The reason for the lack of awareness nearby was explained by Henry Townshend: 'it being a brick building burnt so all inward that he and his wife, great with child, and all his family, being 3 in number, were all burnt to death, and all his goods except some copper. Another merchant, who lay in his house and to be married that week and parted that night from his mistress at 12 of the clock, was also burnt'.[7] Pepys made notes of other fires in the early 1660s, at an inn off Lombard Street – where he watched the merchants and mercers 'carry away their cloths and silks' from their warehouses – and 'in the great uniforme pile of buildings in the middle of Cheapside'.[8]

Explosions of gunpowder were less frequent but destructive of both life and property. Gunpowder is stable when left untouched, but is very sensitive to flame and the risk is greatest when it is being moved, stored, or taken from its barrels to be divided into smaller packets and prepared for use. The worst disaster of that kind during the period occurred one January evening in 1650 at the premises of Robert Porter in Tower Street. He had twenty-seven barrels of gunpowder in his house; twenty of them had been sold to a ship's master and as they were to be collected the next day they had been brought into the shop. The cause of the detonation was not known, because none of the five people in the house was left alive. The explosion, 'did blow up suddenly many houses, and shatter and deface many more'. Five houses fronting the street were wrecked and ten others in an alley to the rear were 'scattered and part beaten downe', with at least a hundred more, 'much shattered and defaced, the tiles blowne off, the glasse windowes broken and much hurt done to them'. The fire that followed raged for two hours until the fire-fighters got it under control, deploying fire-engines, 'which did great service'. The explosion killed sixty-seven people, 'left children found and not owned at the charge of the parish', and destroyed property and goods valued at £60,000. The windows of All Hallows church, opposite Porter's house, were 'wholly all broken and blowne out' and the tower was so badly damaged that it had to be rebuilt, in 1659.[9]

A destructive explosion in 1654 on a ship in the Thames, laden with textiles 'to a great value', was caused by a pot of pitch that was being heated on deck, which caught fire. As the flames spread the crew cut the ship's ropes so that it drifted away from other vessels until it beached on the Southwark side, near St Olave's church. The fire eventually reached the gunpowder, which 'being all blown up at once made a terrible noise, and shook the houses thereabouts; The Church received much harm for besides the glasse all broken, one beam, and some Iron Barrs were broken, which have done much hurt within it'. The eight people killed were mostly hit by flying debris. By chance, another ship blew up on the following day, damaging houses near the shore.[10]

Such catastrophic detonations were rare, but the risks were recognised. The disaster in 1650 prompted parliament to order that the Committee of the Army and the corporation should consult to decide, 'the best ways and means for avoiding all mischiefs and Inconveniences that may happen by Powder, and other combustible Matter, in private Houses and other Magazines within the City of London'.[11] During the Second Dutch War, in March 1666 a committee was appointed to suggest a storage place for gunpowder and a safer route to and from the Tower than the one then used. Its recommendations were implemented, but gunpowder continued to be moved in vehicles along London's streets.[12]

The disaster that occurred six months later had its origins not in a detonation of a powder magazine, but an accident in a bake-house, in

Pudding Lane. It belonged to Thomas Farriner, who held the post of Conduct of the King's Bakehouse and was supplying the navy with biscuit. The fire began in his bake-house early in the morning of Sunday 2 September 1666. The family was woken by smoke some time after one o'clock and, unable to get downstairs because of the smoke, they escaped through an upstairs window and along a gutter to an adjoining house. A maid could not steel herself to follow them on their perilous route and was killed.

The cause of the fire was not ascertained, although it was Farriner's practice to put some fuel next to the oven, or even within it, to ensure that it would be dry enough to re-light the fire in the morning. He insisted that the fire in the oven had been extinguished at about ten o'clock the previous evening, only one grate had any smouldering embers at midnight, and they had been raked over, and the doors and windows were closed to prevent draughts through the building.

Evelyn wrote that during August and September there was a 'long & extraordinary' drought during 'a long set of faire & warme weather'.[13] The danger was particularly great at the time of the fire because of an easterly gale, which fanned the flames and made fire-fighting difficult and hazardous. Furthermore, stocks of fuel were high in preparation for the coming winter. Yet it seems that the fire did not spread rapidly at first, for a next-door neighbour removed his goods from his house before it caught fire. But the flames gradually spread to nearby premises and by about three o'clock in the morning they could be seen by Pepys's maids in Seething Lane, 500 yards away. They were up late making preparations for a feast that Samuel and Elizabeth were hosting on the following day. One of the maids, Jane Birch, was concerned enough to wake her master and mistress, 'to tell us of a great fire they saw in the City'. Pepys got up and looked out and 'thought it to be on the back side of Markelane at the furthest; but being unused to such fires as fallowed, I thought it far enough off, and so went to bed again and to sleep'. Mark Lane was the next street westwards from Seething Lane, and so Pepys thought the fire to be closer than it was at that stage. Franciscus de Rapicani was in London as a travelling companion of a Swedish nobleman and spent that night at Lincoln's Inn, much further away: 'We had hardly been in bed for an hour when, about midnight, we heard a great noise of drums; we jumped out of bed and from the window could see nothing but a great fire beside the Thames.'[14]

When Pepys got up again at about seven o'clock and checked on its progress, he judged it to be, 'not so much as it was, and further off. So to my closet to set things to rights after yesterday's cleaning.'[15] As it was a Sunday morning, others may have reacted in a similar way and begun their routine chores rather than investigate the fire's progress. And fewer people were up and about early than would have been the case on a weekday. Despite the alarms during the night, and the flames, smoke, sound and smell of burning, news of the fire seems to have spread slowly. Ringing the church bells was a way of raising the alarm in such an emergency, but the sound of bells would be expected on a Sunday. Not until late morning did William Taswell, a schoolboy at Westminster, become aware of the outbreak: 'between ten and eleven forenoon, as I was standing upon the steps which lead up to the pulpit in Westminster Abbey, I perceived some people below me running to and fro in a seeming disquietude and consternation; immediately almost a report reached my ears that London was in a conflagration'.[16]

After the alarm was raised the lord mayor, Sir Thomas Bludworth, arrived at the scene with his officers. At first he was not greatly concerned at the danger, for he was said to have remarked that, 'a woman might piss it out'. When he was advised to authorise the demolition of four houses and a shop close to the fire, he demurred, asking, 'When the houses have been brought down, who shall pay the charge of rebuilding them?' This very point had been addressed in a case in King's Bench in 1660, when the judges had ruled that the 'law of necessity' dispenses with actions that otherwise are unlawful, 'as to throw down any neighbour's house for preventing the spread of fire'. Pepys had discussed the issue with Sir Richard Ford, one of the sheriffs, in the aftermath of the fire in Cheapside in 1664. Ford told him that the lord mayor and sheriffs, 'have power of commanding the pulling down of any house or houses to defend the whole City'.[17] Why Bludworth should not have known this or been informed of it, or simply recognised the risk and acted decisively, is not clear. Pepys certainly blamed him for his pusillanimity, as the fire spread and the scale of the unfolding disaster became clear. When Pepys appreciated the extent of the conflagration he went to Whitehall to alert the king and received instructions to order the lord mayor to pull down buildings to create fire-breaks. He then set off in search of Bludworth: 'At Last met my Lord Mayor in Canning Streete, like a man spent, with a hankercher about his neck. To the King's message, he cried like a fainting woman, "Lord, what can I do? I am spent! People will not obey me. I have been pulling down houses. But the fire overtakes us faster than we can do it." That he needed no more soldiers; and that for himself, he must go and refresh himself, having been up all night.' Pepys was critical, yet he took time off from watching the fire's progress to entertain his guests, as planned: 'we had an extraordinary good dinner, and as merry as at this time we could be'.[18]

The fire continued to spread remorselessly, 'the wind mighty high and driving it into the city, and everything, after so long a drougth, proving combustible'. According to de Rapicani, on that first day, 'it was thought that about a hundred houses were being burnt every hour', and Sir Heneage Finch later wrote that, 'in six hours it became a large stream of fire, at least a mile long, that could not possibly be approached or quenched'. The king and Duke of York arrived and gave orders to pull down houses, 'but little was or could be done, the fire coming upon them so fast'.[19]

Pepys returned to watch the fire and was alarmed by what he saw. The flames spread westwards, beyond St Magnus church and London Bridge, as far as the Steelyard. In this riverside area the houses stood, 'so very thick thereabouts, and full of matter for burning, as pitch and tar, in Thames-street – and warehouses of oyle and wines and Brandy and other things'. Pepys could not see anyone trying to quench the flames:

Everybody endeavouring to remove their goods, and flinging into the River or bringing them into lighters that lay off. Poor people staying in their houses as long as till the very fire touched them, and then running into boats or clambering from one pair of stair by the water-side to another. And among other things, the poor pigeons I perceive were loath to leave their houses, but hovered about the windows and balconies till they were some of them burned, their wings, and fell down.[20]

John Rushworth commented on the apparent shortage of fire-fighters: 'when Cheapside was on fire, not tenn men stood by helping or calling for help'. The citizens seemed more concerned with saving their belongings than their houses. As Pepys walked along Watling Street in search of Bludworth he met, 'every creature coming away loaden with goods to save – and here and there sick people carried away in beds. Extraordinary good goods carried in carts and on backs.'[21]

Some took their possessions to the churches, hoping that the stone buildings might be fire-proof, although of course their goods simply added to the kindling and churches were gutted as well as the other buildings. Some took them to the houses of friends or relatives, but when those houses were threatened by the flames, they had to be moved again. Citizens who lived near the river could put their possessions on to boats. Pepys saw the Thames, 'full of lighter[s] and boats taking in goods, and good goods swimming in the water', and Evelyn described it as, 'coverd with goods floating, all the barges & boates laden with what some had time & courage to save'.[22] For those who lived away from the waterside, that was not an option and they needed labourers to carry their goods, or load them on to vehicles. Carts and wagons could be obtained only at very high prices, and the congestion in the streets, as people piled goods outside their houses, made it difficult to move vehicles along them. Householders had to decide not only what was most valuable but what could be carried, and some escaped with scarcely any possessions. When Taswell left the abbey he saw on the river, 'four boats crowded with objects of distress. These had escaped from the fire scarce under any other covering except that of a blanket.'[23]

The pattern of that first day was continued during the nights and days that followed, for as long as the gale continued there was no chance of checking the flames, or saving any building. Pepys's resentment at Bludworth's failure to pull down buildings grew. On the Tuesday he wrote to Sir William Coventry: 'The fire is now very neere us as well on Tower Streete as Fanchurch Street side, and we little hope of our escape but by that remedy, to the want whereof we doe certainly owe the loss of the city, namely, the pulling down of houses, in the way of the fire.'[24] It was not only Pepys who blamed Bludworth for his inaction in the early stages. According to Robert Stephens, after the fire, 'many blame the Lord Mayor for not pulling houses downe time enough'. They included the Earl of Clarendon and the writer of a lampoon who observed that the City was burned, 'All though a strong man and a stoute / Did say at first hee'd pisse it out'.[25]

But once the fires were well established, fire-breaks were ineffective. Evelyn noted how the flames spread quickly, 'leaping after a prodigious manner from house to house & streete to streete, at greate distance one from the other'. The strong wind blew burning debris ahead of the front of the fires, setting buildings alight. And the lack of secure party walls between buildings, and interconnections between them, enabled the fire to spread within a row of structures and break out some distance from the apparent front of the fires. Pepys experienced the effects: 'with one's face in the wind you were almost burned with a shower of Firedrops ... so as houses were burned by these drops and flakes of fire, three or four, nay five or six houses, one from another'. He heard that at Bishopsgate, 'where no fire had yet been near, and there is now one broke out – which did give great grounds to people, and to me too, to think that there is some kind of plot in this'.[26]

Many found this suspicious and were prepared to give credence to rumours of arsonists, who were alleged not only to have started the fire in Pudding Lane but were continuing to set others. Those arsonists could only be enemies, interpreted as Catholics and foreigners, with the Dutch and French the most suspect because their countries were at war with England. The arson could well be a prelude to an uprising or invasion, and so stories spread that an army, Dutch or perhaps French, or both, was marching on London. Foreigners were said to be carrying fire-balls or other means to start fires. Thomas Vincent reported that the trained-bands were called out, 'watching at every quarter for outlandish men, because of the general fears and jealousies, and rumours that fire-balls were thrown into houses by several of them, to help on and provoke the too furious flames'.[27]

Taswell summarised this mood as, 'The ignorant and deluded mob … hurried away with a kind of phrenzy.' Some foreigners were attacked at random and Pepys wrote, 'it hath been dangerous for any stranger to walk in the streets'. Taswell recalled that, 'A blacksmith, in my presence, meeting an innocent Frenchman walking along the street, felled him instantly to the ground with an iron bar.' He also saw a crowd loot a French painter's shop and then wreck the building, and his brother told him of a Frenchman who was, 'almost dismembered in Moorfields, because he carried balls of fire in a chest with him, when in truth they were only tennis balls'.[28] A friend of de Rapicani had a very narrow escape. He was walking in the street when he was:

> seized by a furious mob, together with the steward who was with him, and was hung up from the projecting sign of a house. The steward, however, proved his salvation, for he made such a commotion with the crowd that they could not decide which of them to hang first. Thus a little time was gained, and they had hardly got the nobleman strung up when a mounted troop of the Duke of York's bodyguard came by; they saw what was going on, rode up, and cut the rope with a sword, threw the crowd's victim onto a horse, and brought him away.[29]

Others were arrested, according to the writer of a pamphlet issued after the disaster: 'Divers strangers, Dutch and French, were during the fire apprehended, upon suspicion that they contributed mischievously to it, who were all imprisoned.'[30] After the fire, in October, a Huguenot, Robert Hubert – a watchmaker and a native of Rouen who had worked in London – was hanged at Tyburn, convicted on his own insistence that he had deliberately started the fire at Farriner's bake-house. This was despite the findings of enquiries that the conflagration had begun accidentally as the result of a mischance, not a conspiracy.

The Duke of York was in overall control of the fire-fighting and the eight fire posts that had been set up on the Monday by the king's order. They were ranged in an arc, from Temple Bar to Coleman Street. A privy councillor or nobleman was put in charge of each post, assisted by three justices of the peace, the parish constables, 100 men and 30 foot soldiers. They could co-ordinate activity, but were powerless to halt the fire, which had broken up into several individual fires. On the Monday Pepys climbed the tower of All Hallows, near the Tower, 'and there saw the saddest sight of desolation that I ever saw. Everywhere great fires. Oyle-cellars and brimstone and other things burning.' Yet some success had been achieved in his neighbourhood, 'by the blowing up of houses and the great help given by the workmen out of the King's yards'.[31] Houses were also demolished to protect the Tower.

The flames could be checked in those areas because they made only slow progress into the wind, still blowing from the east. But downwind fire-fighting was more difficult and dispiriting; fire-breaks were established but burning debris was blown over them.

Thomas Vincent graphically described how, 'you might see in some places whole streets at once in flames ... and then you might see the houses tumble, tumble, tumble, from one end of the street to the other with a great crash, leaving the foundations open to the view of the Heavens'.[32] The major buildings were destroyed as well as the flimsy ones. The Royal Exchange was burnt, Guildhall was engulfed, the livery companies' halls and the churches were gutted, and St Paul's caught fire and was left 'a sad ruine'. Flames broke through into St Faith's church beneath the cathedral, destroying the booksellers' stocks which they had stowed there, hoping that the fire would not reach them. Evelyn gave a dramatic summary of what he witnessed:

above ten thousand houses all in one flame, the noise & crakling & thunder of the impetuous flames, the shreeking of Women & children, the hurry of people, the fall of towers, houses & churches was like an hideous storme, & the aire all about so hot & inflam'd that at the last one was not able to approch it, so as they were force'd to stand still, and let the flames consume on which they did for neere two whole miles in length and one in bredth: The Crowds also of Smoke were dismall, & reached upon computation neere 50 miles in length.[33]

The intense heat, foul smoke, flying debris, collapsing buildings, incessant wind and growing fatigue did hinder the fire-fighters. To a fatalist like Vincent their attempts were useless in any event. The fire, beginning on the Sabbath and following so soon after the plague, showed once more that God's wrath was directed against the sinful city: 'London's sins were too great, and God's anger against the city was too hot, so easily and presently to be quenched and allayed ... the fire hath received its commission from God to burn down the city, and therefore all attempts to hinder it are in vain.'[34]

They were ineffectual so long as the gale continued to blow; only when the wind dropped could the fires be brought under control and gradually extinguished. That finally happened on the Wednesday, the fourth day, but even then, 'There was yet no standing neere the burning & glowing ruines neere a furlongs Space.' Only as the smoke cleared and the ruins cooled could the extent of the destruction be assessed. Evelyn attempted to do that, by 'clambring over mountains of yet smoking rubbish', and found it a most uncomfortable experience, 'the ground & aire, smoake & fiery vapour, continud so intense, my haire being almost seinged, & my feete unsufferably surbated'. Added to the discomfort was the unpleasantness caused by, 'the Voragos of subterranean Cellars Wells & Dungeons, formerly Warehouses, still burning in stench & dark clowds of smoke like hell'. Only the widest streets were passable, the narrower ones were, 'quite fill'd up with rubbish, nor could one have possibly knowne where he was, but by the ruines of some church, or hall, that had some remarkable towre or pinnacle remaining'.[35] Rushworth walked the full length of the area destroyed by the fire, from St Dunstan's-in-the-West to the Tower, 'over heapes of rubbish and smoake, not one howse standing nor church but all Burnt, and most of the Bells melted'.[36]

The king and the Duke of York were praised for their efforts. Sir Heaneage Finch described how:

> when the citizens had abandoned all further care of the place, and were intent chiefly upon the preservation of their goods, [they] undertook the work themselves, and with incredible magnanimity rode up and down giving order for blowing up of houses with gunpowder to make void spaces for the fire to die in, and standing still to see those orders executed, exposing their persons not only to the multitude but to the very flames themselves and the ruins of buildings ready to fall upon them and sometimes labouring with their own hands and give example to others.[37]

According to Rushworth, 'the Duke of York hath wonn the hearts of the people with his continuall and indefatigable paynes day & night in helpeing to quench the Fire, handing Bucketts of water with as much diligence as the poorest man that did assist, if the Lord Maior had donn as much, his Example might have gone Far towards saveing the citty'.[38]

Despite the efforts of the royal brothers, not all of their courtiers were sorry to learn of the disaster that had struck their old enemy, which had supported parliament in the Civil War and had not acted to prevent the execution of Charles I. One of them even described it as being to the king's advantage, indeed it was:

> the greatest blessing that God had ever conferred upon him, his restoration only excepted: for the walls and gates being now burned and thrown down of that rebellious city, which was always an enemy to the crown, his majesty would never suffer them to repair and build them up again, to be a bit in his mouth and a bridle upon his neck; but would keep all open, that his troops might enter upon them whenever he thought necessary for his service, there being no other way to govern that rude multitude but by force.

His comment 'did not please the king, but was highly approved by the company'.[39]

After the fires had been doused, an appraisal of the loss could be made. Sir Heneage Finch wrote to Viscount Conway, telling him that, 'all London almost within the walls and some part of it which was without the walls now lies in ashes'.[40] The City from the Tower to the Temple and as far north as the city wall was burned. St Paul's cathedral, 87 churches, 6 consecrated chapels, 52 livery companies' halls, the Custom House, the Royal Exchange, Blackwell Hall, Newgate prison, Bridewell, two debtors' prisons, the Sessions House and 13,200 houses were destroyed and the Guildhall was gutted. Yet only six deaths had occurred during the fire. At least 65,000, and perhaps almost 80,000, Londoners were made homeless; for many of them the destruction of their homes was a shattering blow. A plausible estimate for the value of the buildings, trade and household goods destroyed is almost £8 million. But the fire had not reached the Strand, Westminster, the northern and eastern suburbs, or Southwark, and Sir William Petty calculated that the houses destroyed were 'but a fifth part of the whole'.[41]

Most citizens who were homeless could find space only in the open areas around the city. Vincent described them as 'the people late of London, now of the fields'.[42] Evelyn was concerned for the conditions of 'the poore Inhabitans dispersd all about St. Georges, Moore filds, as far as higate, & severall miles in Circle, Some under tents, others under miserable Hutts and Hovells, without a rag or any necessary utinsils, bed or board'.[43] Yet all of them quickly found somewhere to stay, as Clarendon described: 'in four days, in all the fields about the town, which had seemed covered with those whose habitations were burned, and with the goods which they had saved, there was scarce a man to be seen'. All of those displaced had found shelter. Property rents and prices rose dramatically as a result and were still high four years later, according to the Venetian ambassador, Piero Mocenigo, who complained that, 'the cost of the most ordinary houses has become excessive since the fire'. And some of those who had been burned out, 'with more expedition than can be conceived, set up little sheds of brick and timber upon the ruins of their own houses ... though they knew they could not long reside in those new buildings'.[44]

Their reaction displayed a positive attitude and optimism for the future. That was also shown by their rulers, who quickly resolved that the city should be rebuilt. On 10 September Henry Oldenburg wrote to Robert Boyle to tell him that, 'I was yesterday in many meetings of the principal Cittizens, whose houses are laid in ashes, who in stead of complaining, discoursed almost of nothing, but of a survey of London, and a dessein for rebuilding.' On the same day a member of Lord Ashley's household wrote to John Locke, 'hear is great talke of bilding this sitty Againe finer then ever it was'.[45]

The regulations already in place would be appropriate for the new buildings, which would be of brick and tile, with uniform frontages. Other improvements could be made, with a new quay along the riverfront, streets widened and the market places taken out of the streets into areas created for them. Within a few days plans showing new street layouts were submitted to the king by Evelyn, Christopher Wren, Robert Hooke, Peter Mills, Valentine Knight and the cartographer Richard Newcourt, who produced two. None was implemented; the practical, tenurial and financial difficulties could not have been overcome without causing a long delay. Talk after the fire that, 'the King and Parliament are to buy the whole land of London and to build upon' described what was required, but the scheme was hopelessly unrealistic, as neither of them, nor the City, could raise anything like the funds needed.[46] But the king directed Wenceslaus Hollar and Francis Sandford to survey the City, and the corporation commissioned a team of surveyors, whose results were presented on a plan drawn by John Leake, completed in March 1667, and engraved by Hollar. The survey was carried out, 'for the better stating thereafter every ones right and propriety'. A special court was established to arbitrate in the many disputes that were expected to arise over such matters as liabilities, tenures, boundaries and rents. It held its first sitting on 27 February 1667.[47]

Two Acts of Parliament governing the rebuilding received the royal assent on 8 February. Four categories of houses were specified, according to their site. The smallest ones, of two storeys and garrets, were those in 'by-streets and lanes'; those of the second sort were of three storeys and garrets in 'streets and lanes of note' and facing the river; those in the next category were one storey higher and fronted the 'high and principal streets'; while the biggest were 'mansion houses for citizens and other persons of extraordinary quality', not necessarily standing in the streets or lanes, but nevertheless also limited to four storeys. All houses had to conform to those categories and the desired appearance was furthered by a ruling that the roof lines within the first three sorts of houses should be uniform. An Act of Common Council issued on 29 April listed the streets and alleys that were to be widened. Public buildings were to be paid for from a duty on coal landed in the port of London.

A potential hindrance to the rebuilding process was that leaseholders were generally required by a covenant in their lease to maintain the property in good repair. They should, therefore, pay for reconstruction, so that they would leave the premises at the end of their lease in the condition in which they had found them. This they would be reluctant to do, for they would be making an investment from which their landlords would gain the most benefit, having a new building erected for them. But, as Lord Crew explained to Pepys on 5 November, 'the Judges have determined in that case whether the Landlords or the Tenants ... shall bear the loss of the fire. And they say that Tenants should, against all Casualtys of fire beginning either in their own or in their neighbour's; but where it is done by an Enemy, they are not to do it. And this was by an Enemy, there having been one Convict[ed] and hanged upon this very score – which is an excellent Salvo for the Tenants, and for which I am glad – because of my father's house'.[48] That was the house in Salisbury Court, and Pepys's reaction would have been shared by many. The ruling effectively accepted that Robert Hubert had begun the fire and as a Frenchman he could be defined as an enemy. It removed the legal doubts about liability for rebuilding.

The planning and legislation did not delay the start of the work, for building would not have been undertaken during the cold winter months, in any case; the rubbish and debris had to be cleared away and sorted for items that could be salvaged, and not enough materials would have been available. Timber had to be brought in and bricks and tiles manufactured, and skilled labour was required. Owners had to make agreements with leaseholders and arrange for funds to pay for their new buildings. All of this would take time and Pepys's comment at the close of 1666, that the City was 'less and less likely to be built again', was unduly pessimistic.[49]

The necessary materials and workmen did become available, the City's surveyors were prompt in setting out the lines of the streets, and the work began in the spring of 1667. As the principal streets were marked out, Pepys's spirits revived and at the end of March he wrote: 'if ever it be built in that form, with so fair streets, it will be a noble sight'.[50] But activity came to a halt in the middle of June and the marking of house sites did not resume until August, after a break during the peak period of the building season. On 12 June the Dutch navy mounted a large-scale raid on the Royal Navy's base in the Medway, burning some vessels and towing away the flagship, the *Royal Charles*. They then blockaded the Thames estuary, bringing London's sea-going trade to a halt and provoking fear and despondency in the city. According to Evelyn, 'this alarme was so greate, as put both County and Citty in to a panique feare & consternation, such as I hope I shall never see more: for every body were flying, none knew why or whither'.[51] Only after the peace treaty was signed on 21 July could confidence return and building pick up once again.

In 1668, 1,450 houses were built and Pepys's optimism grew after a conversation with Sir Denis Gauden, a victualler for the navy, 'who by the way tells me how the City doth go on in several things toward the building of the public places; which I am glad to hear, and gives hope that in a few years it will be a glorious place'.[52] By the end of 1670 some 6,000 houses had been erected. A further 2,000 were added over the next two years, and in 1672 the erection of new houses was almost completed. Another crisis then intervened. In January payments from the Exchequer were halted because of the crown's chronic financial problems, and in March another war with the Dutch was begun, in alliance with France.

Fewer houses were built than had been destroyed. Demand had fallen and a survey in 1673 showed that tenants had not been found for almost 3,500 of the houses built after the fire. Admittedly that was during the war, when trading was difficult, but the City's population had been falling since c.1640; the fire gave momentum to an existing process. In a sample of eight parishes, there was a fall of 22 per cent between 1638 and 1695. A part of the reason for the decline was that the regulations successfully prevented the return of tenements in the back streets and courts. The alleys and courts themselves were rebuilt, even though a royal proclamation issued just a week after the fire was extinguished had planned to remove them, and Richard Newcourt had intended to do away with the 'multitude of bye-lanes, rooks and alleys, huddled up one on the neck of another'. They were rebuilt because affordable housing within the City was needed and that need took precedence over aesthetic considerations.

Most of the livery companies' halls were also rebuilt, between 1668 and 1673, although a few were not finished until the late 1670s. The Custom House, Blackwell Hall, St Paul's School and the new Royal Exchange were completed during 1671, and the lord mayor's feast was again held in Guildhall that year, with a pageant entitled 'London's Resurrection to Joy and Triumph'. By 1674 only Bridewell of the major public buildings destroyed had not been finished.[53] To commemorate the fire, the City erected the Monument, close to the site of Farriner's bake-house. This tall, slender Doric column topped by a flaming urn was completed in 1676. A further Rebuilding Act, in 1670, provided for the building of fifty-one churches, to replace the eighty-seven which had been destroyed. Their design was overseen by Wren and all were completed by 1696, although the towers and spires were added later in many cases. Wren's spectacular new cathedral took far longer; begun in 1675, the first service in the rebuilt St Paul's was held in 1697, but the building was completed only in 1710.

New projects undertaken by the City were the canalisation of the Fleet River, which was lined with warehouses, and the construction of a quay 40 feet wide along the Thames, although that scheme was completed only in parts and not as a continuous grand quay, as envisaged. Nor was the hoped-for uniformity along the street frontages achieved and it was more a wish than reality to write, as the Revd R. Kirk did c.1690, that, 'Since the burning, all London is built uniformly, the streets broader, the houses all of one form and height.'[54] The streets were wider and some of them were straighter, but uniform frontages had not been achieved because of the variety of house-fronts built by the individual owners and builders. The plots were small and single ownership of a run of contiguous frontages was rare. There were, too, differences in the finishes of the bricks and in the decoration, balconies and ~~doorways. In streets built on an incline the stepped effect of the buildings~~ broke up the line of the frontages and roofs. Some materials used were of poor quality. Pepys recorded in December 1668: 'I hear this day that there is fallen down a new house, not quite finished, in Lumberdstreet, and that there have been several so, they making use of bad mortar and bricks.'[55]

Yet visitors' reactions were generally favourable. In 1671 Mocenigo wrote that, 'the city is renewed, magnificent and sumptuous, after an interval that was no longer than required for the removal of the debris left by the fire.'[56] Adam Ebert, in the summer of 1678, commented on the new buildings and the revival of traffic: 'All houses newly-built since the Fire are bright red with flat roofs and a balcony over the entrance. There the occupier and his wife sit in summer, drinking to their neighbours opposite and smoking tobacco, while innumerable carriages drive past, making a frightful din (especially at night).'[57] Henri Misson's reaction, in the 1690s, was favourable, if not entirely enthusiastic: 'ever since the great Fire, the People of London have built in a manner polite enough … Now the Houses are built with Brick, with even Fronts, without Magnificence, indeed, or any Thing like it, but with Symmetry and Neatness enough.'[58] English writers were less restrained. In 1673 Edward Chamberlayne gave a positive view of the fire's impact:

> the Buildings are become infinitely more beautiful, more commodious, and more solid (the three main vertues of all Edifices) then before, nay, as if the Citizens had not been any way impoverish'd, but rather enrich by that huge Conflagration, they may be said to be even wanton in their Expences upon the stately Italian *Facciata's* or Fronts of their new Houses, Churches, and Halls.[59]

When John Strype issued his revised edition of John Stow's Survey of London, in 1720, he also struck a positive note: 'it was in the Space of Four or Five Years well nigh rebuilded. Divers Churches, the stately Guildhall, many Halls of Companies, and other Publick Edifices; all infinitely more Uniform, more Solid, and more Magnificent than before: So that no City in Europe (nay, scarcely in the World) can stand in Competition with it.'[60]

As well as the aesthetic effects, writers came to acknowledge the economic benefits. The fire provided a stimulus in the demand for building materials and labour, which Sir William Petty estimated to have added £1 million to the economy in each of the four years when the new houses were being built, 'without lessening any other sort of Work, Labour, or Manufacture'.[61] The need to replace the merchandise that had been destroyed also generated business. In 1714 Bernard Mandeville used the example of the post-fire reconstruction to illustrate 'the usefulness of private losses and misfortunes to the public', writing that:

> if the carpenters, bricklayers, smiths, and all, not only that are employed in Building but likewise those that made and dealt in the same manufactures and other merchandises that were burnt, and other trades again that got by them when they were in full employ, were to vote against those who lost by the fire; the rejoicings would equal, if not exceed, the complaints.[62]

A few years later, Daniel Defoe conveyed the scale of the business generated: 'It is incredible what a Trade this made all over the whole Kingdom, to make good the Want and to supply that Loss.'[63]

As the bulk of the rebuilding drew to a close, another major fire provided further work for builders and suppliers. On Friday 26 May 1676, 'before Break of day', a fire broke out in Southwark High Street, described by the lawyer Littleton Powys in a letter to his uncle:

> Upon last Thursday night there broke out a great fire in an oylmans house in Southwark near London Bridge & it happening amongst old timber houses in narrow streets, it burnt all last fryday & could not be stopped till it had burnt at least 6 hundred houses and truly all Southwark & even London Bridge was in great Danger, but that by the mercy [of] God & mighty Labour & Diligence the fire at last was conquered about 10 of Clock upon fryday night.[64]

The street contained several large inns, with their stocks of hay and straw; the fire ran along both sides, destroying 624 houses, and it 'much defaced the Church & utterly consum'd the School-House'.[65] The loss was valued at £84,375. A similar number of houses had been destroyed by a fire in Northampton in the previous year, and the response there was to follow the example of London and obtain an Act of Parliament to regulate the rebuilding. Southwark now did the same.

The Act for Southwark established a fire court. Its judges attempted to enforce the provisions of the Act, which ordered that, 'all encroachments and purprestures upon the High Street, and most especially such as are or shall be from the foot of London Bridge to the lane called Compter Lane ... shall be regulated, reduced and reformed by the ... Court'. That was a distance of 400 yards. Reconstruction was swift; the preamble to the rebuilding act, passed on 16 April 1677, stated that, 'many Tenants and Under-tenants, late Occupiers of the said Houses, for the Continuance of their Trade and to encourage the Rebuilding, have built up and finished several Houses of much better Use and Ornament than ever the same were before'. The inns were rebuilt and there was no great change in the social composition of the district. Southwark was not a fashionable area. Most houses were rebuilt by October 1677, when a survey discovered eighty-seven illegal encroachments. Their owners were instructed to remove them, but the governors of St Thomas's hospital prevaricated and were indicted for contempt of court. A part of their problem was that the tenants of those properties threatened with demolition, mostly small shops, which the governors intended to amalgamate and rebuild as viable premises, were 'soe tenacious of their interests as that they could not bee brought to quitt their Termes in the remaining ground'.[66] The issue was resolved only when the tenants, 'pulled downe their houses and shopps (as wee suppose to prevent or mitigate the Fine the next Sessions would have bin inflicted as they feared upon them)'. But that was not until November 1681, four years after the judges had ordered the removal of the encroachments. As part of the rebuilding that followed, the hospital's gate to the street was decorated with stone figures, 'which may invite contributions to the relief of the poore'.[67]

The speed of the rebuilding in Southwark reflected the demand for housing across the city. In April 1667 Pepys was told of new streets set out in Moorfields, properly paved, and with houses built on ground leased by the corporation for just seven years. He investigated and sure enough, 'did find houses built two storeys high, and like to stand, and must become a place of great trade till the City be built'.[68] He was displeased, as he feared that such developments would be inimical to the City's recovery. But shopkeepers already were moving, not north into Moorfields, but west, in search of wealthy customers, especially the aristocracy and gentry occupying the new developments in the West End. In the following summer he and Elizabeth bought some linen at a shop in the Strand, where the shopkeeper had, 'come out of London since the fire; who says his and other tradesmen's retail trade is so great here, and better then it was in London, that they believe they shall not return, nor the City be ever so great for retail as heretofore'.[69]

The entrepreneur and improver Andrew Yarranton attributed the City's problems to the difficulty of providing security for business loans. He believed that had a register of houses been created in the immediate aftermath of the fire, it would have gone some way to solving the problem, for if someone proposed a property as security for a loan, ownership could have been quickly checked in a register at Guildhall. Had that been done, 'there needed not one House to stand empty and untenanted, as now they do; nor the Trade to have departed out of the City, as it hath done since the Fire'.[70] His explanation simplified the economic complexities of post-fire London, but the trend was undeniable and was confirmed by a writer seven years later. He complained that some shop-keepers, 'have (since the fire) set up in Covent Garden, and on that side of the City; by which means many of the houses and Shops are not tenanted, and those which are, the Rents of them are exceedingly fallen'. He proposed a drastic solution to halt the trend, explaining that, 'there are some Trades whose Commodities are such, that it would be very little more trouble for any one to go into the City to buy them, than to go to Covent Garden, such as Woollen, or Linnen cloth, Stuffs, or Hangings for Rooms, or Plate, or the like: if then all such trades were prohibited from setting up on that side of the City, it would presently fill their Shops and Houses with people, and their City with trade'.[71]

Although some retailers moved away, the merchants remained in the City, some of them building impressive houses on sites that they had been able to enlarge after the fire by acquiring adjoining premises. A list compiled in 1677 and entitled *A Collection of the Names of the Merchants living in and about the City of London* contains the names of 1,953 merchants and traders. It includes 58 goldsmiths and 38 trading in textiles and based in Blackwell Hall. Of those listed, 24 had served or were to serve as lord mayor. The merchants were not tempted to move to the suburbs or nearby villages, and they were not part of the society developing in the West End.[72]

Most of the suburbs remained unfashionable, although continuing to grow. The poorer buildings which proliferated in those districts were more likely to take fire than the substantial ones in the wealthier areas, but fires continued to break out even where the buildings were now of brick and tile. Despite the regulations controlling building materials, the availability of fire-fighting equipment and awareness of the horrific consequences of negligence, in the wake of the Great Fire, occasional outbreaks could not be prevented. John Tillison reported a fire in 1673 in Shadwell that began in a brewhouse and destroyed almost a hundred houses, 'all very old', only forty of which were rated for taxation, 'all the rest being poor'. In a local echo of the rebuilding after the Great Fire, when the landlord marked out the line of the street, alleys and quay, they were 'made wider & more convenient than before'.[73] The Navy Office and adjoining buildings in Seething Lane were much grander and escaped the Great Fire, but were burnt out during the night of 29 January 1673. The blaze was described in the Navy Board's minute book as, 'an unhappy fire, which in six hours time Laid in ashes the said office, with Severall of the houses about it'.[74] It spread to thirty nearby houses. Six years later, during the evening of 26 January 1679, a fire at Pump Court in the Middle Temple demonstrated a problem when tackling a blaze in freezing weather, and some ingenuity by the fire-fighters: 'The Thames being frozen, there was great scarcity of water: it being so bitter a frost, the water hung in isecles at the e'ves of the houses. The engines plaid away many barrels of beer to stop the fire: but the cheif way of stopping the fire was by blowing up houses.'[75] In the following March there were four fires to report on one Sunday: a chimney fire near St Clement's church 'in sermon time', which caused a panic among the congregation that 'endangered many limbs & occasioned some miscarriages'; a blaze that began in a draper's shop in St Paul's churchyard and destroyed two 'good houses'; one in Creed Lane that required the attendance of eight fire-engines and their crews; and one in Fetter Lane that was 'almost as soon out as in'.[76]

The last great conflagration of the century in London broke out in Whitehall Palace, on 4 January 1698. A blaze in 1691 had done much damage in the southern part of the large and rambling complex of buildings and the fire in 1698, according to the antiquary John Pointer, 'burnt down all the Body of the Palace and Long-Gallery, with the lodgings adjoining'.[77] From his house in Pall Mall, Charles Hatton saw 'a great fire towards Westminster', but was unable to get into the palace when he arrived there. He later explained that:

The fire broke out betwixt 3 and 4 of ye clocke in a garret … occasioned by a Dutch serving maide laying a sack of charcoale soe nere ye fire it all tooke fire, and ye servants hoped to quench it without any help from others, but it increas'd soe violently it occasion'd ye ruine of ye whole pallace. All persons were intent to save their goods, and all ye gates were lock'd up to prevent ye mob coming in; and, when ye houses were blown up, most of wch were blown up very high, ye timber and rafters lay bare, and ther wanted hands to remove ym, soe yt, instead of stopping ye fire, it help'd to increase it.[78]

His account suggests that a small domestic fire developed into such a destructive blaze because it had not been taken seriously enough at the outset; the maids attempted to douse it themselves, without calling for help. The palace gates were closed to prevent looters from getting in to take advantage of the confusion, and so there were not enough fire-fighters, as those inside the buildings were more concerned to save their goods than tackle the flames. And attempts to create fire-breaks by blowing up buildings were, 'done soe unskilfully and violently, it doth great hurt but noe Good'. A further parallel with the Great Fire was that the fire was blamed on a foreigner, albeit one from an ally, the United Provinces, rather than, as in Hubert's case, a country with which Britain was at war. There was some irony in the fact that the principal royal palace and the centre of government, from which emanated royal proclamations and the Privy Council's orders concerning fire regulations, was itself burnt down.

The banqueting house, the Court Gate, the Holbein Gate, the King Street Gate and some other sections of the buildings survived, but the greatest part was destroyed. Wren surveyed the site, 'in order to rebuild the same: his Majesty designs to make it a noble palace'. He produced two plans for William III and erected a new council chamber adjoining the banqueting house. After her accession in 1702, Anne also planned to build a new palace there, appointing William Talman as architect. But money was short and St James's Palace had to suffice, while the site at Whitehall stood unused and dotted with ruins.[79] Those courtiers who had greeted news of the Great Fire with a certain satisfaction would have been chastened if they could have known that the palace on which their own lives centred was to be destroyed a generation later, and that, while the City was rebuilt, their palace was not. Its vestiges stood in a large area of waste ground well into the next century.

7

A Wasp's Nest

Lingering resentment over the events of the Civil War and regicide was only one of the tensions that troubled relations between the citizens and the court. The Restoration religious settlement and the enforcement of penal measures against nonconformists fuelled the citizens' ill feeling, and many were offended by the all-too-obvious licentiousness of the court. They were also increasingly concerned by the apparent influence of Roman Catholics and, as the years passed and the king did not produce an heir, the likelihood that his brother James, an avowed Catholic from 1673, would become king. Those tensions flared up into a crisis in the late 1670s, with the court's supporters and critics acting out their rivalries on London's streets. This rumbled on into the next decade and, as part of the political manoeuvrings, the City's charter was withdrawn. The capital witnessed another upheaval in 1688, when James, who had become king, fled and London was once again occupied by an army.

The antipathy evident in the courtiers' reaction to the news of the Great Fire was indicative of their attitude. For their part, many citizens viewed with distaste the immorality of Charles and James, and the courtiers' extravagance, debauchery, indolence and frivolity. Pepys was aware of the behaviour at court as early as the summer of 1661, and was afraid of the impact it might have on the conduct of government business: 'at Court things are in very ill condition, there being so much aemulation, poverty, and the vices of swearing, drinking, and whoring, that I know not what will be the end of it but confusion'. A few days later, when he was told of 'the vices of the court', he noted that, 'the pox is as common there … as eating and swearing'. Things had not changed by the end of the reign, according to Evelyn, who, although loyal to the Stuart monarchy, found it difficult to stomach what he witnessed. Shortly before Charles's death he wrote that: 'I saw this evening such a sceane of profuse gaming, and luxurious dallying & prophanesse, the King in the middst of his 3 concubines, as I had never before.'[1] Pepys and Evelyn had to go to Whitehall because of their official duties, but the lives of most citizens did not impinge upon those of the courtiers. Yet they could not fail to know about the goings-on at court, through gossip and pamphlets which criticised and lampooned both it and the conduct of government. And they were occasionally made more directly aware of the courtiers' scandalous behaviour by incidents such as the murder of a watchman, carrying out his duties, by a group of aristocratic young rakehells that included the Duke of Monmouth, Charles II's illegitimate son.

Londoners did express their resentment occasionally, such as during the Bawdy House riots in March 1668. These disturbances continued the tradition of smashing up brothels over the Easter period. But that year they were given an extra edge when the apprentices proclaimed, 'that if the King did not give them liberty of conscience, that May-day must be a bloody day'. More directly, they also threatened that, 'ere long they would come and pull White-hall down'. Presumably their logic was that the palace was another, and indeed larger, bawdy house. This caused great alarm, as Pepys witnessed:

> to White-hall, where great talk of the tumult at the other end of the town about Moorefields among the prentices, taking the liberty of these holidays to pull down bawdy-houses. And Lord, to see the apprehensions which this did give to all people at Court, that presently order was given for all the soldiers, horse and foot, to be in armes; and forthwith alarmes were beat by drum and trumpet through Westminster, and all to their colours and to horse, as if the French were coming into the town.

He went to Lincoln's Inn Fields, where the soldiers were drawn up, 'and my Lord Craven commanding of them, and riding up and down to give orders like a madman'. When some apprentices were arrested and imprisoned in the gaol at Clerkenwell, others came 'and brake open the prison and release them'. The extravagant reaction to what was a common practice during the Easter holiday highlighted the tensions between the citizens and the court, significantly focused on the issue of brothels.[2]

Implementation of the penal code against non-Anglicans, both nonconformists and Catholics, had a more direct and continuous impact on many citizens. Perhaps as many as one in five Londoners were dissenters during the post-Restoration period, a significant minority that was subject to restraints and harassment. But that varied, with periods of relative tolerance alternating with crackdowns. Both the king and the Earl of Clarendon favoured some toleration, although political circumstances prevented them from practising that policy for long, and Clarendon fell from power in the wake of the Second Dutch War and the humiliation of the raid on the Medway and blockade of London. And so nonconformists learned to live with persecution. Some disguised their beliefs by swearing the stipulated oaths, attending Anglican services and taking communion when required. Others preferred to worship separately, in meeting houses or even their own homes, risking arrest and imprisonment. By the 1680s London contained an estimated 425 meeting houses and, in St Martin's-in-the-Fields alone, services were held in 'the house of an unknown person', 'the house of Elizabeth Cambridge', 'the house of John King, mason', 'the meeting-house in the house of Mrs. Meggs' and 'in the house of Anthony Wythers'.[3]

In the aftermath of the Great Fire, the Quakers acquired a lease of ground in White Hart Court, off the west side of Gracechurch Street, near Lombard Street. Here they built a meeting house, concealed from the street by other buildings, which was ready for meetings in 1668. George Fox, their founder, was arrested there in 1670, and William Crouch was fined £10 for attending a meeting there in June 1683 and the same, not inconsiderable, amount for a similar offence ten months later. Also in 1683, Daniel Quare, a clock- and watch-maker, and five other Quakers had goods confiscated that were valued at £145 17s 6d, for attending a meeting at White Hart Court.[4]

Such persecution bore important fruit. In August 1670 the Quakers William Penn and William Mead were arrested at a crowded meeting held in Gracechurch Street, having been prevented from entering their meeting house. They were charged with unlawful assembly and disturbing the peace. The Old Bailey jury acquitted them, although they were guilty of 'speaking in Gracious Street'. That was not the verdict which the court required and so the judge put the members of the jury under great pressure – they were even imprisoned without food or water – but they remained defiant. In pressuring a jury to give the 'required' verdict, the judge was acting in accordance with existing practice. But that practice was now overruled and the outcome of the jurors' refusal to co-operate was to establish the primacy of the jury's decision in English law.

Hostility to the dissenters partly reflected latent fear of them as a potentially subversive force. An anti-government conspiracy in the north of England in 1663 coincided with one in Dublin, in which Thomas Blood was instrumental. A plan to seize Dublin castle failed, but Blood, a nonconformist, with a number of his associates, attempted another bold stroke in December 1670, when they almost succeeded in capturing the Duke of Ormond, Lord Lieutenant of Ireland, in London, as he made his way home to Clarence House. Ormond was taken from his coach but managed to break free and when the conspirators shot at him, they missed. Blood then planned an even more audacious coup, to seize the crown jewels from the Tower. Adopting the name Dr Ayliffe, he ingratiated himself with the assistant keeper of the jewels, Talbot Edwards, so successfully that Edwards agreed to his daughter's marriage with Blood's supposed nephew, actually his son. On the day of the wedding, 9 May 1671, Blood and his son arrived at the Tower with three accomplices and, when being shown the jewels, overpowered Edwards, who was wounded in the struggle. They took the jewels and were returning to their horses 'thro all the guards', when Edwards managed to free himself and, joined by his son, who had providentially returned home from overseas just at that time, raised the alarm. The thieves were captured. Blood was imprisoned and was interviewed by the king, the Duke of York and Prince Rupert. Despite the nature of that crime and his earlier attempt to seize Ormond, he was set free and pardoned, to general astonishment. Evelyn was perplexed: 'How he came to be pardoned, & even received to favour, not onely after this, but severall other exploits almost as daring, both in Ireland and here, I could never come to understand.' The explanation may have been that the court took the opportunity to use him as a go-between, to make contact with 'the Sectaries & Enthusiasts' that he knew, as the government considered granting greater toleration for nonconformists.[5]

Apprehension of the latent influence of the dissenters reflected a more general uneasiness. Even coffee-houses were viewed with suspicion by the court and its adherents, as hotbeds of political opposition and perhaps sedition. The lawyer Roger North described them as places of 'Comon Assemblys to discours of Matters of State, News & Great persons, as they are nurserys of Idleness, & pragmaticallness'. A royal proclamation of 29 December 1675 declared them to be 'the great resort of Idle and disaffected persons' that had 'produced very evil and dangerous effects' and ordered all coffee-house keepers to stop selling their beverages, with effect from 10 January following. But, on examination, the government realised that the licences already issued could not be summarily withdrawn, and so it had to countermand the proclamation and publish a new order allowing them to trade for a further six months. The issue then died away and the coffee-houses survived.[6]

Such concerns of the government were far exceeded by the citizens' widespread dread of a Catholic takeover. Perhaps that would be achieved through an uprising, in the aftermath of a disaster such as the Great Fire. But it could be attained more subtly; after all, the queen and heir were Catholics, as were some leading courtiers. And recent events could be interpreted to fit the fears. The notion that the Great Fire had been started deliberately as a prelude to an invasion or coup had not been quashed. John Graunt, a Catholic, was alleged to have turned off the flow of water from the New River Head, to reduce the amount available for fighting the fire. And the fact that Hubert was a Protestant was no obstacle to such an interpretation, for he was said to have been converted while in prison and died a Catholic. How that could have been part of his motivation for setting fire to Farriner's bake-house some weeks earlier was not explained. Nor did it need to be, for the evidence could be adapted to the fears. But it was an undeniable fact that if the king did not produce an heir, then his brother would come to the throne, the first Catholic monarch since Mary Tudor, whose reign was inextricably associated with the persecution and burning of Protestants. In February 1683 Robert Humes of Stepney was convicted of saying that, 'Popery is coming into this Kingdome, and if the Duke of Yorke should succeede his brother, hee would be a worse popish tyrant then ever Queene Mary was.'[7]

A strong political movement developed to exclude James from the succession. If Charles had been married to Lucy Walter, the Duke of Monmouth's mother, then the duke was the legitimate heir, and he was a Protestant. Hence the rumour reported in April 1680 and described as:

a strange Story published yesterday in Coffee Houses, of which … it was said, that Cosens Bishop of Durham had left a paper seal'd in Sir Gilbert Gerrard's hands, with a charge not to open it till the King was dead, but he had been of late wrought on to open it, and finds it a certificate of that Bishop's having married the King to the Duke of Monmouth's Mother, this I had from a Person of Honour, who heard it published in the Coffee house'.[8]

An alternative to legitimising Monmouth was to exclude James from the succession, so that his daughter Mary would succeed Charles. She married, in November 1677, the Stadholder William of Orange, effective ruler of the United Provinces, a Calvinist and inveterate enemy of Louis XIV. Sir Richard Newdigate was notified that, when the news of the marriage was released, 'the rejoicing in London by ringing of bells, bonfires etc. was great'.[9]

Opponents of the court – with the Earl of Shaftesbury and Duke of Buckingham prominent in the Lords and William Lord Russell and Algernon Sidney in the Commons – made exclusion a major issue in the late 1670s and early 1680s and introduced a bill in three successive parliaments to achieve their objective. Both they and their opponents issued vehement and vitriolic propaganda. Narcissus Luttrell explained that the exclusionists were called by their opponents, 'whigs, fanaticks, covenanteers, bromigham protestants, &c.; and the former are called by the latter, tories, tantivies, Yorkists, high flown church men'. Oliver Heywood simplified the categories when he noted that, 'instead of Cavalier and Roundhead, now they are called Torys and Wiggs'.[10] Whigs were Presbyterian rebels from the west of

Scotland, in the late 1640s, and Tories were dispossessed outlaws in Ireland. Both labels stuck and were retained as the names of the two major political groups until the nineteenth century.

The situation was complicated and inflamed by the Popish Plot, a fabrication by Titus Oates, an Anglican clergyman, and Israel Tonge, whose particular obsession was the Great Fire. The king was first told of their allegations in August 1678. Essentially, these were that there was a Jesuit plot to assassinate him and burn London, with uprisings in England and Ireland and even a French invasion. On 6 September Oates swore to a deposition consisting of forty-three articles before the City justice of the peace Sir Edmund Berry Godfrey, a well-known and respected figure, not least because he had remained in London during the Great Plague. Before the end of the month an expanded version had been given to the Privy Council. Then, on 12 October, Godfrey disappeared, and five days later his body was found in a ditch at Primrose Hill. He had been strangled and then stabbed with his own sword; valuables on the body showed that robbery was not the motive and the assumption was that he had been killed by Catholic conspirators to prevent him from revealing what he knew of their practices and plans. Evelyn explained that, 'the Murder of Sir Ed: Godferie (suspected to have ben compassed by the Jesuite party, for his intimacy with Coleman (a buisy person whom I also knew) & the feare they had he was able to have discovered some thing to their prejudice) did so exasperate, not onely the Commons, but all the nation'.[11] On 21 October the king told the Commons that, 'I have been informed of a Design against my Person, by the Jesuits; of which I shall forbear any Opinion, lest I may seem to say too much, or too little.' The Commons interviewed Oates, Tonge and others, investigated the murder of Godfrey and seized the papers of Edward Coleman, secretary to the Duke and Duchess of York, a sensitive post, who had been named by Oates as a suspect. Eleven days after being informed by the king of the plot, the Commons declared: 'That this House is of Opinion, that there hath been, and still is, a damnable and hellish Plot contrived and carried on by the Popish Recusants, for the Assassinating and Murdering the King; and for subverting the Government; and rooting out and destroying the Protestant Religion.'[12]

Oates and Tonge were taken seriously, despite the nature of the allegations, inconsistencies in their accounts, their past lives and personalities. A search of Coleman's papers did reveal correspondence that was deemed to be treasonable and he was convicted and executed on that evidence. This, as Evelyn wrote, gave Oates 'such esteeme with the Parliament', that his other, increasingly far-fetched, allegations were also given credence and more than thirty others were subsequently tried and executed, even though, in

Evelyn's opinion, 'Such a mans Testimonie should not be taken against the life of a Dog.' Gilbert Burnet explained that, because of Godfrey's murder, 'Oates's evidence was ... so far believed that it was not safe to seem to doubt it'.[13] That was borne out by the case of Edward Sackville, an MP, who was sent to the Tower and expelled from the Commons in March 1679, because, 'he has gone about to make it be believed, that there is no Popish Plot, by vilifying and disparaging the Evidence given for the Discovery thereof, and contemning the Proceedings of Parliament thereupon; and endeavouring to stifle the Belief of the Murder of Sir Edmundbury Godfrey by the Papists'.[14]

As news of the plot and Godfrey's murder became known, precautionary steps were taken in London. The trained bands were put on alert, the gates were kept closed, posts and chains were erected in the streets, and houses of leading Catholics were searched for weapons. Parliament's committees enquiring into the plot were told of priest-holes discovered in some houses years earlier and caches of arms that had been hidden in others. At Bridlington they heard that, 'daily carts are loaded with arms found in papists' houses and carried to the Tower'.[15]

Many now came forward with tales and accusations, hoping to gain favour or influence, perhaps protect themselves, or displace or take revenge on someone by alleging that they were a Catholic. Pepys's connection with the Duke of York attracted suspicion. He was accused in the Commons of being a closet Papist and in May 1679 resigned his post as Secretary to the Admiralty. He spent six weeks in the Tower, suspected of passing naval information to the French, although he was released without charge. One of his clerks, Samuel Atkins, was 'by a most manifest contrivance' arrested and tried for being an accessory to Godfrey's murder, but was acquitted. As Pepys wrote, the charge, 'cannot be thought to pass in the world at so jealous a time as this without some reflections upon me as his master'. Presumably for the same reason, his musician friend Cesare Morelli was alleged to be a Jesuit. Morelli was able to send Pepys a list of men who, 'all could agree in my not having been known at Lisbon as a priest, much less as a Jesuit'. Pepys did not think that was sufficient and advised him to recollect 'the places and conditions' where he had been over the past years, because 'those who have the wickedness to begin that lie, will not forbear to assert it as often as they shall judge it apropos to do me and you mischief with'. Those were dangerous days, even for a Protestant such as Pepys, and more so for someone with Catholic connections.[16]

For the majority of Londoners, the winter of the Popish Plot was one of foreboding and fears of arson. According to the Presbyterian divine Richard Baxter, they organised, 'private Watches in all streets ... to keep their houses from firing'.[17] When the Duke of York went to help direct operations at a blaze in the Temple, he had to leave because of the abuse, some calling him 'a Popish dog'.[18] A maid servant set fire to her master's house in Fleet Street after a row over the cooking of dinner, in 1680, and a pamphleteer took the opportunity to warn readers, in *The Jesuites Firing-Plot Revived*, of the 'many Firing Plots' recently carried out by 'the cunning Jesuites ... in the which for the most part they Employ Silly Servant-Maides'.[19]

In January 1679 the king prorogued the Cavalier Parliament and later dissolved it, after eighteen years. Although the first impact of the plot subsided, the Whig leaders now took up the issue of exclusion and he prorogued the new Parliament, on 27 May, to prevent the progress of a bill, 'to disable the Duke of Yorke to inherit the Imperial Crown of this Realm'. In so doing he incidentally halted a bill to renew the Act of 1662, 'for preventing Abuses in Printing seditious, treasonable, and unlicensed Books and Pamphlets; and for Regulating of Printing and Printing Presses'. And so the powers in that Act, for licensing and censoring of publications, came to an end. The consequence, described by Gilbert Burnet, was that, 'many virulent pamphlets both against the Court and clergy were published, wherein the Nonconformists had so great a hand that they provoked the other party to write with the like vehemence against them'.[20] The number of books and pamphlets published certainly increased sharply, from 1,174 in 1678 to 1,730 in 1679 and 2,145 in 1680. London was the centre of publishing and printing and many of the titles were issued in the city. Distribution of exclusionist material was organised by the Whig clubs, of which there were twenty-nine in London, based in taverns and coffee-houses. The best-known was the Green Ribbon Club, at the King's Head tavern in Chancery Lane.[21]

The Green Ribbon Club played an important part in organising the pope-burning processions in 1679, 1680 and 1681, which drew enormous crowds. These were held on 17 November, Queen Elizabeth's accession day. Commemoration of the discovery of the Gunpowder Plot was still observed on 5 November, and in 1679, 'there was a great bonfire made in the Palace Yard at Westminster, and many of the Books, Garments, Crucifixes and other Popish Trinkets were there publickly burnt, with the Acclamations of the People'.[22] But the pope-burning events were more elaborate, with expensively made effigies and pageants, and they attracted the largest crowds. In 1679, after the procession through the City, an estimated 200,000 people watched the burning of the effigies at Temple Bar. That was the place for the bonfires in the following year, and in 1681 the climax was in Smithfield, an emotional choice because it was the site of many of the burnings of Protestants during Mary Tudor's reign.

A pamphleteer reminded his readers of those evil times, when members of the laity were, 'torn to pieces, and tied to a Stake in the midst of flames at Smithfield, and other places'.[23] Temple Bar, too, was significant, as it stood at the boundary between the City and Westminster, on the principal ceremonial route. Charles II had insisted that the corporation replace the old, and increasingly unsound, structure as part of the process of improving the City in the aftermath of the Great Fire. The new one, erected in 1672 to Christopher Wren's designs, was a triumphal arch, in Portland stone, with statues of the Stuart monarchs Charles I and Charles II on the Westminster side, and James I and his queen, Anne of Denmark, facing the City.

The London Whigs celebrated on other occasions, such as Monmouth's arrival in the city in November 1679, in defiance of his father: 'The Bells & Bone-fires of the Citty at this arrival of D:M: publishing their joy to the no small regret of the Court'.[24] When the Duke of York returned, the following February, the court's supporters staged a similar response: 'there were many Bonfires on Tuesday night made in and about the City for Joy of his R. Highness's arrival'. This led to a scuffle at a bonfire outside a Frenchman's door in the Strand. When some gentlemen on his balcony waved their hats and shouted, 'God save the D. of York', some boys about ten or twelve years old around the fire replied, 'God bless the D. of Monmouth also!' The gentlemen 'came down and drew their swords and made the Boys flie. But a little after some lusty fellows came down to the fire, who broke their swords and beat them soundly and broke the windows of the house'. The crisis produced low-level brawling and bullying in London, and incidents such as the one in which two lords, a Captain Billingsly and a dozen others went into a coffee-house in Covent Garden to provoke the Whigs there by shouting, 'Damn the Whigs for Rogues'. When they were ignored, they 'took hold of one Party, a Tailor, as he was going and asked him whether he was a Whig or a Tory, and he crying "a Whig!" they burnt his periwig, and Billingsly kicked him downstairs, of which he threatens to complain to the Council'.[25]

The highly charged atmosphere proved too much for the Earl of Halifax, as he explained in a letter to Henry Savile, in January 1680:

> Our world here is so over-run with the politicks, the fools' heads so heated, and the knaves so busy, that a wasp's nest is a quieter place to sleep in than this town is to live in, which maketh me so weary of it that you must not wonder if you hear that, notwithstanding my passion for London, that hath been little inferiour to yours for Paris, I go very early this spring into the country.[26]

The Whigs were getting the better of the demonstrations and were in a majority on the corporation. The lord mayor and both sheriffs were Whigs, as were a majority of the common council, and the City's four MPs. The sheriffs returned the juries, which in practice had been done by the under-sheriffs, who were attorneys and so could be managed by the court. But as Burnet wrote, 'a new practice ... that produced very ill consequences' was introduced, with the sheriffs themselves taking the role, which the court regarded 'with a jealous eye, as done on design to pack juries in order to screen the party in all prosecutions'. For example, 'though several printers were indicted for scandalous libels upon the Government, yet the grand juries were so packed that they always returned an Ignoramus upon the bills against them'.[27] They also blocked indictments for treason brought against leading opponents of the court.

The Whig majority at Guildhall confirmed that the Great Fire had been the result of a papist plot, when, in 1680, common council ordered that an inscription be added to the Monument, stating that, 'the City of London was burnt and consumed with fire by the treachery and malice of the Papists'. In the following year the Court of Aldermen agreed that there should be an inscription on the Monument concerning 'the fireing of this City by the Papists', with another on 'the house where the fire began'. That added to the building on the site of Farriner's house stated: 'Here, by the Permission of Heaven, Hell brake loose upon this Protestant City, from the malicious Hearts of barbarous Papists, by the hand of their Agent HUBERT', while the statement on the Monument was equally uncompromising: 'This pillar was sett up in perpetuell remembrance of the most dreadful Burning of this Protestant City, begun and carried on by the treachery and malice of the Popish faction ... in order to the effecting of their horrid plot for the extirpating the Protestant religion and English liberties, and to introduce Popery and slavery'.[28]

Those inscriptions were put up during the mayoralty of Sir Patience Ward, but he was to be the last Whig lord mayor for the time being. The most senior alderman after Ward was Sir John Moore, a Tory who had attracted criticism because he had presented an address to the king, thanking him for his proclamation justifying his dissolution of the third Exclusion Parliament. The king had summoned it to meet at Oxford, a royalist city, and had dissolved it after eight days; he did not summon another. In an attempt to forestall Moore, two other aldermen were nominated for the post, and so a poll was held, which Moore won with a comfortable majority.

The corporation had earlier overcome attempts by the crown to influence the choice of sheriffs, when the court's candidates were defeated at the elections in 1680 and 1681. Common Hall went so far in 1681 as to thank the outgoing sheriffs for their 'continual provision of faithful and able juries'. The effect of such juries on the crown's policies was again illustrated after the arrest and imprisonment of Shaftesbury on suspicion of high treason, in July of that year. In November his case came before a grand jury, largely consisting of exclusionists and Whigs, which was to decide whether he should be sent to trial. The hearing provoked demonstrations in his support. After the depositions were given in, the court adjourned for dinner and when the witnesses against the earl returned to court they were accosted, according to one of them, by 'thousands of people with long poles, half-pikes and halberts in their hands hindering our passage, calling us rogues and rascals'.[29] Such intimidation was not necessary and the jury duly brought in a verdict of ignoramus, which was followed by celebrations and bonfires in the City. Shaftesbury was released from the Tower on 28 November, and 'because the rabble in the city had lighted bonfires on the day the jury acquitted him, the justices of London and Middlesex had now strict orders to prevent the like tumultuous doings'.[30]

The king showed his approval of Moore's election by dining at the feast on lord mayor's day. He had done so throughout the 1670s, until 1678, when he was absent, as he was in 1679 and 1680, at the inauguration of Whig lord mayors. In 1679 the *True Domestick Intelligence* reported: 'His Majesty dined not at the New Lord Mayor's Feast, though invited above a week before the time; but most of the courtiers did, and the forraign Ministers.' The *Domestic Intelligence* carried the lord chief baron's comments, when in his 'discourse of this great office [he] was pleased to intimate that the City ought yet to be carefull of the designs of the Romish party, whose Jesuits and Priests are never idle in contriving and promoting the destruction of his Majestie's person and Government'. At the following year's celebrations for Ward's mayoralty the three new songs were, 'the first in praise of the Merchant Taylors; the second, the Protestant's Exhortation; and the third, the plotting Papist's Litany'.[31]

Moore's mayoralty saw a confused and bitterly contested election for sheriffs, which took several weeks. The outcome was that both men chosen were Tories, the election of Thomas Papillon and John Du Bois, the Whig candidates put forward by Common Hall, having been set aside. A poll was also required for the choice of lord mayor to succeed Moore. Sir William Pritchard, the senior alderman who had not passed the chair, was a Tory and the crown's preferred candidate, and he was chosen. The Tories were now in a strong position on the corporation. Those who sailed close to the wind during demonstrations, in print or by speaking publicly against the government, would not now have the security of having their case heard by a grand jury that would throw out the charge.

The crown had mounted another challenge to the corporation, that of questioning the validity of their charter. This was also done in the case of other cities and boroughs. Technical flaws could be detected by the crown's lawyers and a charter then declared forfeit, to be replaced by a new one giving the crown powers over the choice of officers. The outcome of the policy when applied to the City of London would be an important test case. And so a *quo warranto* writ was issued, in January 1682, summoning the lord mayor and commonalty to appear in the court of King's Bench to demonstrate the basis on which they held their privileges and rights. The case was not heard until February 1683 and judgement, for the crown, was delivered in June.

The lord mayor, sheriffs and aldermen went to the king, to discover what action would be taken, now that the charter was suspended. Charles received the delegation at Windsor and Evelyn witnessed the occasion:

> my Lord Keeper made a speech, to them, exaggerating the dissorderly & royotous behaviour in the late Election & polling for Papillon & Du Bois, after the Common hall had been formaly disolv'd, with other misdemeanors, Libells on the Government, &c for which they had incurr'd upon themselves his Majesties high displeasure; and that but for this submission, and under such Articles which the King should require their obedience to: he would certainely, Enter Judgement against them; which hitherto he had suspended: which were as follows: That they should neither Elect Major, Sheriff, Alderman, Recorder, Common Serjeant, Towne-Cleark, Coroner or Steward of Southwark, without his Majesties approbation; and that if they presented any, his Majestie did not like, they should proceede in wonted manner to a second choice, if that were disapprov'd his Majestie to nominate them; & if within five daies they thought good to assent to this, all former miscarriages should be forgotten &c: & so they tamely parted, with their antient priveleges, after they had dined and ben treated by the King &c:[32]

His ultimatum was debated by common council and when put to the vote, 104 were for acceptance and 85 were against. Evelyn judged this to be, 'a signal & remarkable period; what the Consequences will prove time will shew'. As a result of the proceedings, the recorder, Sir George Treby, was displaced and, according to Evelyn, 'an obscure lawyer set in his place', and eight of the 'richest & prime Aldermen' were removed, the remainder were made only justices of the peace '& wearing no more Gownes or Chaines of Gold'. Evelyn had the opportunity to play a part in the purging of the corporation, but declined, as he disapproved. He was, he noted in his diary, 'not a little sorry, his Majestie was so often put upon things of this nature, against so great a Citty, the Consequences wheroff might be so much to his prejudice'. Having summarised the changes, he added that, 'the pompe & grandeur of the most august Cittie in the World chang'd face in a moment, & gave much occasion of discourse, & thoughts of heart, what all this would end in, & prudent men were for the old foundations'.[33] Similar action was taken against the livery companies, to establish the crown's right to control the membership of their governing bodies.

As the king reasserted his authority and the political pendulum swung his way, the Tory elements among the citizens and apprentices grew in confidence. They held processions, roasted rumps, burned effigies of Presbyter Jack and attacked Whig demonstrators. Their days for demonstrations to show their loyalty were 29 May, the king's birthday, and the queen's birthday, 25 November. Nevertheless, the exclusionist crowds were still powerful and on the day of the Gunpowder Treason celebrations in 1682 they retaliated forcefully when some Tories attempted to put out bonfires, to chants of 'a York, a York'. The Whig apprentices 'sowndly beat off these persones that were putting out their fires'. They then paraded through the streets and attacked the premises of Tories, including the house of Sir Roger L'Estrange, the leading Tory propagandist, and that of Nathaniel Thompson, publisher of Tory newspapers and pamphlets. The crowd also vented their rage on inn signs that offended them, such as the Cardinal's Head and Duke of York's Head in Cheapside, and the Mitre in Stocks Market. They were numerous enough to drive off the trained-bands that had been called out to suppress them and so only a few arrests were possible. But this proved to be the last such riot of the exclusion crisis, for four days later a government order banned bonfires and fireworks during the days of public celebrations, and it was enforced effectively.[34]

Shortly after the lord mayor, aldermen and sheriffs had been told of the king's actions regarding the charter, news broke of the Rye House Plot to assassinate the king and his brother. This was to be done as they returned from the races at Newmarket, but miscarried because a fire in the town caused them to leave much earlier than planned. When information on this 'Protestant Plot' was given by Josiah Keeling, a London oilman and 'most perverse Fanatick', the government acted swiftly and arrested not only some prominent Whigs, but others who had opposed the government. Lord William Russell and Algernon Sidney were convicted and executed in the aftermath; Shaftesbury had gone into exile in Holland in the previous November. Ward, Papillon and Slingsby Bethel, a Whig who served as sheriff in 1680–1, had also moved there for safety and were living in Utrecht. The Whigs were left virtually leaderless and their propagandists now came under pressure. Newdigate's supplier of news wrote to him on 14 June that, 'Tuesday being the time that Judgment was given against the Charter of

London, I had well nigh finished my Letters, when an order came from the Lord Mayor into my house and seized all the said Letters together, which my Wife and Servants say 'twas done to divers others besides.' Early in July he was told that, 'all our discourse now is who are seized and who are committed'.[35] Henry Care was the most influential Whig writer and in early July his printer, James Astwood, was fined for printing Care's *Weekly Pacquet* without authority. Harassed and weary, Care ceased issuing the paper on 13 July. He subsequently switched his allegiance and wrote for James and the Tories.[36] Pressure was also brought to bear on nonconformist meetings. In 1683, Newdigate was told that, 'The Quakers are extreme stubborn. Their Meeting House in Grace Church Street being kept shut, they in great numbers resorted thither in the street, bringing forms, chairs etc., and one beginning to speak he was taken away either by the Constables or Soldiers, but immediately his Room was supplied by another and so successively, and some were committed.'[37]

Such passive opposition to persecution could not weaken the government's grip on London. When Charles died, in February 1685, his brother succeeded to the throne as James II and, as was customary, was proclaimed king in the city, without any hostile reaction. And when Monmouth raised a rebellion in the West Country four months later, Londoners remained quiescent, despite their earlier admiration of him as their Protestant hero. Without the support of the leading Whigs and Londoners, or risings elsewhere, Monmouth was defeated and went to the block in July. So sure was the government of its control of the capital that, 'Now were also those words in the Inscription about the Pillar (intimating the Papists firing the Citty) erased and cut out.'[38]

James attempted to introduce toleration for his co-religionists, extending that policy to Protestant dissenters, which was designed to weaken Anglican influence. It allowed them to worship free from harassment, and to hold offices and positions from which they had been debarred, unless they took the requisite oaths. In 1687 he issued his first Declaration of Indulgence, which suspended the religious tests and penal laws against Catholics and dissenters. The *quo warranto* proceedings had allowed Charles's government to ensure that members of the Church of England held office in the cities and boroughs. James now turned this round and removed Anglicans, replacing them with dissenters, but was disappointed by the outcome. When he returned from a progress, according to Burnet, 'he changed the magistracy in most of the cities in England in favour of the Dissenters, but was surprised to find that the new Lord Mayor and aldermen of London took the Test, and ordered the observation of Gunpowder Treason day to be continued'. That was indeed a rebuff, for he could reasonably have expected those celebrations to be cancelled, in return for ending the persecution of dissenters. Burnet added that they, 'continued the service of the Church of England in Guildhall Chapel, notwithstanding the King sent them a permission to use what form of worship they pleased'.[39] The lord mayor chosen in 1687, Sir John Shorter, insisted on 'going to the Sacrament and taking the Test', because he was 'required by law to take the Oath of Allegiance and Supremacy'. He and the others nominated by the king were anxious to observe the law and did not take advantage of the Declaration of Indulgence, to the irritation of the court.[40]

Not all of those nominated by the king were willing to serve. Sir George Treby was twice offered his former position of Recorder, but declined on both occasions. He took the opportunity to tell the king, in a private audience, that his policies had alarmed the people, 'with the apprehension of the loss of their religion'.[41] The Anglican aldermen were ejected in August 1687 and others were nominated, including the Baptist William Kiffin. He had been involved in City politics from the 1640s and was elected sheriff in 1670, but ruled unable to hold the office, as a nonconformist. Kiffin now declined to serve as an alderman and accepted only when he faced the prospect of a huge fine for refusing, serving from October 1687. He limited his involvement to, 'such things as concerned the welfare of the city and the good of the orphans, whose distressed condition called for help; although we were able to do little towards it'. He also recalled that:

> We had frequently orders from the King to send to the several companies, to put great numbers of the Livery Men out of the privilege of being Livery Men, and others to be put in their rooms. Most of those who were so turned out were Protestants of the Church of England. There has been a list of seven hundred at a time sent to be discharged, although no crime was laid to their charge. From this, all men might see to what a deplorable state this city was like to be in.[42]

James nominated Catholics to other places from which they were barred, claiming that the sovereign had a dispensing power to set aside the laws that prevented them from holding those positions. Not all carried influence or profit. One intended beneficiary was Andrew Popham, who was nominated by the king to an almsman's place in the Charterhouse, where he did have the right to nominate almsmen. But nominees were required to present certificates that they had taken the oaths of allegiance and supremacy, and the Anglican communion. Popham's case prompted a debate at the next meeting of the hospital's governors. When the Master pointed out that the Act of Parliament establishing the hospital contained a clause to that effect, 'One Governour answer'd, What is this to the purpose? To whom the late

Duke of Ormond reply'd, He thought it was very much to the purpose, For an Act of Parliament was not so slight a thing, but that it should deserv'd to be consider'd. Hereupon, after some discourse, the Question was put again, Whether Andrew Popham should be admitted or no: and it was carried in the Negative.' The matter was raised again subsequently, but neither Popham nor Philip de Cardonel, another of the king's nominees, was admitted. The case was significant, given the Charterhouse's status as England's largest almshouse, and the seniority of its governors, who were 'Persons of the greatest quality' in the government and the church. The narrator of the affair praised them, for 'tho' they had no precedent, at that time, to follow, [they] made a vigorous resistance to this encroaching power. Whereby they did good Service also to the Publick, in that low station of a private hospital.'[43]

Dissatisfied with the response to the Declaration of Indulgence, James issued a second one in April 1688, 'with the addition that he would adhere firmly to it, and put none in employment but such as would concur in maintaining it'. The bishops were instructed to send copies to the clergy and direct them to read it to their congregations.[44] But both they and the clergy were inclined to resist and, indeed, according to Burnet, 'only seven in London, and not above two hundred all England over, read it'. William Sancroft, the Archbishop of Canterbury, and six of the bishops petitioned the king, explaining their reasons for not obeying the order sent to them. After repeating their stance in an audience with the king, they were despatched to the Tower, pending trial. Burnet described the Londoners' reaction, in extravagant terms:

Never was the City, in the memory of man, in such a fermentation as upon this occasion. The banks of the river (for the bishops went by water) were crowded with people, kneeling down, and asking their blessings, and with loud shouts expressing their good wishes and hearty concern for their preservation. In the Tower the soldiers and officers did the same, and a universal consternation appeared in all peoples' faces.

They received much support while they were imprisoned. George Kenyon wrote to his father, telling him that: 'I was this day in the Tower to see them at prayers. People crowd so many to see them, that the soldiers are forced to keep all the gates shut, and, did they not, I beleeve the Tower would scarce hold the numbers that flock there.' Duly brought to trial, the bishops were, 'at last acquitted, to the inexpressible joy of the City, the army, and the whole nation.'[45]

Having alienated the Anglicans without having conciliated the dissenters, the king's position became increasingly difficult. Furthermore, the birth of a son and heir on 10 June raised the likelihood that James would be succeeded by a Catholic, perhaps indeed by a Catholic dynasty. Rumours had already begun to circulate in the spring that the birth would be faked, and the fact that the baby was a boy was used to support the notion that it had been fabricated, the baby having been smuggled into the queen's bed. On the day that the bishops were acquitted, 30 June, six peers and the Bishop of London, Henry Compton, signed a letter inviting William of Orange to intervene, as the husband of the heiress to the throne, until the birth of James's son. He was most willing to comply and set about reconciling opinion within the United Provinces and negotiating with other states to gain their acceptance, or least acquiescence, while his army was engaged in such a difficult operation. Warnings of William's military preparations reached James towards the end of August, and by the middle of September Evelyn, 'found the Court in the uttermost consternation upon report of the Pr: of Oranges landing, which put White-hall into so panic a feare, that I could hardly believe it possible to find such a change'.[46] Henri Misson later summarised the events of 1688, with the justificatory comment that, 'I was an Eye-witness of most of the Things that I advance here, and had certain Knowledge of the rest'. He recalled that James's spirits were raised when he received a report that the expedition had been scattered by a storm, but that was soon contradicted and so, 'the Joy of Whitehall chang'd into Consternation, on the Evening of the very same Day, 30 Octob'. William's army landed at Torbay on 5 November, the traditional day for Protestant celebration, and when the news reached Whitehall it, 'put the King & Court into greate Consternation'.[47]

A critical press had again sprung up, which James attempted to stifle. Misson's reaction to the king's proclamation 'to hinder the spreading of false News' was that: 'He might as easily have hinder'd the Course of the Thames; and which was worst of all, he was now no longer fear'd. Besides the Manuscript News-Papers, and the common London Gazette, there were a great many others publish'd daily; the Orange Gazette, the Orange Intelligence, Universal Intelligence, Publick Occurrences, English Courant, London Mercury, Observator, &c. all fill'd with Truth and Falsehood mixt'.[48] Publications and prints critical of the court were also brought in from Holland. In the summer of 1688 the Londoner William Westby complained that the Dutch, 'heighten and aggravate all things by their pamphlets which are privately brought over and sold at great prices which hint irreverent reflections on the government and endeavour to spirit away the affections of the people and debauch their love to their prince'.[49]

In an attempt to reconcile the City, on 6 October he had restored its charter, withdrawn five years earlier. But when the Lord Chancellor,

George Jeffreys, went to Guildhall with the charter, 'the people made no huzzahs at the sight of the seal', and some of those nominated as aldermen refused to serve. So did Sir William Pritchard, appointed as lord mayor. But the common sergeant, town clerk and other officers ejected under the *quo warranto* proceedings were re-instated, and on 1 December common council met, for the first time since 1683. The king made a further bid to appease opinion in the capital, reported in a laconic tone by Misson: 'James II. Being mov'd with a sudden Commiseration for the Poor of the City of London, orders, by Proclamation, that a Collection should be made for them, 16 Nov. 1688.'[50] But feelings had been running high for some time, occasionally breaking out into anti-Catholic demonstrations. A sermon by 'an impertinent Jesuite' at the end of September provoked some of the congregation to such an extent that, according to Evelyn, 'they pulled him out of the Pulpit, & treated him very coursely, insomuch as it was like to create a very greate disturbance in the Citty'. Towards the end of October he noted: 'A Tumult in Lond on the rabble demolishing a popish Chappell set up in the City'. That was an attack on the Jesuit's chapel and college in Bucklesbury, where the crowd broke into the chapel and 'took out many of their vests, copes, ornaments and trinkets some say to the value of £400 and burnt them'. The buildings were then set alight.[51]

After news of the invasion reached London, there was another anti-Catholic outburst on a Sunday, when:

> the rabble got together to pull down the Popishe chapel at St. James', and broke the windows, &c., but the Lord Craven and guards coming, and promising to blow it up next day, they were dispersed; but yesterday, as the preists were removing their goods, they seized on two cartloads and burnt them on Holborn Hill and in Smithfeild; whereupon the guards were sent to suppress them, with orders to fire with bullet, which they did, and killed 4 or 5, and forced the rest to retreat.[52]

James went to Salisbury to join his army and oppose William's march on London. But some of his supporters defected, including senior officers, and he returned to Whitehall. Burnet's summary of the problems now facing the king included the phrase, 'the City in an ungovernable fermentation'. Those who gathered in the coffee-houses were not immune from the tension. On 5 December Robert Hooke noted in his diary that there were, 'jealousies of much danger to the City. Great confusion of reports, noe certainty'.[53]

The sense of confusion was increased when James, unable to find a political solution, left London on the night of 10–11 December, intending to escape to France. Burnet's assessment was confirmed by the disorders that erupted when the news broke: 'the apprentices and rabble, supposing the priests had persuaded him to it, broke out again with fresh fury upon all suspected houses, and did much havoc in many places'.[54] A more specific account described how, 'the Mob, grown bolder than ever, arm themselfes with Sticks and all Sorts, and plunder and pull down the Convent of St John's in Smithfield; two Popish Chappels, one near Lincolns-Inn-Fields, and the other in Lime-street; the Houses of the Embassadors of Spain, Venice, and Tuscany; the Printing-House of Henry Hill, and some Houses belonging to private Papists'. St John's was singled out, 'on a report of gridirons, spits, great cauldrons, &c. to destroy protestants', and the premises of Henry Hills because he was the king's printer, who had decamped just a couple of days earlier. According to the *English Currant*, the crowd, 'destroy'd Mr. Henry Hills Printing-House; spoil'd his Forms, Letters, &c and burnt 2 or 300 Reams of Paper, printed and unprinted'.[55] The crowds then, 'proceeded from place to place, pulling down and burning Popish chapels and mass houses, carrying the images and crosses in triumph'.[56] They also attacked, 'severall popish Lords & Gent: houses, especially that of the Spanish Ambassador, which they pillaged & burnt his Library'.[57] The French embassy was protected by soldiers of the trained-bands. The antiquary John Aubrey was distraught when he wrote to Anthony Wood, in Oxford, telling him of the destruction, 'at the Spanish Ambassador's, at Wild House, where were burnt MSS & antiquities invaluable, such as are not left in the world'.[58]

The peers then in London met at Guildhall, to form a provisional government, and ordered the king's forces to withdraw from the capital. The Guildhall Declaration which they issued stated that they sought protection for the laws and freedoms, James having withdrawn from the kingdom, and declared their support for William and Mary, and Protestantism. On the following day, apprehensive of further disorders, and perhaps also alarmed by a rumour that disbanded Irish troops would march on London, they ordered the placing of cannon 'in the Park, Charing Cross, at the entrance into Piccadilly from Hyde Park side, and other proper places, that the foot guards should stand to their arms in St. James's Park, and the horse guards the same'. They also authorised the trained-bands to fire on the crowds, if necessary.[59] Their fears were shared by the Londoners themselves, who, on the same day, 13 December, were seized with a panic, 'that they should have their throats cut by the French and by the Papists'. Once again, they feared that crisis and confusion were the prelude to a French invasion. A Catholic uprising in London co-ordinated with an attack by a hostile army was a concern that had intermittently gripped the citizens for the previous fifty years or more. And so householders came out into the streets with their weapons in case there was an insurrection and that night placed lighted candles in their windows.[60]

The queen had also left Whitehall on 10 December, disguised as a laundry maid, and took her son with her. She reached Calais on the following day, but, inconveniently, James had not managed to escape, being recognised at Faversham and returned to London on 16 December. Despite his recent flight and its consequences, many citizens were relieved that he had returned and so, 'In his passage through the City he was welcomed by great numbers with loud acclamations of joy.'[61] But the peers were critical of his conduct and the possible effects of the vacuum he had created; he had not only fled without making any political arrangements but had also dropped the Great Seal into the Thames. The Earl of Ailesbury, a gentleman of the bedchamber, was said to have told him, 'that your going away without leaving a Commission of Regency, but for our care and vigilance the city of London might have been in ashes'. Indeed, one of his supporters later regretted James's failure to make a stand, as 'he wanted not incouragement by the Bonefires and Huzzahs with which the City received him' and some defiance on his part would have, 'raised the Spirit of his Army, and of the Papists who were then very numerous in London'. Even the peers were apprehensive of the scale of support for James and, when his departure was being arranged, Halifax opposed plans for him to go through London and across the bridge, 'Saying their going through the Citie might cause disorder and move compassion'.[62] But eventually all was settled and James left on 18 December.

William reached London that day and his troops entered the city without opposition, 'The Eng: souldiers &c. sent out of Towne to distant quarters: not well pleased'.[63] But William's troops were welcomed by the crowds, including 'diverse ordinary women in Fleet Street' and a woman outside Ludgate, who 'gave diverse ordinary baskets full of oranges to the Prince's officers and soldiers as they marched by to testify her affection towards them'. Bells were rung and bonfires were lit, accompanied by 'all the public demonstrations of joy imaginable'.[64] The fears of many citizens were now allayed. There had been no uprising or attacks on the Protestants; it had been the Catholics whose property had been wrecked. Some compensation was paid, according to Misson: 'The Foreign Ministers had full Satisfaction made them for the Loss they suffer'd by the Insolence of this enraged Mob.'[65]

To resolve the constitutional impasse, William summoned an assembly, which the lord mayor, aldermen and fifty members of common council were invited to attend, although the mayor, Sir John Chapman, had been incapacitated by a stroke. The assembly met on 26 December and agreed that a Convention should be summoned. At the elections to the Convention, in January, those chosen to represent the City were Sir Patience

Ward, returned from exile, Sir Robert Clayton, William Love and Thomas Pilkington – who had been imprisoned for three years for his objections to the procedures in the elections to sheriff in 1682. On 13 February William and Mary accepted the offer of the crown and were proclaimed, 'with wonderfull acclamation & general reception, Bonfires, bells, Gunns &c'.[66] Sir George Treby had accepted his former position as Recorder on 10 December and during the following months the *quo warranto* proceedings were reversed, with the City's and livery companies' rights and privileges restored. And the inscription blaming Catholics for the Great Fire was again added to the Monument.

Political stability had returned at last. But perceptive observers, in the coffee-houses and elsewhere, realised that the change of monarch would bring other changes in its wake. Charles and James had kept Britain out of the continental wars since 1674, but it did not require great acuity to realise that William's foreign policy would be quite different.

8

This Smoky, Obstreperous City

Within a few months of William's accession, war was declared on France. This had widespread support within the political nation, for Louis XIV's aggrandising policies were now regarded as a greater threat than the United Provinces' commercial strength, which had been the chief concern of James and his advisors. War was expensive and the cost could be met only by drawing, as never before, on the resources of the City's wealthy goldsmith-bankers and merchants. This was to produce far-reaching changes in the financial sector of London, as the city continued to grow and develop.

The merchants were prospering, for overseas trade was buoyant during the second half of the century, strengthened by the Navigation Acts of 1651 and 1660, which ruled that imports to England must be carried in English vessels or those of the country of origin. To a considerable extent that meant London ships, as the capital remained dominant in overseas trade. The political economist John Houghton wrote, in 1695, that, 'the general Customs of London, are as eleven to fifteen of the whole kingdom'.[1] Between 1663/9 and 1699–1700 exports from London increased from just over £2 million to £2,773,000, and the value of the re-export trade more than doubled, from £900,000 to £1,986,000, during a period of low inflation. Imports also increased, especially in the colonial trades. For example, the volume of tobacco shipped from Maryland and Virginia to London was 7 million lbs in 1662–3, but 22 million lbs in 1699–1700, when two-thirds was re-exported. A strong domestic demand also developed, as smoking became popular, and as the price fell, tobacco ceased to be a luxury. Sugar imports to London from the West Indies, which had been negligible before 1640, rose from 148,000 cwt in 1664/9 to 371,000 cwt in 1699–1700.[2] Perhaps one in five of the capital's workforce was engaged in shipping and other riverside occupations. The other ports feared London's continued, and as they saw it increasing, share of trade. A proposal in 1695 to create a Council of Trade prompted Bristol's merchants to object that if it were to consist of Londoners, 'they will endeavour to overrule things so as they shall best conduce to the bringing all trade to that great city, without respect to the other ports', and in effect, 'London would swallow up the trade of England'.[3]

For domestic business, too, London remained supreme and was without a rival as the fashionable place to shop. Merchandise was more expensive there than locally, yet even a member of the Scottish aristocracy chose to shop in London rather than Edinburgh, for furnishings, clocks, coaches and sedan chairs, and clothes, because of the social imperative to wear the most up-to-date fashions. The increasing number of connections by road reflected its widening trade. In 1681 stagecoach services linked the capital with 88 towns; by 1705 that had risen to 180 towns. Thomas Delaune listed the coach and carriers' services in his *The Present State of London*, published in 1681. This was a practical guide, describing the services by towns; from St Albans, 'Widow Trott's Wagons come to the Cock in Aldersgate-Street, on Mondays and Fridays and goes out on Tuesdays and Saturdays'.[4] Stagecoach services were profitable. Aware that the service between London and Norwich had, 'for several Years last past, been so ill performed, that the Passengers travelling therein, have been very much Incommoded, and the Journeying by the said Coaches rendred very Irksome and Burdensome', in 1695 more than 200 investors got together and 'by a Joynt Stock set up a new and more convenient Stage', leaving three days a week from the Four Swans in Bishopsgate. They were so confident of success that they allocated a share of the profits to charity.[5] The postal service, too, was developing, so that by the mid-1690s, mail was delivered daily to 148 towns and villages within 10 miles of London. And, within the metropolis, according to Henri Misson: 'Every two Hours you may write to any Part of the City, twice a Day to the more distant Parts of the Suburbs.'[6]

That prosperity was threatened by war, which was potentially disruptive and so unwelcome to the merchants, because of the risk of loss of vessels and cargoes to privateers. Roughly 500 vessels had been lost during the Second Dutch War (1665–7) and perhaps 700 during the Third (1672–4). The answer was for the merchantmen to sail in convoys escorted by men-of-war. The merchants disliked this, because of the time lost while a convoy was assembled and the speed at which it sailed, which was necessarily that of the slowest ship. But the system benefited London, as the House of Commons was told during a debate on the cloth trade in 1693, four years after the outbreak of war. More had been exported from London in 1689–91 than in the three preceding years, but less from the other ports: 'it stands with reason that more should be exported from the port of London during the war because of the danger of the seas from privateers, etc. whom to avoid they send up their goods to London and export them hence, because of the conveniency of convoys which go from hence.'[7]

Even the use of convoys could not prevent losses, by capture and shipwreck, and so interruptions to supplies, which had a visible effect in London's shops by the middle of the decade. In June 1693 the convoy from Smyrna was attacked by a French fleet which engaged the escorting warships and captured or destroyed sixty-six of the merchantmen, 'most of them richly laden'. A few weeks later 'divers merchants and citizens' presented a petition to the lord mayor and aldermen, 'relating to the obstruction of trade by sea, and misfortunes that have befallen their ships, to their great impoverishment'. The petition was rejected, but was indicative of concerns about the impact of the war on trade. Evelyn heard, in March 1694, of another blow that had struck the Turkey trade: 'dismal newes of the disaster befalen our Turky merchants Fleete by Tempest, to the almost utter ruine of that Trade'. Narcissus Luttrell noted that the loss was estimated at £400,000 and that the merchants in that trade, 'have shutt up their shops and warehouses from vending any Turky commodities, and silk is risen 8s. per lb'.[8] In September 1695 Pepys wrote to Mrs Steward, a cousin by marriage, telling her that:

> Here's a sad town, and God knows when it will be better, our losses at sea making a very melancholy Exchange at both ends on't; the gentlewomen of this (to say nothing of the other) sitting with their arms across, without a yard of muslin in their shops to sell, while the ladys (they tell mee) walk pensively by, without a shilling (I mean a good one) in their pockets to buy.

Even supplies of low-value raw materials from within England were affected. In January 1694 the impact on the price of such a modest item as tobacco-pipe clay from Poole in Dorset was noted, with the comment that it 'sold in peaceable Times at about eighteen Shillings a Ton, but now in this time of War is worth about three and twenty Shillings'.[9]

Poor harvests, as well as war, contributed to the problems which made the 1690s a difficult period for metropolitan consumers. Foodstuffs were more expensive than in any other decade of the century and prices were particularly high in 1692, 1693 and 1695-9. This had a greater impact in London than elsewhere, with prices in the metropolitan area roughly 10 per cent higher than in southern England and the south Midlands.

Pepys's mention of a 'good' shilling referred to the debasement of the silver coinage, by wear, but more seriously by clipping. The clipping of metal from the rimless edges of coins and melting down the fragments was profitable when the silver price was higher than the coins' nominal value. The process had been gathering momentum since the 1670s and was increased by the demand for silver to pay for the war. Clipping was, of course, illegal, but so many people were doing it that only a few could be detected. On one day in July 1695 Luttrell recorded that 'Moor the tripeman' had been hanged for the offence and that 'a rich chandler of Lambeth and a housekeeper in Long Acre were seized for clipping'.[10] It became such a problem that the public lost confidence in the coins in circulation and weighed them rather than accept their face value, an irritating process that slowed down any transaction.

The impact of losses of shipping and the growing problems with the coinage were frustrating for the government, because the City's financial community was its chief source of loans. The crown's revenues were reduced almost at the outset of the reign by the abolition of the hearth tax, which had been introduced by the Restoration regime in 1662 and had always been unpopular. Although there were exemptions for almshouses, hospitals, some categories of industrial hearths and poor householders, it was regarded as bearing disproportionately on the less well-off and was also disliked because the collectors had the power to enter houses to check the number of hearths. As early as 1 March 1689, William, in a politically adroit move, notified parliament that as 'the Revenue of the Hearth-money is very grievous to the People', he was agreeable 'either to a Regulation of it, or to the Taking of it wholly away'. Not surprisingly, parliament chose the latter course; the Act which abolished the tax included the phrase that it, 'is in itself not only a great oppression to the poorer sort, but a badge of slavery upon the whole nation, exposing every man's house to be entered into and searched at pleasure by persons unknown to him'.[11]

The crown's revenues fell by approximately £200,000 by the abolition of the hearth tax, or almost 11 per cent of anticipated revenue. The excise and other sources of revenue remained, supplemented by new ones, including poll taxes and a window tax, introduced in 1696 and not abolished until 1851. Of much shorter duration was the levy introduced in 1694 on births and burials, with a charge on marriages that was graded according to social and economic status, and a tax on bachelors. Unpopular and not collected assiduously, these failed to raise the sums anticipated. In 1698 the Receiver-General for London, Middlesex and Westminster was rebuked for, 'great neglects … in not examining the produce and duplicates of the Duties … and in failing to afford the receipts of the same as directed … and that thereby the amount of said Duties has fallen considerably short of what might be reasonably expected'.[12] But the biggest source of revenue came to be the land tax, known as the aid, providing almost a third of the crown's revenues.

The political economists Charles Davenant and Gregory King differed when considering whether London was taxed effectively and so paid its due share of taxation. King thought that in country parishes, 'there is scarce an assessor but knows every man, woman, and child in the parish, but it is otherwise in London ... where an assessor shall scarce know 5 families on each side of him'. Davenant, on the other hand, when discussing the sums collected on the aid, believed that it could raise £3 million per annum, 'if it were levied in other parts of England with the same care and exactness as it is in London, Westminster, and Middlesex, which are under the eye and influence of the government'.[13]

The shortfall between revenue and expenditure had to be borrowed from the City's goldsmith-bankers. Sir George Downing, Secretary to the Treasury Commissioners from 1667 to 1672, had been frustrated by this and condemned them as, 'cheats, blood-suckers, extortioners ... the causes of all the King's necessities, and want of monies throughout the kingdom'. Clarendon made plain the connection between the bankers and the City's politics with the observation that, at the time, they, 'did not consist of above the number of five or six men, some whereof were aldermen, and had been lord mayors of London, and all the rest were aldermen, or had fined for aldermen'.[14] Downing's ideal would have been for the loans to have been raised directly. For their part, the leading goldsmith-bankers were so reliant on the king that when repayments of the loans were suspended in 1672, the Stop of the Exchequer, five of them went bankrupt shortly afterwards. Clearly, relations between the City's financiers and the crown were uneasy, with grounds for mistrust on both sides.

Nothing was done before Downing's death in 1684, partly because large-scale borrowing was not a pressing issue while the crown's revenues were increasing and the country was at peace. That changed in 1689 and the need for funds to pay for the war generated a number of schemes. By an act of parliament of 1693 creditors who lent to the government were to be repaid from a separate exchequer fund raised on a specific part of the excise, and so not on the pledge of the king but on the security of parliament. The scheme, proposed by Charles Montagu, was the beginning of the national debt and was followed by a project devised by the City merchants William Paterson and Michael Godfrey for a national bank. Their proposals were well received and Montagu, appointed Chancellor of the Exchequer in April 1694, piloted the necessary legislation through parliament, despite encountering considerable opposition. The tonnage act of April 1694 provided for a loan of £1.2 million, with interest at 8 per cent, to be paid from duties levied on shipping and alcohol. Subscribers were to be incorporated as a bank and given power to borrow further sums on the security of parliamentary taxation, and the bank could deal in bullion and bills of exchange, and issue paper money. The full amount was raised within eleven days from 1,268 subscribers and on 27 July 1694 Britain's first joint-stock bank was incorporated as 'The Governor and Company of the Bank of England'.

The first governor was Sir John Houblon (lord mayor, 1695–6), who subscribed £10,000 to the flotation. He was one of seven of the initial twenty-four directors who were of Huguenot descent, as were almost 10 per cent of the subscribers. Houblon was a member of the Grocers' Company and from November 1694 the bank's staff were housed at the company's hall off Poultry, described by Daniel Defoe as being in 'a very convenient place, and, considering its situation, so near the Exchange, a very spacious, commodious place'. It remained there until 1734, when the bank's first purpose-built office was completed, on the site of Sir John's mansion on the north side of Threadneedle Street.[15]

The bank was a Whig creation, opposed by some leading Tories and described as 'fit only for republics'. Godfrey, the first deputy governor, and 'an eminent merchant', responded with a robust defence, justifying the bank as 'one of the best establishments that ever was made for the good of the kingdom', raising sums for the government more cheaply than could have been done otherwise. Among its benefits to the economy, he predicted that: 'The Bank will reduce the interest of money in England to 3*l*. per cent per annum in a few years, without any law to enforce it, in like manner as it is in all other countries where banks are established, whereby the trade of the nation may be driven upon more equal terms with the rest of our neighbours, where money is to be had at so much lower rates than what we in England have hitherto paid.'[16]

As part of the war effort, the government requested that the bank should send remittances to pay the army campaigning in Flanders. The governors agreed and in May 1695 they decided to establish an agency in Antwerp. Godfrey was one of three governors who went there to arrange it. They then dined with the king at the siege of Namur, and 'afterwards they waited upon him into the trenches to view the same', where Godfrey, peering over the works at the defences, was decapitated by a cannonball. On the news of his death the value of the bank's stock fell immediately, by 2 per cent.[17]

In addition to the loss of such an able governor, the bank faced the problems caused by the much-needed recoinage, carried out in 1696. The old, clipped silver coins were withdrawn and reissued at their nominal value, fixed at the recoinage under Elizabeth, in 1560–1. This process was later described by Hopton Haynes, who was employed at the Royal Mint, as the 'reform by the late grand coynage', but the immediate effect of the process, which necessarily took time, was a shortage of coin, commented upon by Evelyn in June 1696: 'Want of current money to carry on not onely

the smalest concernes, but for daily provisions in the Common Markets.'
Export of silver 'daily transported into Holland' and money sent to pay
the armies in the Low Countries were also blamed for 'breeding such a
scarsity, that tumults are every day feared'. The bankers were accused of
not releasing money held on deposit, 'having gotten immense riches by
extortion, [they] keepe up their Treasure, in Expectation of a necessity of
advancing its value'. The truth was that the value of coins in circulation was
smaller after the recoinage than before, by about one million pounds, but
banknotes were becoming more common, almost a half of them issued by
the Bank of England. In July 1696 the bank could not meet its obligations
to its creditors on the continent, and so the government had to take loans
from Dutch sources. In January 1697 Evelyn noted: 'Mony yet so scarse
&c: the Parliament are in greate distresse to furnish another Summers
Campagne.'[18] The Treaty of Ryswick, which ended the war, was signed in
the following September.

The Bank of England survived the crisis, as did the Bank of Scotland,
but not their competitors. The deflation and problems with circulation that
followed the recoinage helped to sink the bank's chief rival, the National
Land Bank, launched by the Tories. It proposed to invest in mortgages
and hoped to attract investment from the landed gentry, who were hostile
to the metropolitan goldsmith-bankers. In 1670 Sir Edward Seymour
had complained that with the growth of banking, Englishmen had been
encouraged to 'carry all their money to London'.[19] The Commons authorised
a deal by which the land bank would lend the government £2 million in
return for an annual income of £140,000, provided that £1 million was
raised by subscription by August 1696. But the financial sector was then
in the throes of the recoinage crisis and the Commons committee which
had considered the proposal ruled: 'That no Person concerned in the Bank
of England shall, at the same time, be concerned in the said national Land
Bank; nor any Person to be concerned in the said national Land-Bank shall,
at the same time, be concerned in the Bank of England.'[20] The restriction,
aimed at keeping the two banks entirely separate, fatally limited the number
of investors able and willing to invest so much at such a difficult time.
Indeed, only three subscribers came forward by the deadline, with a total
of just £2,100, and the land bank failed. The notion that wealth was derived
from land was not convincing in the new context of late seventeenth-
century finance, and the joint-stock model was preferred.

Despite the problems of the rival banks and the recoinage, the Bank of
England played a crucial role in the government's financing of the Nine
Years War and the period that followed. The war was hugely expensive,
costing three times as much annually as the Second Dutch War had done in

the 1660s. Between William's accession and his death in 1702, revenue was £58.7 million and expenditure £72 million, a deficit of £13.3 million.

The bank was one of many joint-stock companies established during the period; before 1690 there were 15 such companies, but by 1695 the number had increased to about 140. And the previous year had seen the launch of a lottery loan. Lotteries had been held throughout the period, despite the small chance of a win. Indeed, Petty described a lottery as, 'a Tax upon unfortunate self-conceited fools; men that have a good opinion of their own luckiness, or that have believed some Fortune-teller or Astrologer, who had promised them great success about the time and place of the Lottery'.[21] Evelyn did not distinguish between lotteries and banks when condemning the financial sector and in June 1696 noted, 'Banks & Lotteries every day set up'. But his coachman had scooped £40 in 1693 from a 'Lottery set up after the Venetian manner'.[22] Lotteries such as that launched in 1695, with the alluring title 'The Profitable and Golden Adventure for the Fortunate', generated much excitement, according to Ned Ward, who complained of the hurry of people, 'with a pleasing expectancy of getting six hundred a year for a crown. Thus were all the fools in Town so busily employed in running up and down from one lottery to another, that it was as much as London could do to conjure together such numbers of knaves as might cheat 'em fast enough of their money.'[23] But the Million Lottery of 1694 offered a long-term return through an annuity and was the first of a number of such 'lottery loans'. A ticket cost £10 and entitled the holder to 'an annuity of one Pound or (by chance) to a greater yearly sum for sixteen years'. This seemed a good investment, with a guaranteed return of at least £16 on £10 invested, although the annuity became difficult to collect after a few years, as the government's financial problems increased.[24]

The great growth in trading of the joint-stock companies' and Bank of England's stocks, investments in the government debt, especially through Exchequer Bills, and lottery tickets, saw the emergence of a group of men who specialised in trading in stocks. They attracted criticism, for being among those members of the financial sector apparently benefiting from high taxation and the war by making money from paper instruments, not from land or goods produced. Landowners felt that they were being penalised, through the land tax, which they blamed for the fall in the price of land. Their attitude, and a speculative boom in 1693–5, was the background to an Act of Parliament of 1697, 'to restrain the number and ill-practice of brokers and stock-jobbers'. The preamble accused them of 'most unjust practices in selling and discounting tallies, Bank stock, Bank bills, shares and interest on joint stock'. The act limited their number to 100; they had to be 'admitted, licensed, approved and allowed by the Lord Mayor

72. In the immediate aftermath of the Great Fire, Charles II appointed Hollar and Francis Sandford to take 'an exact plan and survey of the city, as it now stands after the calamity of the late fire'. Hollar's plan based on this survey was published before the end of the year. It shows the extent of the area swept by the fire and the buildings within the burnt area. The City wards are identified by capital letters.

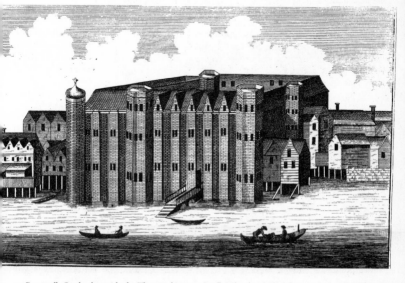

73. Baynard's Castle alongside the Thames, between Paul's Wharf and Blackfriars, was built by Humphrey, Duke of Gloucester, c.1428. The fire-fighters hoped that its stone walls would resist the flames and the building might act as a fire-break, but it was gutted and was not rebuilt.

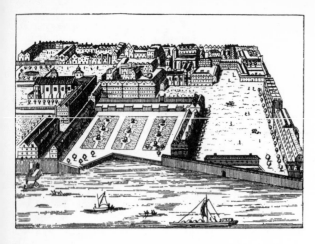

74. The fire was eventually stopped when a part of the Temple had been destroyed. The open spaces of its gardens provided a fire-break, and the wind had dropped sufficiently for the fire-fighters to finally halt the flames.

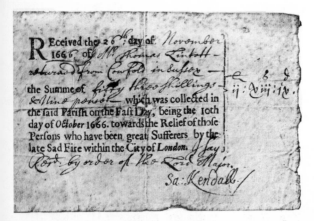

75. Collections were taken across the country to help the victims of the Great Fire. This receipt is for £2 13s 9d collected at Cowfold in Sussex. But the charitable collections brought in only £16,201; the losses were probably close to £8 million.

76. London lying in ruins, drawn by Wenceslaus Hollar.

Top: 77. The Great Fire presented the opportunity of rebuilding the City with a new layout and six plans were prepared. Wren presented his proposal to the king as early as 11 September. It does not respect existing street lines or property boundaries. This copy of the plan was drawn in the nineteenth century.

Above: 78. John Evelyn's first plan included the whole of the area within the walls, because he was unaware of the extent of the destruction until Hollar's plan appeared in December 1666. Evelyn then revised his proposals to take account of that information. As with Wren's proposal, the whole area would have had to be acquired so that the new layout could be set out, and the new building lots then sold. The practical and financial difficulties were too great for any of the post-fire schemes to be adopted. This copy of the plan was drawn in the nineteenth century.

Above right: 79. Sir Christopher Wren (1632–1723), from a portrait by Godfrey Kneller of 1711. Wren was one of the king's appointees to a commission of six members that reported to the rebuilding committee of the Privy Council. He became the principal architect of post-fire London, entrusted with the design of the new churches and St Paul's cathedral.

Above left: 80. John Dryden's poem on the events of 1666, the year of wonders, was addressed to 'the Metropolis of Great Britain, The most renowned and late flourishing City of London'. Dryden described the city as 'a Phoenix in her ashes' and summarised its problems in the mid-1660s as caused by 'an expensive, though necessary War, a consuming Pestilence, and a more consuming Fire'.

81. The new Royal Exchange built after the fire was designed by Edward Jerman, the City surveyor, who died in November 1668. Erected on an enlarged site, it was completed in 1671 and, like its predecessor, was destroyed by fire, in January 1838.

82. A feature of the post-fire planning was the removal of markets from the streets into new market places to ease congestion. The Stocks Market was built on the site of the church of St Mary Woolchurch Haw, to the side of Poultry. In front of the market was an equestrian statue on a plinth, commissioned by the Polish ambassador in London, to present to his king, John Sobieski, to commemorate his victories over the Turks. It depicted the king on horseback, with a Turk being trampled under his horse's hooves. The ambassador failed to pay for it, however, and it stood in its packing on Tower Wharf, until bought by the wealthy goldsmith-banker Sir Robert Vyner. Sobieski's head was replaced by one of Charles II and the trampled Turk was transformed into a likeness of Oliver Cromwell.

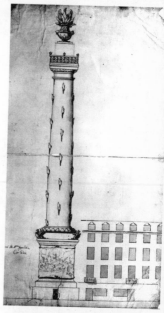

Above: 83. The Monument as built, a fluted Doric column of Portland stone, 202 feet tall, which is surmounted successively by a drum, a dome and a flaming gilt urn. An internal staircase leads to a square balcony above the capital. The basement was constructed to hold a large zenith telescope for astronomical observations, although it proved unsuitable for the purpose.

Above right: 84. Another design for the Monument to commemorate the Great Fire had representations of flames emerging from the pillar, which was to be surmounted by a flaming urn topped by a phoenix. This is endorsed: 'With His Maties Approbation, Chr Wren'.

Right: 85. The Great Plague and Great Fire were blamed by some clergymen and moralists on the sinfulness of Londoners. Because the fire began in Pudding Lane and ended at Pie Corner, on the edge of Smithfield, this figure of a fat boy was humorously put up at Pie Corner. The inscription on the tablet below the figure reads: 'This Boy is in Memmory Put up for the late FIRE of LONDON Occasioned by the Sin of Gluttony 1666'.

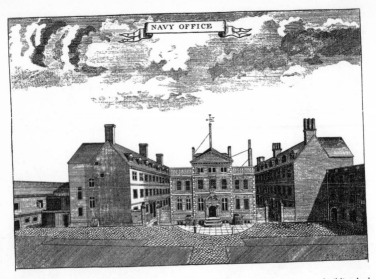

86. The Navy Office in Seething Lane was destroyed in a fire in 1673. By 1683 a new building had been erected on the former site, re-oriented to face Crutched Friars. John Strype described it, in 1720, as 'a noble Structure'. Pepys worked at the Navy Office and also lived there until the fire; he then moved to Buckingham Street.

87. The courtyard of the George Inn in Southwark. Many of the buildings in Southwark High Street were destroyed by fire in 1676 and the galleried range of the George, facing the courtyard, probably dates from the rebuilding, soon after the fire.

Above left: 88. Tablets with street names were set up during the rebuilding after the Great Fire. This one, in Warwick Lane, is dated 1668. The figure may represent Guy, Earl of Warwick; the Beauchamp earls of Warwick had a house in the vicinity from the mid-fourteenth century.

Above right: 89. The medieval church of Christ Church, Newgate Street was the second largest church in medieval London; only St Paul's was bigger. The post-fire church, designed by Wren, was much shorter, and was erected in 1677–87, with the steeple added in 1703–4. The church was destroyed in the Second World War and not rebuilt, but the tower and steeple survived.

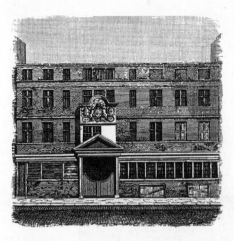

90. The compter in Wood Street was one of the City's prisons for debtors, established after the compter in Bread Street was closed in 1555. During Venner's rising in 1661, the insurgents demanded the release of the prisoners from the compter, and there was a sharp fight outside the building between them and the trained-bands. It was closed in 1791.

91. St Paul's was so badly damaged in the Great Fire that it could not be rebuilt and a royal warrant of July 1668 authorised the demolition of the ruins. Wren was entrusted with the design of its replacement. The rebuilding did not begin until 1675, when the king's warrant authorising construction was issued; the foundation stone was laid on 21 June. This drawing is of the south elevation of the 'warrant design'. Above the crossing is a shallow dome with a tall drum above it, topped with a lofty steeple of six stages.

92. St Mary le Bow was destroyed in the Great Fire and rebuilt to Wren's designs. The body of the church was completed in 1673, with the tower and spire added in 1676–80 and costing almost a half of the total of £15,421. The church was built above the eleventh-century crypt, but Wren erected the new tower on Cheapside, connected to the church by a vestibule. The spire is 224 feet high, second only to St Bride's in height among the City's churches. It is topped by a weathervane in the form of a dragon, made in 1679.

Above: 93. The Popish Plot allegations were discredited and Oates was subsequently arrested and in 1685 he stood trial for perjury. He was sentenced to life imprisonment and on 19 May stood in the pillory in Palace Yard, Westminster. Londoners had turned against him and he was pelted with eggs and miscellaneous rubbish.

Right: 94. Political events were depicted on sets of playing cards. In this set from 1684, by the engraver William Faithorne, the king of hearts shows Titus Oates in 1678, giving Charles II information on the Popish Plot, which was to create a political storm.

King

Dr. Oates diſcouereth ẙ Plot
to ẙ King and Councell.

95. The Sessions House in the Old Bailey was where twenty-nine regicides were tried in October 1660; ten of them were executed. The building was destroyed by the Great Fire and replaced by the structure illustrated here, completed in 1673 and set back from the street behind a courtyard. Until 1737 the courtroom was open to the yard, to allow air to circulate, which was thought to reduce the risk of members of the court being infected by prisoners with typhus, or gaol fever.

96. Johannes Kip's perspective view of *c*.1688–94 of the Charterhouse, where Thomas Sutton's charity, consisting of an almshouse and school, had been established in 1611. The houses facing the square in front of the chapel stand on the site of Rutland House. Sir William Davenant's productions of *The First Days Entertainment at Rutland-House* and *The Siege of Rhodes* were performed in 1656, 'At the back part of Rutland House in the upper end of Aldersgate Street'.

97. James II's accession was greeted with enthusiasm, the political tensions of the previous years now apparently over. His coronation, on 23 April 1685, was preceded by a procession from Westminster Hall to the abbey that included the state trumpeters and drummers, the choirs of Westminster Abbey and the Chapel Royal, and a wind band.

The Lord Mayor & Court Of Aldermen

99. Marcellus Laroon's illustration is of a Quaker meeting; the Quakers were among the nonconformist congregations in London who were intermittently persecuted during the reign of Charles II. But nonconformists were granted toleration by James II, as part of his policy designed to achieve religious and political freedom for his Roman Catholic co-religionists.

98. Power in the City rested largely with the lord mayor and aldermen, and for much of the Exclusion Crisis the Whigs were dominant in City politics. But with the withdrawal of the charter and the election of a Tory lord mayor, they were displaced by the Tories during the mid-1680s. The illustration is the frontispiece to Thomas DeLaune's *The Present State of London* of 1681. A nonconformist writer, DeLaune was convicted of sedition in 1684 and imprisoned in Newgate, where he was joined by his wife and two children. The conditions were so foul that all four of them died there.

100. In the late seventeenth and early eighteenth centuries the aristocratic palaces on the south side of the Strand were demolished, to be replaced by housing developments. The palace built for the first Duke of Buckingham, York House, was pulled down in 1676 leaving only its water-gate, built in 1626–7. Behind the water-gate is Buckingham Street, where Pepys lived from 1679 until 1701.

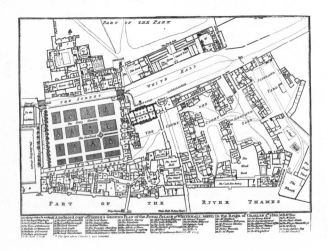

101. This plan of Whitehall Palace in 1680 shows the full extent of the palace complex, between St James's Park and the Thames.

102. The coronation of William III and Mary II, illustrated in the publication of a song, 'The Protestants Joy; An Excellent New Song on the Glorious Coronation of King William and Queen Mary'. It was sung to the tune also used for 'The Subject's Satisfaction; being a new song of the proclaiming of King William and Queen Mary the 13th of February'. Popular music played a part in the Glorious Revolution, especially through the widespread popularity of 'Lillibullero'.

103. William was offered the throne at a ceremony in the Guildhall on 13 February 1689 and he and Mary became joint monarchs. This illustration shows their coronation procession, on 11 April 1689.

Above left: 104. Mary of Modena (1658–1718), who married James, Duke of York, in 1673. Before James came to the throne in 1685 Mary had given birth to four children (all had died in infancy) and had suffered three miscarriages. On 10 June 1688 she gave birth to a boy, James Francis Edward, the heir to the throne; but his father lost that throne before the end of the year. The portrait is by William Wissing (1656–87), who was much favoured by James and Mary.

Above right: 105. Ludgate was rebuilt in 1586 and repaired after the Great Fire. The building was used as a debtors' prison for citizens, where they were held in comfortable conditions, or so it was alleged. The gate was demolished in 1760.

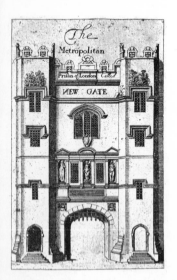

Above left: 106. Newgate was damaged by the Great Fire and at first the fabric was patched up before the corporation decided, in 1672, to rebuild the most damaged sections. The west front was then rebuilt, to the designs of Robert Hooke. The gate was demolished in 1777, the last of the City gates to be removed.

Above right: 107. Aldersgate was rebuilt in 1617 and damaged during the Great Fire. It was repaired in 1670, but demolished in 1761.

Cripplegate was rebuilt in 1491 and used as a storehouse and prison. In 1760 it was sold to a carpenter, for £91, ondition that he would demolish it.

Moorgate was rebuilt in 1415 and, although the Great Fire did not reach it, the gate was again rebuilt in 1672, a vehicular arch flanked by narrow pedestrian ones. Daniel Defoe described it as 'a very beautiful gateway' explained that the arch was so high, almost 20 feet, to allow the City's trained-bands to march through to the llery Ground 'with their pikes advanced'. The use of pikes had since become obsolete and Defoe admitted 'this es the gate look a little out of shape, the occasion of it not being known'. The gate was demolished in 1762.

Bishopsgate was rebuilt in 1479 by the Hansa merchants of the Steelyard. It was again rebuilt in 1733–4, but ew structure was demolished in 1760.

Aldgate was rebuilt in 1606–9, during the reign of James I, and a figure of him in gilt armour was placed ath the battlements. Daniel Defoe commented in 1722 that the gate 'looks still very well'. It was demolished 61.

112. A range of industries and crafts was practised in London, including those producing high-value goods, such as the silversmith's workshop shown in this illustration of 1700.

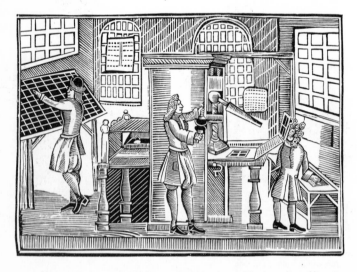

113. London was the centre of publishing and printing, boosted by the ending of licensing and censoring of publications in 1679. This engraving shows a printing office c.1710.

This page: 114 a, b, c, 115, & 116. Marcellus Laroon's *The Cryes of the City of London* (1687) shows the kind of produce that was sold around the streets, including vinegar, strawberries, Dutch biscuits, eels and chickens.

This page: 117, 118, & 119. Other items hawked by the street sellers were *The London Gazette*, which under Charles II and James II was virtually the official newspaper, songs and writing ink.

Opposite page: 120, 121, 122, & 123. Street sellers also sold useful household items such as fine lace and pots and pans, and second-hand clothes, while the chimney-sweep and his boy went around the streets to attract business.

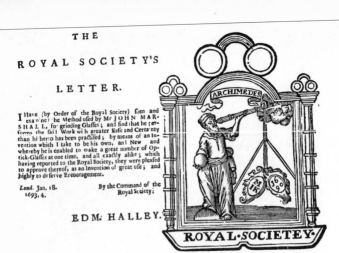

THE ROYAL SOCIETY'S LETTER.

I Have (by Order of the Royal Society) feen and examined the Method ufed by Mr JOHN MAR-SHALL, for grinding Glaffes; and find that he performs the faid Work with greater Eafe and Certainty than hitherto has been practifed; by means of an Invention which I take to be his own, and New and whereby he is enabled to make a great number of Optick-Glaffes at one time, and all exactly alike; which having reported to the Royal Society, they were pleafed to approve thereof, as an Invention of great ufe; and highly to deferve Encouragement.

Lond. Jan. 18. 1693, 4.

By the Command of the Royal Society;

EDM: HALLEY.

Note, There are feveral Perfons who pretend to have the Approbation of the ROYAL SOCIETY; but none has, or ever had it, but my felf; as my Letter can teftifie.

124. John Marshall (1659–1723) was a maker of optical instruments, who, from 1693, was based in Ludgate Street. A letter of approval by Edmond Halley on behalf of the Royal Society was used by Marshall on his trade card.

125. The Nursery in Golden Lane was a training place for actors, opened in 1671 by Sir William Davenant's widow, Mary. It was still being used for that purpose in 1682, when John Dryden mentioned it in *Mac Flecknoe*: 'Near these a Nursery erects its head, Where Queens are formed, and future Hero's bred; Where unfledged Actors learn to laugh and cry, Where infant Punks their tender voices try, and little Maximins the Gods defy.'

Above: 126. This drawing of the interior
of the Dorset Gardens Theatre illustrates
a performance of Elkanah Settle's *Empress
of Morocco*, which opened on 3 July 1673
and was said to have run for a month. The
carvings on the ornate proscenium arch were
by Grinling Gibbons, and the coat of arms is
that of James, Duke of York.

Right: 127. The Dorset Gardens Theatre at
the southern end of Salisbury Court, facing
the Thames, was opened in 1671. It was
also known as the Duke's Theatre. After
1682 it ceased to be used regularly for plays,
although operas were staged there. In 1689 it
was renamed the Queen's Theatre, in honour
of Mary II. By *c.*1700 the theatre had fallen
out of use and the building was demolished
in 1709.

A COLLECTION OF THE NAMES OF THE MERCHANTS

Licenſed *Octob.* 11. 1677.

ROGER L'ESTRANGE.

A COLLECTION
OF THE
NAMES
OF THE
MERCHANTS
Living in and about
The City of LONDON;

Very Uſefull and Neceſſary,

Carefully Collected for the Benefit of all Dealers that ſhall have occaſion with any of them; Directing them at the firſt ſight of their name, to the place of their abode.

LONDON, Printed for *Sam. Lee,* and are to be ſold at his Shop in *Lumbard-ſtreet,* near *Popes-head-Alley* : And *Dan. Major* at the *Flying Horſe* in *Fleetſtreet.* 1677.

Hereunto is added an Addition of all the Goldſmiths that keep Running Caſhes.

A.

JOhn   Addis *and Company at the Sun in Lumbard ſtreet.*

B

JOhn   Bolitho *and Mr. Wilſon at the Golden Lion in Lumbard ſtreet.*

John   Ballard *at the Unicorn Lumbard ſtreet.*

Job   Bolton *at the Bolt and Tun in Lumbard Street.*

Richard   Blanchard } *at the Mary-*
and   } *gold in Fleet-*
Child   } *ſtreet.*

Thomas.

C

THomas Cook } *at the Griffin in*
and   } *Exchange Alley.*
Nicholas Cary }

Mr.   Cutbert *in Cheapſide.*

Mr.   Coggs *in the Strand at the Kings-head.*

Mr.   Churchill *at the in the Strand.*

D

CHar. Duncomb } *at the Graſhop-*
and   } *per in Lumbard*
Richard Kent } *ſtreet.*

E

JOhn   Ewing } *at the Angell*
and   } *and Crown in*
Benj.   Norington } *Lumbard ſtr.*

Mr.   Eaſt *at the in the Strand.*

F

THomas Fowles *at the Black Lion in Fleetſtreet.*

Joſeph

H

Joseph and Nath. Hornboy at the Star in Lumbard street.

H

John Hind } over against the
Thomas Carwood } Exchange in Cornhill.

Benj. Hinton at the Flower de Luce in Lumbard street.

James Herriot at the Naked Boy in Fleetstreet.

James Hore at the Golden Bottle in Cheapside.

I

James Johnson at the Three Flower de Luces in Cheapside.

K

Tho. Kilborne and Capill } at the Kings-Head in Lumbard street.

Mr. Kenton at the Kings-Arms in Fleetstreet.

Mr. Ketch at the Black-Horse in the Strand.

L

Henry Lamb at the Grapes in Lumbard street.

James Lapley at the Three Cocks Cheapside.

M

John Mawson and Comp. at the Golden Hind in Fleet str.

N

Henry Nelthorpe at the Rose in Lumbard street.

P

Tho. Price at the Goat in Lumbard street.

Peter Percefull and Stephen Evans } at the Black Boy in Lumbard street.

I 2   Mr.

Thomas

R

Thomas Pardo at the Golden Anchor in Lumbard street.

R

Tho. Rowe and Thomas Green } at the George in Lumbard street.

S

Humph. Stocks at the Black-Horse in Lumbard str.

John Sweetaple at the Black-Moors-Head in Lumbard street.

John Snell at the Fox in Lumstreet.

Michael Schrimpshaw at the Golden Lion in Fleetstreet.

Richard Stayley in Covent Garden.

T

John Temple and John Seale } at the Three Tunns in Lumbard Str.

John Thursby at the Ball in Lumbard street.

I 3   Bar.

W

Bar. Turner and Samuel Tookie } at the Fleece in Lumbard street.

W

Major Joh. Wallis at the Angell in Lumbard street.

Peter Wade at the Mearmaid in Lumbard street.

Peter White and Churchill } at the Plough in Lumbard street.

Thomas White at the Blew Anchor in Lumbard street.

Thomas Williams at the Crown in Lumbard street.

Robert Ward and John Townely } at the Ram in Lumbard str.

Bethlehem Hospital.

129. At the dissolution of the monasteries the site of the priory of St Mary Bethlehem outside Bishopsgate was granted to the City, which continued it as a mental asylum. In 1674 the governors decided to replace the old buildings and a new site was chosen at Moorfields, along London Wall. The new building, designed by Robert Hooke, was completed in 1676. It was 550 feet long and John Evelyn praised it as 'magnificently built, & most sweetly placed in Morefields'.

130. Pepys moved into a house in Buckingham Street, York Buildings, in 1679. There he organised his library, which housed his collections of books, manuscripts, ballads, theatre bills, prints and drawings. The bookcases were specially made and were the first in England to have glazed doors, to protect the books, which were shelved by size. In 1693 and again in 1700 he oversaw the compilation of a catalogue of his collection, which he bequeathed to his old college, Magdalene College, Cambridge.

By the King.

A PROCLAMATION
Against NEW BUILDINGS.

CHARLES R.

 Hereas in the Fields commonly called the Wind-Mill-Fields, Dog-Fields, and the Fields adjoyning to So-Hoe, and several other places in and about the Suburbs of London and Westminster, divers small and mean Habitations and Cottages have been lately Erected upon New Foundations, and more of that kind are daily preparing, not onely without any Grant or Allowance from his Majesty, but some of them against his Majesties Expresse Commands, signified by his Surveyor-general: Which kind of Buildings are likely to prove common and publick Nusances, by being made use of for the most Noysom and Offensive Trades, already too much Increased, and by turning the Government of those parts more Unmannageable: But especially by Choaking up the Aire of his Majesties Pallaces and Parks, and endangering the Infection, if not the total loss of those Waters, which by many Expencefull Drains and Conduits, are Conveyed from those Fields to his Majesties Pallace at Whitehall; Whereof some Decay is already perceived by his Majesties Serjeant Plummer, and more is daily feared: Therefore for prevention of such growing Mischiefs, whereby his Majesties Pallaces may be greatly Annoyed, the Houses of the Nobility and Gentry very much Offended, the Parishes Over-charged, the performing of the City-Buildings very much hindred, and the health both of City and Suburbs exceedingly endangered: Our Majesty by Advice of his Privy Council, hath thought fit to Publish this his Royal Proclamation, and doth hereby Straightly Charge and Command all manner of persons whom it doth or may concern, That they forbear to Erect, or cause to be Erected any more New Buildings in the Suburbs of London or Westminster, or to Finish any Buildings in the said Suburbs already begun, without his Majesties Licence in that behalf, under his Great Seal first had and obtained: To the end, That if any more New Buildings be thought fit by his Majesty to be carried on, they may be Built Formerly and Regularly, according to such Design and Order as may be best sute with the Publick Benefit and Conveniency, as they will answer the contrary at their perils. And if any shall presume to Offend against his Majesties Royal Command herein Declared, his Majesty will cause such Buildings to be Abated and Thrown down, and the persons of such Offenders to be Arrested and Fined, and further proceeded against according to the utmost Rigour and Severity of Law.

Given at Our Court at Whitehall, the Seventh day of April, 1671.

GOD SAVE THE KING.

In the SAVOY,

Printed by the Assigns of *John Bill* and *Christopher Barker*, Printers to the Kings most Excellent Majesty, 1671.

Above: 131. St Margaret, Lothbury, was rebuilt in 1440. That church was destroyed by the Great Fire and a new one was constructed in 1683–92, finished in Portland stone. The tower is slightly later, from 1698–1700, topped by a slender lead spire which rises 140 feet. After the Great Fire the churches of St Mary Colechurch and St Martin Pomeray were not replaced and the parishes were united with St Margaret's. *Right*: 132. This royal proclamation of 1671 was issued in response to new developments in 'the fields commonly called the Wind-Mill-Fields, Dog-Fields, and the fields adjoyning to So-Hoe, and several other places in and about the Suburbs of London and Westminster'. It adopted the terminology of a report on those developments prepared by Wren. This was the last such proclamation against new buildings in London.

The Parish Church of St James at Garlick hith

Above: 133. St James Garlickhithe was destroyed during the Great Fire. In 1676–82 the church was rebuilt, with the three-stage tower added in 1685 and the spire in 1712–17. The church became known as 'Wren's lantern', because the design produced a light and airy interior.

Below: 134. The original house in the north-west corner of Lincoln's Inn Fields was destroyed by fire in 1684 and replaced by a new one, with the upper rooms on its north side built on arches over Great Queen Street. This fine building was a typical aristocratic London house of the period. The Duke of Newcastle bought the house in 1705 and it subsequently became known as Newcastle House. It is seen here in a photograph of the early twentieth century.

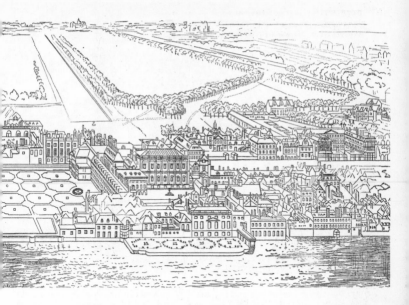

135. Whitehall Palace before its destruction by fire; the buildings at its southern end were damaged in 1691 and the remainder were gutted by a blaze in 1698. The Banqueting House, the Court Gate and Holbein Gate survived, and the Banqueting House was converted by Wren into a chapel, before the end of 1698. Plans to build a new palace proved to be too expensive and parts of the site were leased to members of the aristocracy who built grand houses along the riverfront.

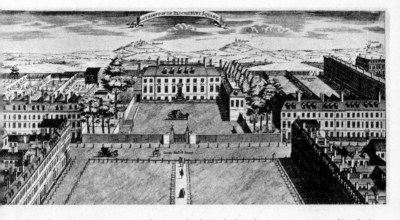

136. Bloomsbury Square was set out in the 1660s for the Earl of Southampton; it was one of London's earliest squares. On its north side was Southampton House, completed in 1660. John Evelyn described the development in 1665 as 'a noble square or Piazza & little Towne'.

137. Burlington House was built on the north side of Piccadilly by Sir John Denham, Surveyor of the Works, who probably began building in 1665, and it was completed by the 1st Earl of Burlington, who bought it in 1667. The chapel to the left of the gardens behind the house is Trinity Church, first erected on Hounslow Heath for the soldiers of James II's army and dismantled and re-erected here in 1691.

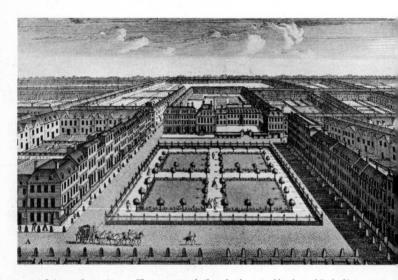

138. Leicester Square in 1727. The square was built on land acquired by the 2nd Earl of Leicester in the 1630s and 1640s. Leicester House was built upon part of the land and the square was set out on the remainder in the 1670s, with Leicester House set back behind a deep courtyard.

Above: 139. Charterhouse Square *c.*1720. Squares were the fashionable form of development for the aristocracy and gentry from the middle of the seventeenth century, so much so that areas that were not squares were given that designation and even, as in this case, depicted as a rectangle, when they were not. Charterhouse Square is in fact an irregular pentagon. *Right*: 140. Charterhouse Square was a largely aristocratic enclave by the mid-seventeenth century, but towards the end of the century the mansions were steadily replaced by houses for the urban gentry. The Countess of Nottingham's mansion in the south-east corner was pulled down and this fine house was built, possibly in 1694. It was demolished in 1864–5.

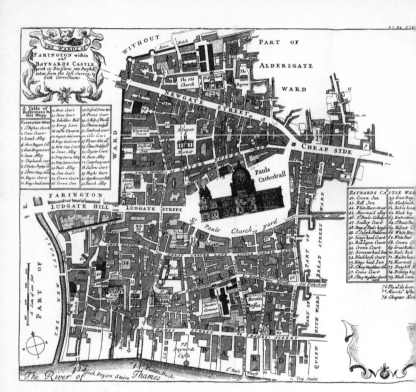

VI OZ FIX

THE WARDS of
FARINGTON within
and
BAYNARDS CASTLE
with its Divisions into Parishes,
taken from the last Survey,
with Corrections

A Table of
References to
this Mapp

Above: 141. The wards of Farringdon Within and Baynard's Castle, in 1720. Christ's Hospital is at the north of the plan and south of it stands Newgate Market, erected after the Great Fire on a block of land acquired by the corporation. Paternoster Row, north of St Paul's, was occupied by mercers and dealers in high-quality silks and lace, but when they moved away it became a centre for publishers and booksellers. South of the cathedral are the Heralds' Office (College of Arms) and Doctors' Commons, the common name for the College of Advocates and Doctors of Law. *Left*: 142. Publication of Pepys's Diary in 1825, albeit in an abbreviated form, was followed by a growing interest in the man and his career. In 1880 Henry Benjamin Wheatley (1838–1917), a Londoner, published a biography of Pepys and in 1893–6 issued an edition of the diary. He also founded the Samuel Pepys Club and was instrumental in the installation of this monument to the diarist, on the south wall of St Olave's, Hart Street, in 1883.

143. The Thames between London Bridge and the Tower, in 1746. Behind the vessels on the river is the varied and exciting skyline produced by the towers and spires of Wren's post-fire churches.

144. The old and new in the City of London are illustrated in this early eighteenth-century print. In the foreground is the open space of Smithfield, where livestock markets and the annual Bartholomew Fair were held. The Great Fire did not reach St Bartholomew's Hospital and its church, St Bartholomew the Less, or the former priory church of St Bartholomew the Great. Behind them are the regular roofs of buildings erected in the area that was destroyed, and St Paul's cathedral.

In a House
formerly standing
on this site lived
SAMUEL PEPYS
1633-1703 Diarist &
ROBERT HARLEY
Earl of Oxford
1661-1724 Statesman
And in this House lived
WILLIAM ETTY
1787-1849 Painter &
CLARKSON STANFIELD
1793-1867 Painter

145. Pepys's celebrity became such that his name was included on the plaque on the site of the house in which he lived in Buckingham Street, close to the York Watergate.

146. A significant link with Pepys's London was restored when Temple Bar was reconstructed. It had been taken down in 1878 and then re-erected in Theobald's Park, but there was growing feeling that it should be returned to London. In 2002 consent for its dismantling and erection on a new site was secured, with the corporation agreeing to cover the costs. The restored Bar was officially opened in November 2004 at the entrance to the new Paternoster Square facing St Paul's.

and Court of Aldermen', pay an admission fee and enter a bond for £500, which would be forfeit in case of misconduct. Unauthorised brokers could be fined up to £100 and made to stand in the pillory. In 1698 stock dealers were expelled from the Royal Exchange, perhaps because of overcrowding, although their rowdy behaviour was also blamed. They then operated in the coffee-houses in and around Exchange Alley, despite attempts by the corporation in 1700 and 1703 to stop them trading there.[25] They favoured Garraway's and Jonathan's, established by Jonathan Miles in 1677. At Jonathan's, in 1698 John Castaing began to issue a news-sheet entitled *The Course of the Exchange and Other Things*, which carried stock prices and appeared twice weekly. This was the first such list of prices.

The traders attracted the venom of Ned Ward, who, at the turn of the century, published a hostile caricature:

> A stock jobber is a compound of knave, fool, shopkeeper, merchant, and gentleman. His whole business is tricking. When he cheats another he's a knave; when he suffers himself to be outwitted he's a fool. He most commonly keeps a visible trade going, and with whatsoever he gets in his shop he makes himself a domestic merchant upon 'Change by turning stock-adventurer. He is led on by mighty hopes of advancing himself to a coach and horses, that he might lord it over his neighbouring mechanics ... He spins out his life between Faith and Hope, but has nothing to do with Charity, because there's little to be got by't.[26]

Ward was a Tory, which may help to explain his hostility to the bankers and financiers in the City, who were apparently rising in wealth and status. For example, he commented that in the aftermath of the recoinage, 'their trade has been in a declining condition, but they have, most of them, so feather'd their nests, that they have no occasion to fear the greatest disadvantages the difficulties of the times can bring them under'. And he recounted a tale which illustrated their extortionate methods, described as 'base and unChristian-like impositions'.[27]

Another financial development of the second half of the century saw the beginnings of fire and marine insurance. Fire insurance was stimulated by the Great Fire and before the end of the 1660s the entrepreneur and developer Nicholas Barbon was granting policies on London properties. In 1680 he launched the 'Insurance Office for Houses', with a prospectus that explained that he and his eleven partners would insure up to 5,000 houses in London. The City's response was to announce that it would also promote an insurance company, attracting Barbon's scorn with the comment that the members of its committee, 'did not well understand the design they were about'. That was not surprising, he wrote, 'for it is not reasonable to expect that they should so well (on a sudden) understand a design as the inventor of it, who had spent much time and study in the contrivance'. Political turmoil in the City may have helped to kill that scheme, although another competitor to Barbon, the Friendly Society, was launched in 1684. A legal battle between its promoters and Barbon ensued, but the Insurance Office – later renamed the Phenix Office – survived and insured more than 5,000 houses between 1686 and 1692, meeting Barbon's target. The business was so profitable that another new office, the Hand-in-Hand, began to insure houses in the 1690s.[28] Shipping news and insurance developed at Edward Lloyd's coffee-house, which he moved in 1691 from near the Custom House to Lombard Street, where it remained until 1785. The first issue of *Lloyd's News* was published there in 1696.

Barbon was also a promoter of the National Land Bank, but attracted most attention as a builder and property developer. He was the son of the Fleet Street leather-seller Praise-God Barebones whose house had been attacked during the Restoration disturbances. Nicholas had taken a degree in medicine at Utrecht University, but soon returned to London and in the aftermath of the Great Fire became the most prominent builder in the city. From the 1670s until his death in 1698 he was involved in building, both setting out new developments and rebuilding neighbourhoods after demolishing existing houses or mansions.

He operated on a large scale. As he explained to Roger North, 'it was not worth his while, to deal litle, that a bricklayer could doe. The gaine he expected was out of great undertakings, which would rise lustily in the whole.' That required considerable capital investment, beyond his means, and so, 'he must compass his designes either by borrowed mony or by credit with those he dealt with, either by fair means or foul'. He was constantly in debt, which he managed by delaying payments to his creditors as long as possible, playing the legal system and settling a debt only when it could no longer be put off, and when the capital and costs were the equivalent of only 3 to 5 per cent, 'which was seldome more then half the charg of borrowing'. To handle his business he 'maintained a gang of clercks, attorneys, scriveners, and lawyers, that were his humble servants and slaves to comand'. If he faced opposition when planning to redevelop the ground on which 100 or so houses stood, 'He sayd he never bought off all, but onely some few of the leaders, and most angry of them'. His tactic was to call a meeting, which he would manipulate so effectively, by the manner of his arrival, appearance and personality, and skill at drawing the sting of their anger, that 'at last they would truckle and take any termes, for peace, and a quiet life'. But his methods did not always placate the opposition and in 1684 his workmen at Red Lion Square were attacked by men from nearby Gray's Inn and were driven off after a skirmish. More seriously, perhaps, 'he had like to have lost his trade by slight building in Mincing Lane, where all the vaults, for want of strength, fell in, and houses came downe most scandalously'. But he survived that crisis and the antagonism which his business methods provoked. According to North, 'all his aim was at profit' and the measure of his success was that he 'livd all the while splendidly', and 'at the upper end of Crane Court in Fleet Street, he had made himself a capitall messuage, where he livd as lord of the mannor'. North described him as, 'the inventer of this new method of building, by casting of ground, into streets, and small houses, and to augment their number with as litle front as possible, and selling the ground to workmen, by so much per foot front, and what he could not sell, build himself. This has made ground rents high, for the sake of mortgaging, and others following his stepps have refined and improved upon it, and made a superfetation of houses about London.'[29]

Barbon and other developers were not hampered by prohibition of new buildings, which was no longer enforced. In a report of 1671 on buildings erected in 'Dog Fields, Windmill Fields, and the Fields adjoyning to So Hoe and severall other Places', Christopher Wren described them as, 'small and meane habitations, which will prove only receptacles for the poorer Sort and the Offensive trades'.[30] A royal proclamation duly forbade further building there without licence. That was the last proclamation of its kind, although the corporation continued to petition parliament for the control of building for a few more years and opposition to new development was still expounded by pamphleteers.

That opposition no longer went unchallenged and was countered by arguments supporting development. One of the pamphlets justifying new building, published in 1678, almost certainly was by Barbon. In it he argued that urban development provided an economic stimulus that benefited nations and governments by 'increasing their revenue and rendering people more easily governed'. Positive effects came from the 'building and enlarging of cities', through the division of labour, which he described as the 'exercise of several arts and calling'. He restated this point in *An Apology for the Builder* (1685) and *A Discourse of Trade* (1690), again arguing that building stimulated the economy, as 'the chiefest promoter of trade', because of the numbers which it employed and those who gained business indirectly, by providing furnishings:

It employs a greater number of trades and people than feeding or clothing: the artificers that belong to building, such as bricklayers, carpenters, plasterers, etc. employ many hands; those that make the materials for building, such as bricks, lime, tile, etc. employ more; and with those that furnish the houses, such as upholsterers, pewterers, etc. they are almost innumerable.

He made a robust case in defence of his native city and against the restriction of building, with arguments that were a clear rebuttal of the long-stated notions that the extravagant metropolis was harmful to the rest of the country. In *An Apology* he asserted that, 'if a great city be the glory of a nation, if it renders a people more easily governed, and increases the prince's revenue, and if it be impossible for a nation to be either rich, strong, or great, without increase of buildings', then those opinions were absurd. Five years later he wrote that: 'The metropolis is the heart of a nation, through which the trade and commodities of it circulate, like the blood through the heart, which by its motion giveth life and growth to the rest of the body; and if that declines, or be obstructed in its growth, the whole body falls into consumption.'[31]

Others were now taking a positive view of a burgeoning and wealthy London. In 1681 John Houghton observed that: 'The bigness and great consumption of London doth not only encourage the breeders of provisions and higglers thirty miles off, but even to four score miles; wherefore I think it will necessary follow, that if London by its bigness, or any other way, should consume as much again, the country within these four score miles would have greater employment; or else, those that are further off will get some with them.'[32] That applied to all materials supplied to the London market. In 1695 Davenant commented that, 'The use of sea coal in London has more than trebled of late years, which is a great advantage to the north.' He went on to summarise the views against and in support of the large and expanding metropolis. Those against asserted 'that the growth of London is pernicious to England; that the kingdom is like a rickety body, with a head too big for the other members'. While those who believed 'that the growth of that city is advantageous to the nation' claimed that:

> no empire was ever great, without having a great and populous city ... the greatness of London will best preserve our constitution, because, where there is a great and powerful city, the prince will hardly enterprise upon the liberties of that people; in the same manner, a rich and powerful city seldom rebels upon vain and slight occasions. On these grounds, and many others, some people are led to think the growth of London not hurtful to the nation; but, on the contrary, to believe that there is not an acre of land in the country, be it never so distant, that is not in some degree bettered by the growth, trade, and riches of that city.[33]

But the argument against restrictions on building was won less by the theories expounded by Barbon and others and more by the impact of an expanding economy and the city's role as political and cultural capital. Prosperity fuelled a demand to which landowners responded by erecting new buildings or redeveloping existing ones. Squares became the favoured form of development for the aristocracy and gentry in the growing West End. Henry Jermyn, Earl of St Albans, set out St James's Square in 1665, justifying his application for a grant from the crown with the statement: 'the beauty of this great town and the convenience of the Court are defective in point of houses fit for the dwellings of noblemen and other persons of quality'.[34] Other developers followed, setting out Bloomsbury Square in the 1660s; Leicester Square, Golden Square and Soho Square in the 1670s; Red Lion Square and Queen Square in the 1680s. North of the City, Devonshire Square was begun in 1678 and a few years later a residential square was set out to the east of the City, initially known as Marine Square, but by the mid-eighteenth century as Wellclose Square. Barbon was the developer of Red Lion Square, Devonshire Square and Marine Square. In contrast to the squares and rectangular grid layouts, near St Giles-in-the-Fields church was Thomas Neale's Seven Dials development, in which 'seaven streetes make a starr from a Doric Pillar plac'd in the middle of a Circular Area'. Neale began the development in 1693 and it was completed by 1710.[35]

Squares were so fashionable that the designation was attached to other developments, in some cases rather dubiously. Charterhouse Yard, an irregular pentagon, was said by James Howell to contain 'many handsome Palaces' in the mid-seventeenth century and was redeveloped as a fashionable bourgeois enclave in the 1680s and 1690s.[36] Its new identity was subsequently confirmed when it was depicted as a rectangular space and became known as Charterhouse Square. A long narrow rectangle among the courts on the north side of Fleet Street that was developed by the Gough family, wool merchants, in the late seventeenth century, came to be designated Gough Square.

Other redevelopments took place on the sites of aristocratic mansions along and to the north of the Strand, again with Barbon heavily involved. Between 1674 and 1718 ten mansions in the Strand area were demolished and replaced by streets and houses. In 1682 Sir George Downing demolished a house near Whitehall Palace, which he had acquired in 1654, and replaced it with a street of twenty-five terraced houses. They were not well built, however, and had inadequate foundations, and just four of the original houses remain in the street which took his name. A generation earlier Petty had feared that old properties could be neglected by their owners, 'until they become fundamentally irreparable, at which time they become either the dwelling of the Rascality, or in process of time return to waste and Gardens again, examples whereof are many even about London'. In fact, demand kept property values and rents so high that such decay was unlikely within the city.[37] New public buildings included Bethlehem Hospital, designed by Robert Hooke (1676), and, beyond the city, the royal hospitals at Chelsea (1682–92) and Greenwich (1694–1705), both designed by Wren. By the 1690s, Misson could write that, 'one may safely venture to affirm, that London, including Westminster, is the biggest City in Europe'.[38]

The growing suburbs required places of worship. Chapels-of-ease were built in Wapping in 1615, in Tothill Fields in 1635–42 and at Shadwell and Poplar in the 1650s. St Paul's, Shadwell, was created as a new parish, out of St Dunstan's, Stepney, in 1669 and other new parishes were Christ Church, Southwark (1671), St Anne, Soho (1678), St James, Piccadilly, (1685) and St John, Wapping (1694). Both St Anne and St James were created out of St Martin's-in-the-Fields, the population of which increased from 19,000 in 1660 to 69,000 in 1685. New parish churches were then erected in Southwark, Soho and Piccadilly. Others were rebuilt. St Clement Danes had become so dilapidated that it was demolished in 1680 and a new church, in Portland stone, was built to Wren's designs. Completed in 1682, it cost almost £15,000. After the Glorious Revolution, in 1691 Trinity Church was built north of Piccadilly, where Conduit Street was to be set out a few years later. Evelyn explained that: 'This church being formerly built of Timber on Hounslow-heath by K. James for the Masse-Priests, being beged by Dr. Tenison Rector of St. Martines, was set up by that publique minded, charitable & pious Doctor.' Thomas Tenison, later Archbishop of Canterbury, also advocated that the district should be made a separate parish, 'in regard, the building & inlargement of that quarter was so many & populous', although that was not done. Another chapel built by a benefactor was the Danish church, erected in 1694–6 in Marine Square and paid for by King Christian V. Ned Ward described it as, 'a very regular and commodious building … a neat and well compact tabernacle', but because the seafaring community worshipped there, it stank of 'pitch and tar'.[39]

With the relaxation of the restrictions on nonconformists, and the surge of Huguenot immigrants from France, in the 1690s meeting-houses were built or restored. By 1700 Spitalfields had nine French churches and a *Maison de Charité* had been established, distributing food to the poor. From 1681 the former pesthouse north of Old Street was used to house sick and elderly Huguenots, many of them refugees. It was replaced in 1718 by the French Protestant Hospital, known as La Providence, built partly with a legacy from Jacques de Gastigny, a member of William III's household. Since the resettlement in the 1650s, the community of Sephardic Jews had grown to the point where a new synagogue was required, replacing that in Creechurch Lane. A site was chosen in Heneage Lane, off Bevis Marks, where the new synagogue was built in 1699–1700 by Joseph Avis, a Quaker, discreetly placed in a court rather than on a street frontage.

As well as places of worship, new buildings for pleasure were also erected. The Theatre Royal was closed between June 1665 and November 1666 because of the Great Plague, and burned down on 25 January 1672. The company then moved to Lincoln's Inn Fields, Sir William Davenant's former company having transferred to the new Dorset Gardens Theatre, erected facing the river at the southern end of Salisbury Court. Davenant planned the building, but he died before the scheme was implemented and the plans were taken up by Henry Harris and the leading actor Thomas Betterton, with Davenant's widow. The theatre was opened in 1671, having cost £9,000. This was the finest playhouse yet built in London, with an auditorium 140 feet by 57 feet that could hold 1,200 patrons. The grand proscenium arch's decorative carvings, of fruit and foliage, were by Grinling Gibbons, his earliest decorative work in London. The portrait-painter Thomas Murray later recalled that, 'the play house in Dorsett garden calld the Dukes house being a building Mr Betterton finding him an ingenious man imployd him to Carve for him the Ornements & decorations of that house particularly the Capitals comishes & Eagles'.[40]

As the theatre was built for the Duke of York's company, his arms were placed above the proscenium and the theatre was commonly referred to as the Duke's Theatre. It was close to Dorset Stairs, for the convenience of those patrons arriving by river. The French traveller François Brunet, who visited c.1676, wrote that:

The auditorium is infinitely more beautiful and functional than those in the playhouses of our French actors. The pit, arranged in the form of an amphiteater, has seats, and one never hears any noise. There are seven boxes, holding twenty persons each. The same number of boxes form the second tier, and, higher still, there is the paradise.[41]

Betterton had been to Paris to investigate theatre design there and introduced innovations at Dorset Gardens. The large stage and back-stage apparatus allowed the use of movable scenery, first used in a production of Elkanah Settle's *The Empress of Morocco* (1673). Other productions there were visually lavish by contemporary standards.

Its early success was partly due to the fire at the Theatre Royal, which was not reopened until 1674. But the productions were expensive and by the early 1680s both theatres were in difficulties, exacerbated by the current political tensions, which deterred patrons from going to places of entertainment. The two companies merged in 1682, performing thereafter at Drury Lane. The Dorset Gardens theatre was later used occasionally for operas and then for fencing, wrestling and acrobatics. It was demolished in 1709.

As in the 1660s, music was an important part of the productions. In the late seventeenth century leading composers, including Matthew Locke and Henry Purcell, composed for the theatre. Purcell's music for Nathaniel Lee's tragedy *Theodosius* (1680) was his first theatre music. He subsequently composed the incidental music for many plays, more than forty between 1690 and his death in 1695, and his three semi-operas were staged at Dorset Gardens: *The Prophetess, or The History of Dioclesian* (1690), *King Arthur* (1691) and *The Fairy Queen* (1692). John Dryden wrote the text of King Arthur and in the preface praised the music, by 'the artful hands of Mr Purcell, who has composed it with so great a genius, that he has nothing to fear but an ignorant, ill-judging audience'. But these were costly productions; neither *Dioclesian* nor *King Arthur* generated enough receipts to recover the outlay, while *The Fairy Queen* cost £3,000 to stage, so that 'the Company got very little by it'.[42]

Independently of the development of theatre music, the first-ever public concerts were inaugurated by the violinist John Banister. In 1667 he lost his position as leader of the twenty-four violins, the string band created by Charles II in imitation of Louis XIV's 'vingt-quatre violins du roy'. He had allegedly complained of the employment of Italian violinists and the appointment of a Frenchman, Louis Grabu, as Master of the Musick. Banister then composed music for the theatre and at the end of 1672 he began to present concerts, 'performed by Excellent Masters'. These were held in a large room at 'the Musick-school, over against the George Tavern in White Fryers', where admission was one shilling. His choice of location was somewhat surprising, for the district, between Fleet Street and the Thames, lay outside the lord mayor's jurisdiction and was a sanctuary for unscrupulous debtors and other ne'er-do-wells, who could operate beyond the law. This outraged respectable citizens, because, as Ned Ward explained, it allowed shopkeepers to obtain credit and then avoid their creditors when payment was due by taking refuge there. He indignantly condemned, 'these infernal territories, where vice and infamy were so long protected and flourish'd without reproof, to the great shame and scandal of a Christian nation'.[43] Yet the area's reputation did not deter the public and the concerts proved to be very popular. In 1675 Banister moved them to Chandos Street in Covent Garden, a very different setting which reflected the genteel background of the clientele.[44]

Another series of concerts was begun in 1678 by Thomas Britton, a coalman, book collector and music enthusiast, in a room over his coal-shop in Jerusalem Passage, Clerkenwell. The room was long and narrow, and was lit only by a window that Ned Ward described as 'very little bigger than the Bunghole of a Cask'. Despite the venue, 'his Musick Meeting improved in a little Time to be very considerable, insomuch, that Men of the best Wit, as well as some of the best Quality, very often honoured his musical Society with their good Company'. The concerts were continued until his death in 1714.[45]

In 1683, and possibly before, a Musical Society met on 22 November, St Cecilia's Day, to commemorate the patron saint of music. This became an annual event and ten years later the Huguenot literary scholar Peter Motteaux described it in *The Gentleman's Journal*: 'most of the Lovers of Music, whereof many are persons of the first Rank, meet at Stationers-Hall in London, not thro a Principle of Superstition, but to propagate that divine Science. A splendid Entertainment is provided, and before it is always a performance of Music by the best Voices and Hands in Town ... This feast is one of the genteelest in the world'. Music also formed a part of the entertainment at the annual feasts held by gentlemen from Yorkshire, Gloucestershire, Kent and Norfolk who were in London. The nature of the Yorkshire feast in March 1690 was summarised in a notice in the *London Gazette*: 'The Annual Yorkshire Feast will be held the 27th instant at Merchant-Taylors' Hall in Threadneedle Street; with a very splendid Entertainment of all sorts of Vocal and Instrumental Musick.' Henry Purcell composed the music that year, setting a text by Thomas D'Urfey, who described it as, 'One of the finest Compositions he ever made, and cost £100 the performing'.[46]

A similar annual celebration was held at the Charterhouse on 12 December, the anniversary of the death of Thomas Sutton, who had established the charity. It consisted of two parts, 'a feast for all the members of the house within it; and another by all those that have had relation to the house that upon summons from 2 stewards yearly chosen come together upon that occasion from all parts Kept in the town'. The feasts were accompanied by 'musicke vocall and instrumentall', provided from the early 1670s by the King's Trumpeters and from 1674 the Gentlemen of the Chapel Royal were paid for performing there. Purcell composed the anthem *Blessed is the Man* for one of these Founder's Day celebrations, probably in 1687.[47] At Josias Priest's school at Chelsea, John Blow's *Venus and Adonis* was performed in 1684, and Purcell's *Dido and Aeneas* in 1689. Priest had been a dancing master, and proprietor of a girls' boarding school in Leicester Fields before moving to the school at Chelsea in 1680, which he took over from two musicians.

Those who wished that they or their children should be adept in the courtly accomplishments had a number of establishments in London from which to choose. Advertisements in John Houghton's *Collections* in 1694 listed five dancing masters, three fencing masters and two French teachers.

Concerts were held at some dancing schools, such as that advertised in the *London Gazette* in November 1685: 'Several Sonata's, composed after the Italian way, for one and two Bass Viols, with a Thorough Bass … are to be performed on Thursday next, and every Thursday following, at Six of the clock in the Evening, at the Dancing School in Walbrook'. The musicians themselves erected, 'a fabric reared and furnished on purpose for public music … called the Music-Meeting; and all the quality and *beau monde* repaired to it'. This was in York Buildings, off the Strand, and it seated 200 people. Concerts were held there twice a week during the season, from October to May. They attracted musicians from Europe, including Margarita de l'Epine, 'The Italian lady (that is lately come over that is so famous for her singing)', the violinist Gottfried Finger, and the composers and teachers August Kühnel, Johann Wolfgang Franck, who had been Kapellmeister at the court of Ansbach, and Pier Francesco Tosi, whose series of concerts in 1693 were advertised to begin on 30 October and then 'continue weekly all the winter'. Jacob Kremberg had held posts at the courts of Halle, Sweden and Saxony, and at the Hamburg Opera, before coming to London, where, according to *The Post Bag* for 20 November 1697, he was to present at Hickford's Dancing School, 'a New Concert of Music by very great Masters, of all sorts of instruments, with fine singing', and 'always with New Compositions'.[48]

Houghton's lists also included twenty-three artists specialising in portraits. They included Michael Dahl, who had moved to London from Sweden in 1682, and the Dutch artists Jan van der Vaart, who arrived in London c.1674, and Harmen Verelst, who settled there in 1682, after working in Rome and Vienna. The 'Mr. Vande Velde, Pickadilly', listed as a specialist in marine painting, was Willem van de Velde, who had arrived in London from the United Provinces in the winter of 1672–3 with his father, who also specialised in seascapes.[49] That such musicians and artists chose to settle in London demonstrated its growing importance as a centre of music and painting in northern Europe.

Various other groups met in London, for convivial celebrations, or perhaps intellectual discussions. Some were formal meetings, such as those of the Royal Society, and others were informal, including gatherings of the wits and literati at Will's coffee-house in Bow Street. Alexander Man's coffee-house near Charing Cross was the most fashionable of London's coffee-houses and the place where, in private rooms, 'the beau-politicians retired upon extra-ordinary occasions to talk nonsense by themselves about state affairs, that they might not be laugh'd at'.[50] The informal meetings included those of the Saturday Academicals, who got together weekly on Saturday afternoons during the 1690s, at Samuel Pepys's lodgings.

The Royal Navy was administered by a commission after Pepys's resignation in 1679, until 1684, when he was reinstated as Secretary. Because of his connections with James II, he again lost his place after the Glorious Revolution and indeed was imprisoned for a time in the Gatehouse prison. He spent most of his retirement at a house in York Buildings, off the Strand, on the site of the Duke of Buckingham's mansion. There Pepys passed his time perusing his collections of books, music and manuscripts, corresponding with scholars from a variety of backgrounds on a range of topics, entertaining and meeting friends, holding discussions and enjoying music. Their gatherings were interrupted during the summers; in 1692 Pepys referred to 'shutting myself up within this lushious Towne a whole Summer long'. More serious disruption followed his move to Clapham in 1701, to live with his former clerk Will Hewer. Evelyn wrote to tell him how he missed the Saturday meetings and the break in visits and conversations, 'especialy since I am come to this smoaky, obstreperous Citty'. Evelyn had become a little bit disconsolate. In 1684 he inspected new developments off Piccadilly and wrote, gloomily, 'to such a mad intemperance the age was come of building about a Citty, by far too disproportionat already to the Nation, I having in my time seene it almost as large more than it was within my memorie'. Four years later he sent Pepys a copy of *Fumifugium*, which he described as, 'the old smoky Pamphlet … which had it taken Effect, might have sav'd the burning of a Great Citty'. In the following year he complained that: 'This greate and August Citty, abounding in so many Witts and Leter'd Persons, has scarse one Library furnish'd and endow'd for the Publique.' And during the harsh winter of 1694–5 he reminisced about the great freeze eleven years earlier, when 'a Citty was built upon the Thames, and we both rod over it in our Coaches'.[51] The Saturday Academicals' meetings did not resume, for Pepys stayed on at Hewer's house, where he died on 26 May 1703.

The meetings of Pepys's circle reflected the intellectual life of late seventeenth-century London, in the exchange of information and ideas, embracing scholars from across the country. And they exemplify London's role as a focus of learning and enquiry. One strand of such investigations had done much to explain London's demography; the size of the population, the numbers of births and deaths, the causes of death and the significance of immigration. Between Pepys's schooldays and his death, its population had continued to increase, despite a devastating plague epidemic and against the national trend. And as the city was not shackled by fortifications, it was free to expand, and so the suburbs spread out, across the adjoining fields, along the Thames and, most innovatively, in the development of the squares in the growing West End. Economic and social pressures had defeated the long-standing policy to restrict its growth, which was abandoned. Aristocratic landlords, setting out their estates, and the new breed of property developer had done much to transform the capital's appearance. Fire had purged not only the City, but also other districts within the metropolis, and had destroyed the large, rambling and architecturally incoherent royal palace at Whitehall. The building types specified after the Great Fire created a degree of standardization in appearance, as buildings of brick-and-tile were erected, with plain, upright front walls, not only in the area rebuilt after the conflagration, but as the norm across London. The scornful comments about its old-fashioned houses and uninteresting architecture, even in the centre of the city, made by visitors in the middle of the century, were no longer appropriate by its end. Indeed, the spacious residential squares came to be admired as an elegant contribution to urban design, and coherent developments, rather than piecemeal building, became more common. And the new red-brick buildings were intermixed with stone churches, their diverse towers and spires creating an eye-catching skyline, with the great new cathedral as a remarkable centrepiece.

London's important role in national politics had been demonstrated through revolutionary changes and different regimes, and, in a struggle with the crown, the City had first lost and then recovered its charter and its privileges. But the City already was becoming synonymous with financial strength rather than the striving for power, and never again was it to endure an occupation by soldiers as part of a national struggle. Political rivalries, partisan and prejudiced crowds, and bloody reprisals did not end with the settlement following the Glorious Revolution, but it became less dangerous to engage in civic politics. And the preoccupations increasingly were with trade, profit and loss, loans and investments, rather than religious and dynastic broils. Its already dominant commercial position was enhanced by the institutions developed during the financial revolution of the 1690s. And Londoners' social and cultural life had widened, with the new coffee-houses, theatres, concert-houses and pleasure grounds.

Pepys lived in a burgeoning metropolis through a time of constitutional crises and political upheaval, riots and religious tensions, frosts, fires and plague. Yet it maintained its primacy in politics, society, fashion, entertainment, trade, business and finance. Politically, socially, economically, intellectually and aesthetically, Pepys's London was a changing, developing, lively and exciting place in which to live, and it emerged from those troubled times as one of Europe's great cities.

Notes

Abbreviations

BL	British Library
CSPVen	*Calendar of State Papers Relating to English Affairs in the Archives of Venice*
Evelyn, *Diary*	E.S. de Beer (ed), *The Diary of John Evelyn*, Oxford: OUP 1959
GL	Guildhall Library
HMC	Historical Manuscripts Commission
LMA	London Metropolitan Archives
ODNB	*Oxford Dictionary of National Biography*
Pepys, *Diary*	R.C. Latham and W. Matthews (eds), *The Diary of Samuel Pepys*, 11 vols, London: Bell & Hyman 1970–83
TNA	The National Archives

Chapter 1
Imperial Chamber & Chief Emporium

1. A.G.H. Bachrach and R.G. Collmer (eds), *Lodewijck Huygens: The English Journal 1651–1652*, Leiden: Leiden University Press 1982, p.37.
2. Samuel Sorbière, *A Voyage to England*, London: 1709, pp.13, 15.
3. Lorenzo Magalotti (ed), *Travels of Cosmo the Third, Grand Duke of Tuscany, through England, during the Reign of King Charles the Second*, London: 1821, p.395.
4. James Howell, *Londinopolis: An Historicall Discourse or Perlustration Of the City of London*, London, 1657, p.404. Guy de la Bédoyère (ed), *The Writings of John Evelyn*, Woodbridge: Boydell 1995, p.136.
5. *A collection of the State Papers of John Thurloe*, 2, 1742, xix, p.239.
6. Howell, *Londinopolis*, p.346.
7. Howell, *Londinopolis*, p.404.

8. *Oxford English Dictionary*, citing A. Huntar, *Treatise of Weights and Measures*, I, p.10: 'The English Myle is more than the Fundamentall, or Italian Myle of paces 56, of English yardes, 93 and 1 inch'.

9. *State Papers of John Thurloe*, 2, 1742, xix, p.239. Lawrence Manley, *London in the Age of Shakespeare*, Beckenham: Croom Helm 1986, p.47.

10. Howell, *Londinopolis*, p.403. Manley, *London in the Age of Shakespeare*, p.47. Magalotti (ed), *Travels of Cosmo the Third*, p.396.

11. John Graunt, *Natural and Political Observations ... upon the Bills of Mortality*, in C.H. Hull (ed), *The Economic Writings of Sir William Petty*, Cambridge: CUP 1899, II, p.385.

12. Howell, *Londinopolis*, Dedication & p.389.

13. Manley, *London in the Age of Shakespeare*, p.47.

14. *CSPVen*, 30, p.308. Sorbière, *Voyage to England*, p.13. Magalotti (ed), *Travels of Cosmo the Third*, p.393.

15. *State Papers of John Thurloe*, 2, 1742, xix, p.239.

16. *CSPVen*, 30, p.309. Maurice Exwood and H.L. Lehmann (eds), *The Journal of William Schellinks' Travels in England 1661–1663*, Camden Soc., fifth series, I: 1993, p.47.

17. Magalotti (ed), *Travels of Cosmo the Third*, p.197. Bachrach and Collmer (eds), *Lodewijck Huygens*, p.57.

18. Howell, *Londinopolis*, p.396.

19. Magalotti (ed), *Travels of Cosmo the Third*, pp.396, 401, 405. Howell, *Londinopolis*, p.397. Sorbière, *Voyage to England*, p.16.

20. Graunt, *Natural and Political Observations*, II, pp.352–3.

21. Philip Bliss (ed), Anthony Wood, *Athenae Oxonienses*, 3, p.905, cited in Barbara Donagan, 'Ford, Sir Edward (1605–1670)', *ODNB*.

22. Bachrach and Collmer (eds), *Lodewijck Huygens*, p.65. Sorbière, *Voyage to England*, p.15.

23. *CSPVen*, 30, p.210. J.A. Chartres, *The Inland Trade 1500–1700*, London: Macmillan 1977, p.45.

24. Ralph Davis, 'English Foreign Trade, 1660–1700', in E.M. Carus-Wilson (ed), *Essays in Economic History*, II, London: Arnold 1962, p.267. Brian Dietz, 'Overseas trade and metropolitan growth', in A.L. Beier and Roger Finlay (eds), *London 1500–1700: The Making of the Metropolis*, London: Longman 1986, pp.115–140.

25. Exwood and Lehmann (eds), *Journal of William Schellinks*, p.54. Bachrach and Collmer (eds), *Lodewijck Huygens*, p.56.

26. Exwood and Lehmann (eds), *Journal of William Schellinks*, p.67.

27. Sorbière, *Voyage to England*, pp.16, 17.

28. Bachrach and Collmer (eds), *Lodewijck Huygens*, p.46. Exwood and Lehmann (eds), *Journal of William Schellinks*, p.54.

29. Sorbière, *Voyage to England*, p.16.

30. Bachrach and Collmer (eds), *Lodewijck Huygens*, pp.43, 105. Howell, *Londinopolis*, p.26. Exwood and Lehmann (eds), *Journal of William Schellinks*, p.50.

31. J.W. Willis Bund (ed), *The Diary of Henry Townshend of Elmley Lovett, 1640–1663*, Worcestershire Historical Soc., 1915, I, p.30. John Towill Rutt (ed), *Diary of Thomas Burton esq*, I, 1653–1657, London: 1828, p.309, n.4.

32. Todd M. Endelman, *The Jews of Britain, 1656 to 2000*, Berkeley and Los Angeles: University of California Press 2002, pp.27, 29.

33. A.H. Niemeyer, *Travels on the Continent and in England*, London: Phillips & Co. 1823, p.v.

34. Magalotti (ed), *Travels of Cosmo the Third*, pp.396–7. Sorbière, *Voyage to England*, pp.8, 46. C.D. Andriesse, *Huygens: The Man Behind the Principle*, Cambridge: CUP 2005, p.210.

35. Howell, *Londinopolis*, p.396.

36. Exwood and Lehmann (eds), *Journal of William Schellinks*, p.48. Bachrach and Collmer (eds), *Lodewijck Huygens*, p.48.

37. Robin Gwynn, *Huguenot Heritage: The history and contribution of the Huguenots in Britain*, Brighton: Sussex Academic Press 2001, p.42.

38. Pepys, *Diary*, III, pp.276–7.

CHAPTER 2
CONGESTION, POLLUTION & ANXIETY

1. Joan Thirsk and J.P. Cooper (eds), *Seventeenth Century Economic Documents*, Oxford: OUP 1972, p.383.

2. *The Works of Sir William Davenant*, I, London: 1673, reissued London and New York, Benjamin Blom 1968, p.354.

3. Lawrence Manley, *London in the Age of Shakespeare*, Beckenham: Croom Helm 1986, p.47.

4. *CSPVen*, 31, p.21.

5. *CSPVen*, 31, p.85. Evelyn, *Diary*, pp.394, 395.

6. Maurice Ashley, *Financial and Commercial Policy under the Cromwellian Protectorate*, 2nd edn, London: Frank Cass 1962, pp.88–90.

7. Maurice Exwood and H.L. Lehmann (eds), *The Journal of William Schellinks' Travels in England 1661–1663*, Camden Soc., fifth series, I: 1993, p.85.

8. John Towill Rutt (ed), *Diary of Thomas Burton esq*, London: 1828, II, p.283.

9. Evelyn, *Diary*, p.398.

10. Rutt (ed), *Diary of Thomas Burton*, II, p.181.

11. Francis Sheppard (ed), *Survey of London, vol.36, Covent Garden*, London:

LCC 1970, p.26.

12. Exwood and Lehmann (eds), *Journal of William Schellinks*, p.58.

13. James Howell, *Londinopolis: An Historicall Discourse or Perlustration Of the City of London*, London, 1657, pp.344, 345.

14. Howell, *Londinopolis*, pp.342, 344. D.J.H. Clifford (ed), *The Diaries of Lady Anne Clifford*, Stroud: Sutton 1990, p.171.

15. *A collection of the State Papers of John Thurloe*, 2, 1742, xix, p.239.

16. C.D. Andriesse, *Huygens: The Man Behind the Principle*, Cambridge: CUP 2005, p.210. *CSPVen*, 33, p.19. Lorenzo Magalotti (ed), *Travels of Cosmo the Third, Grand Duke of Tuscany, through England, during the Reign of King Charles the Second*, London: 1821, p.393.

17. Samuel Sorbière, *A Voyage to England*, London: 1709, p.13.

18. *The Works of Sir William Davenant*, I, pp.351–4.

19. 'Observations, both Historical and Moral, upon the Burning of London', *Harleian Miscellany*, III, London: 1809, p.305.

20. Guy de la Bédoyère (ed), *The Writings of John Evelyn*, Woodbridge: Boydell 1995, pp.131–2, 136.

21. Helen Truesdell Heath (ed), *The Letters of Samuel Pepys and his Family Circle*, Oxford: OUP 1955, pp.13–15.

22. Howell, *Londinopolis*, p.393.

23. C.H. Firth and R.S. Rait (eds), *Acts and Ordinances of the Interregnum, 1642–1660*, London: HMSO 1911, II, pp.1223–34.

24. Howell, *Londinopolis*, p.394.

25. LMA, GL, MS 4069/1 Cornhill Wardmote Book, 1571–1651, f.242v.

26. *The Harleian Miscellany*, VI, London: 1810, p.401. Corporation of London MSS, Precept to Alderman of Bridge Without, 24 Oct. 1642. *Mercurius Politicus*, 18 Oct. 1658.

27. LMA, GL, MS 4069/1 Cornhill Wardmote Book, 1571–1651, f.238.

28. Howell, *Londinopolis*, p.394.

29. John Cordy Jeaffreson (ed), *Middlesex County Records: Volume 3: 1625–67*, 1888, p.226.

30. *State Papers of John Thurloe*, 2, 1742, xix, p.239. Howell, *Londinopolis*, p.391.

31. H[ugh] P[eter], *Good Work for a Good Magistrate*, London: 1651, pp.105–8.

32. de la Bédoyère (ed), *Writings of John Evelyn*, pp.131–2, 136.

33. P[eter], *Good Work*, pp.105–8.

34. Eric Bennett, *The Worshipful Company of Carmen of London*, London: Carmen's Company 1952, pp.50–1.

35. Exwood and Lehmann (eds), *Journal of William Schellinks*, pp.55–6.

36. John Taylor, *Old Parr*, 1635, cited in *Oxford English Dictionary*.

37. Jeaffreson (ed), *Middlesex County Records: vol.3*, p.227.

38. Magalotti (ed), *Travels of Cosmo the Third*, p.401.

39. *The Works of Sir William Davenant*, I, p.358. Andriesse, *Huygens*, p.210.

40. J.J. Jusserand, *A French Ambassador at the Court of Charles the Second*, London: Fisher Unwin 1892, p.160.

41. A.G.H. Bachrach and R.G. Collmer (eds), *Lodewijck Huygens: The English Journal 1651–1652*, Leiden: Leiden University Press 1982, p.65.

42. de la Bédoyère (ed), *Writings of John Evelyn*, p.131.

43. Evelyn, *Diary*, p.434.

44. William L. Sachse (ed), *The Diurnal of Thomas Rugg 1659–1661*, Camden Soc., 3rd series, XCI, 1961, p.64. Pepys, *Diary*, I, pp.93, 95.

45. E.M. Symons, 'The Diary of John Greene (1635–57)', *English Historical Review*, XLIV, 1929, pp.106–7. Bachrach and Collmer (eds), *Lodewijck Huygens*, pp.54–5.

46. Lady Newdigate-Newdegate, *Cavalier and Puritan in the Days of the Stuarts*, London: Smith, Elder 1901, pp.234–5. Evelyn, *Diary*, pp.764–6.

47. Evelyn, *Diary*, pp.765–6.

48. Evelyn, *Diary*, p.437.

49. Valerie Pearl, 'Social Policy in Early Modern London', in Hugh Lloyd-Jones, Valerie Pearl and Blair Worden (eds), *History and Imagination: Essays in Honour of H.R. Trevor-Roper*, London: Duckworth 1981, pp.116–17.

50. W.H. Manchee, *The Westminster City Fathers, 1585–1901*, London: Bodley Head 1924, p.8.

51. Howell, *Londinopolis*, pp.392, 394.

52. Jeaffreson (ed), *Middlesex County Records, vol.3*, pp.217, 270.

53. Evelyn, *Diary*, p.336.

54. W.L. Bennett (ed), *Epistolae Ho-elianae: The Familiar Letters of James Howell*, I, London: Nutt 1892, p.56.

55. Howell, *Londinopolis*, p.392.

56. Jeaffreson (ed), *Middlesex County Records: vol.3*, p.254.

57. Magalotti (ed), *Travels of Cosmo the Third*, p.402.

58. Pepys, *Diary*, II, p.60.

59. Jeaffreson (ed), *Middlesex County Records, vol.3*, pp.ix, 185, 230, 259, 260, 266, 269.

60. *CSPVen*, 30, p.184.

61. *CSPVen*, 29, pp.38, 58, 63.

62. Jeaffreson (ed), *Middlesex County Records, vol.3*, p.224.

63. Bachrach and Collmer (eds), *Lodewijck Huygens*, p.54. Howell, *Londinopolis*, pp.399–400. *CSPVen*, 29, p.142.

64. Evelyn, *Diary*, p.366.

65. Bachrach and Collmer (eds), *Lodewijck Huygens*, pp.43, 60.

66. Simon Thurley, *Somerset House: The Palace of England's Queens 1551–1692*, London Topographical Soc., No.168, 2009, p.58.

67. *CSPVen*, 30, p.308.

68. Rutt (ed), *Diary of Thomas Burton*, III, p.540n.

69. Jeaffreson (ed), *Middlesex County Records, vol.3*, pp.251, 252, 264, 271, 272.

70. *CSPVen*, 31, p.219.

71. *The World's Mistake in Oliver Cromwell*, London: 1668, p.11.

CHAPTER 3
LONDON & THE RESTORATION

1. Godfrey Davies, *The Restoration of Charles II 1658–1660*, Oxford: OUP 1955, p.118.

2. Samuel Sorbière, *A Voyage to England*, London: 1709, p.16.

3. A.G.H. Bachrach and R.G. Collmer (eds), *Lodewijck Huygens: The English Journal 1651–1652*, Leiden: Leiden University Press 1982, pp.79–80.

4. Bachrach and Collmer (eds), *Lodewijck Huygens*, pp.42, 55, 60.

5. Lorenzo Magalotti (ed), *Travels of Cosmo the Third, Grand Duke of Tuscany, through England, during the Reign of King Charles the Second*, London: 1821, p.400.

6. Cited in *Oxford English Dictionary*.

7. *Journal of the House of Commons*, VII, 1802, p.797.

8. Reginald R. Sharpe, *London and the Kingdom*, II, London: Longmans, Green 1894, p.556.

9. William L. Sachse (ed), *The Diurnal of Thomas Rugg 1659–1661*, Camden Soc., 3rd series, XCI, 1961, pp.5–6.

10. F.J. Routledge (ed), *Calendar of the Clarendon State Papers, IV, 1657–1660*, Oxford: OUP 1932, p.322.

11. *Journal of the House of Commons*, VII, p.773.

12. Sachse (ed), *Diurnal of Thomas Rugg*, p.7.

13. *CSPVen*, 32, p.92.

14. Thomas Sprat, *The History of the … Royal Society*, London: 1667, pp.57–8.

15. R.C. Temple and L.M. Ansty (eds), *The Travels of Peter Mundy in Europe and Asia 1608–1667*, V, London: Hakluyt Soc. 1936, p.113.

16. Sachse (ed), *Diurnal of Thomas Rugg*, p.9.

17. John Towill Rutt (ed), *Diary of Thomas Burton esq*, IV, March–April 1659, 1828, p.365.

18. Tim Harris, *London Crowds in the Reign of Charles II. Propaganda and politics from the Restoration until the exclusion crisis*, Cambridge: CUP 1987, p.41.

19. *CSPVen*, 32, p.89. E. Hockliffe (ed), *The Diary of the Rev. Ralph Josselin 1616–1683*, Camden Soc., 3rd series, XV, 1908, p.132.

20. Davies, *Restoration*, p.160.

21. R.G. Howarth (ed), *Letters and the Second Diary of Samuel Pepys*, London: Dent 1932, p.14.

22. Sachse (ed), *Diurnal of Thomas Rugg*, pp.13–14.

23. Howarth (ed), *Letters*, p.15. Sachse (ed), *Diurnal of Thomas Rugg*, pp.13–14. Temple and Ansty (eds), *Travels of Peter Mundy*, V, p.110.

24. Temple and Ansty (eds), *Travels of Peter Mundy*, V, p.111.

25. Sachse (ed), *Diurnal of Thomas Rugg*, pp.9, 16–19.

26. Routledge (ed), *Clarendon State Papers*, IV, pp.467, 477, 487.

27. Evelyn, *Diary*, p.399.

28. *CSPVen*, 32, p.101.

29. Sachse (ed), *Diurnal of Thomas Rugg*, p.19.

30. Evelyn, *Diary*, pp.401–2.

31. Sachse (ed), *Diurnal of Thomas Rugg*, p.16.

32. Sachse (ed), *Diurnal of Thomas Rugg*, p.22.

33. Pepys, *Diary*, I, pp.39–40.

34. Sachse (ed), *Diurnal of Thomas Rugg*, p.35.

35. *Journal of the House of Commons*, VII, pp.837–8.

36. Temple and Ansty (eds), *Travels of Peter Mundy*, V, p.113. Pepys, *Diary*, I, pp.48, 51.

37. Oliver Lawson Dick (ed), *Aubrey's Brief Lives*, Harmondsworth: Penguin 1972, p.367.

38. Sachse (ed), *Diurnal of Thomas Rugg*, p.25. Pepys, Diary, I, p.49.

39. Ruth Spalding (ed), *The Diary of Bulstrode Whitelocke 1605–1675*, Oxford: OUP for the British Academy 1990, p.568.

40. James A. Garfield (ed), *Clarendon Historical Society*, series II, Edinburgh: 1884, pp.366–70.

41. Pepys, *Diary*, I, p.52.

42. Temple and Ansty (eds), *Travels of Peter Mundy*, V, pp.113–14.

43. Pepys, *Diary*, I, p.52.

44. Dick (ed), *Aubrey's Brief Lives*, pp.367–8.

45. Gilbert Burnet, *History of His Own Time*, London: Dent 1979, p.30.

46. Pepys, *Diary*, I, p.52. Sachse (ed), *Diurnal of Thomas Rugg*, p.73.

47. Sachse (ed), *Diurnal of Thomas Rugg*, pp.51, 60, 71.

48. *Journal of the House of Commons*, VII, pp.837–8.

49. Cited in Michael Foss, *The Age of Patronage: The Arts in Society 1660–1750*, London: Hamish Hamilton 1971, pp.19, 210 n.2.

50. Pepys, *Diary*, I, p.63.

51. *Journal of the House of Commons*, VII, pp.848–9.

52. Sachse (ed), *Diurnal of Thomas Rugg*, p.60. Pepys, *Diary*, I, p.89.

53. Sachse (ed), *Diurnal of Thomas Rugg*, pp.67, 73.

54. Sachse (ed), *Diurnal of Thomas Rugg*, p.80.

55. Sachse (ed), *Diurnal of Thomas Rugg*, pp.89–90. Evelyn, *Diary*, p.406. Temple and Ansty (eds), *Travels of Peter Mundy*, V, pp.117–18. G. Huehns (ed), *Clarendon: Selections from The History of the Rebellion and The Life by Himself*, Oxford: OUP 1978, p.370.

56. Temple and Ansty (eds), *Travels of Peter Mundy*, V, p.116.

57. Huehns, *Clarendon*, p.370.

58. A.B. Worden (ed), Edmund Ludlow, *A Voyce from the Watch Tower*, Camden Soc., fourth series, 21, 1978, p.158.

59. Worden (ed), *A Voyce from the Watch Tower*, p.248.

60. *CSPVen*, 32, p.203.

61. Huehns, *Clarendon*, p.379.

62. J.W. Willis Bund (ed), *The Diary of Henry Townshend of Elmley Lovett, 1640–1663*, Worcestershire Historical Soc., I, pp.93, 95.

63. Pepys, *Diary*, I, pp.190, 195, 210, 261.

64. *CSPVen*, 32, p.204.

65. Pepys, *Diary*, I, pp.282, 289.

66. Evelyn, *Diary*, p.407.

67. Jerry Brotton, *The Sale of the Late King's Goods*, London: Macmillan 2006, p.329.

68. Pepys, *Diary*, I, p.282.

69. Evelyn, *Diary*, p.412.

70. Pepys, *Diary*, I, pp.265, 269–70.

71. Temple and Ansty (eds), *Travels of Peter Mundy*, V, p.127.

72. B.S. Capp, *The Fifth Monarchy Men*, London: Faber, 1972, pp.77, 81.

73. *CSPVen*, 32, p.239. Willis Bund (ed), *Diary of Henry Townshend*, I, p.66. Richard L. Greaves, 'Venner, Thomas (1608/9–1661)', *ODNB*.

74. Sachse (ed), *Diurnal of Thomas Rugg*, p.140. Pepys, *Diary*, II, p.9. Worden (ed), *A Voyce from the Watch Tower*, pp.277–9. Willis Bund (ed), *Diary of Henry Townshend*, I, pp.6–7.

75. Sachse (ed), *Diurnal of Thomas Rugg*, p.142.

76. Temple and Ansty (eds), *Travels of Peter Mundy*, V, p.129. Willis Bund (ed), *Diary of Henry Townshend*, I, pp.66–7.

77. Pepys, *Diary*, II, p.9.

78. Temple and Ansty (eds), *Travels of Peter Mundy*, V, pp.130–1.

79. Maurice Exwood and H.L. Lehmann (eds), *The Journal of William Schellinks' Travels in England 1661–1663*, Camden Soc., fifth series, I: 1993, pp.70, 82. Alexander Gordon, rev. Jane Baston, 'James, John (d. 1661)', *ODNB*.

80. Evelyn, *Diary*, p.411.

81. Pepys, *Diary*, I, pp.315–16.

82. Sachse (ed), *Diurnal of Thomas Rugg*, p.132.

83. Willis Bund (ed), *Diary of Henry Townshend*, I, p.65.

84. Pepys, *Diary*, IV, pp.373–4.

CHAPTER 4
THE PLEASURES OF THE TOWN

1. George Laurence Gomme, *The Gentleman's Magazine Library: Manners and Customs*, London: Eliot Stock 1883, p.118.

2. Evelyn, *Diary*, p.430.

3. Maurice Exwood and H.L. Lehmann (eds), *The Journal of William Schellinks' Travels in England 1661–1663*, Camden Soc., fifth series, I: 1993, pp.66–8.

4. Evelyn, *Diary*, p.419.

5. Lorenzo Magalotti (ed), *Travels of Cosmo the Third, Grand Duke of Tuscany, through England, during the Reign of King Charles the Second*, London: 1821, p.354. Exwood and Lehmann (eds), *Journal of William Schellinks*, p.71.

6. Pepys, *Diary*, IV, pp.341, 355.

7. J.J. Jusserand, *A French Ambassador at the Court of Charles the Second*, New York & London: Fisher Unwin 1892, pp.77–9.

8. Jusserand, *French Ambassador*, p.67.

9. Pepys, *Diary*, III, p.268.

10. Pepys, *Diary*, II, pp.187–9. *CSPVen*, 33, pp.54–5. Jusserand, *French Ambassador*, pp.26–8.

11. Evelyn, *Diary*, p.381.

12. Pepys, *Diary*, II, p.172; III, p.80.

13. TNA, SP29/91/94.

14. Exwood and Lehmann (eds), *Journal of William Schellinks*, p.62. Pepys, *Diary* IV, p.298.

15. Pepys, *Diary*, I, p.53.

16. Exwood and Lehmann (eds), *Journal of William Schellinks*, pp.51–2, 86.

17. A.G.H. Bachrach and R.G. Collmer (eds), *Lodewijck Huygens: The English Journal 1651–1652*, Leiden: Leiden University Press 1982, p.94.

18. Exwood and Lehmann (eds), *Journal of William Schellinks*, p.83.

19. Samuel Sorbière, *A Voyage to England*, London: 1709, pp.71–2.

20. Magalotti (ed), *Travels of Cosmo the Third*, p.316.

21. Cited in Ian Borden, 'The Blackfriars Gladiators: Masters of Fence, Playing a Prize, and the Elizabethan and Jacobean Theater', University of Nebraska, School of Theatre and Film, 2006, p.142. R.J. Mitchell and M.D.R. Leys, *A History of London Life*, London: Longmans 1958, p.140.

22. Pepys, *Diary*, IV, pp.167–8.

23. J.W. Willis Bund (ed), *The Diary of Henry Townshend of Elmley Lovett, 1640–1663*, Worcestershire Historical Soc., 1915, I, pp.31–2.

24. Evelyn, *Diary*, p.540.

25. Pepys, *Diary*, IV, pp.427–8. Magalotti (ed), *Travels of Cosmo the Third*, pp.312–13.

26. Exwood and Lehmann (eds), *Journal of William Schellinks*, p.93.

27. Pepys, *Diary*, IX, pp.3–4.

28. Evelyn, *Diary*, pp.433, 519–20.

29. Cited in Liza Picard, *Restoration London*, London: Weidenfeld & Nicolson 1997, p.208.

30. *The Works of Sir William Davenant*, I, London: 1673, reissued London and New York: Benjamin Blom 1968, p.354.

31. Henri Misson, *Memoirs and Observations in his Travels over England*, London: 1719, p.307. Magalotti (ed), *Travels of Cosmo the Third*, p.399.

32. James Howell, *Londinopolis: An Historicall Discourse or Perlustration Of the City of London*, London, 1657, pp.398–9.

33. Exwood and Lehmann (eds), *Journal of William Schellinks*, pp.60, 71.

34. Magalotti (ed), *Travels of Cosmo the Third*, pp.174, 200.

35. Cited in A.F. Scott, *Every One A Witness: The Stuart Age*, London: Scott & Finlay 1974, p.129.

36. Exwood and Lehmann (eds), *Journal of William Schellinks*, p.84.

37. Evelyn, *Diary*, p.336.

38. *A Character of England as it was lately presented in a Letter to a Noble Man of France*, cited in Ben Weinreb and Christopher Hibbert, *The London Encyclopaedia*, London: Macmillan 1995 edn, p.832.

39. Pepys, *Diary*, III, p.95.

40. Evelyn, *Diary*, p.425. Exwood and Lehmann (eds), *Journal of William Schellinks*, p.58.

41. Pepys, *Diary*, VIII, p.240.

42. Sorbière, *Voyage to England*, p.62. Magalotti (ed), *Travels of Cosmo the Third*, p.405.

43. Sorbière, *Voyage to England*, pp.125, 145.

44. John Cordy Jeaffreson (ed), *Middlesex County Records: Volume 3: 1625–67*, 1888, pp.189–90.

45. Pepys, *Diary*, I, p.88. Bachrach and Collmer (eds), *Lodewijck Huygens*, p.105.

46. Pepys, *Diary*, VI, p.44.

47. William L. Sachse (ed), *The Diurnal of Thomas Rugg 1659–1661*, Camden Soc., 3rd series, XCI, 1961, p.10. Pepys, *Diary*, I, p.253.

48. W.D. Robson-Scott, *German Travellers in England 1400–1800*, Oxford: Blackwell 1953, p.104. *Old Lombard Street*, London: Sir Joseph Causton & Co. 1912, pp.34–5.

49. Oliver Lawson Dick (ed), *Aubrey's Brief Lives*, Harmondsworth: Penguin 1972, pp.283–4.

50. Pepys, *Diary*, I, pp.13, 14, 17, 20–1.

51. Dick (ed), *Aubrey's Brief Lives*, p.284. Pepys, *Diary*, I, p.61.

52. Pepys, *Diary*, IV, pp.434, 438; V, pp.12, 14–15, 27–8, 34, 35, 37, 63.

53. Anthony Powell, *John Aubrey and His Friends*, London: Hogarth Press 1988,

p.183. Stephen Inwood, *The Man Who Knew Too Much: The Strange and Inventive Life of Robert Hooke 1635–1703*, London: Macmillan 2002, p.153.

54. Charles Webster, *The Great Instauration: Science, Medicine and Reform 1626–1660*, London: Duckworth 1975, pp.51, 94, 223.

55. Cited in Marie Boas Hall, 'Oldenburg, Henry [Heinrich] (c.1619–1677)', *ODNB*.

56. Powell, *John Aubrey*, p.153.

57. Thomas Sprat, *The History of the … Royal Society*, London: 1667, pp.87–8.

58. Magalotti (ed), *Travels of Cosmo the Third*, p.186.

59. Oliver Lawson Dick (ed), *Aubrey's Brief Lives*, Harmondsworth: Penguin Books 1972, p.274. Sprat, *Royal Society*, p.67.

60. A.G.H. Bachrach and R.G. Collmer, eds, *Lodewijck Huygens: The English Journal 1651–1652*, Leiden: Leiden University Press 1982, p.105.

61. Cited in Michael Foss, *The Age of Patronage: The Arts in Society 1660–1750*, London: Hamish Hamilton 1971, p.7.

62. Roy Sherwood, *The Court of Oliver Cromwell*, Willingham: Willingham Press 1989, p.137.

63. Jeaffreson (ed), *Middlesex County Records: Volume 3: 1625–67*, p.258.

64. Pepys, *Diary*, I, p.59.

65. TNA, C10/99/21; C33/217, f.137v.

66. Curtis Price, 'The Siege of Rhodes' in Stanley Sadie (ed), *The New Grove Dictionary of Opera*, 4, Oxford: OUP 1992, pp.366–7.

67. Evelyn, *Diary*, p.397.

68. Judith Milhous and Robert D. Hume (eds), *A Register of English Theatrical Documents 1660–1737*, I, Carbondale and Edwardsville: Southern Illinois University Press 1991, p.1.

69. Sorbière, *Voyage to England*, p.69.

70. Magalotti probably was writing about the Lincoln's Inn building, although he described it as the King's Theatre: Magalotti (ed), *Travels of Cosmo the Third*, pp.190–1. Sorbière, *Voyage to England*, p.69.

71. Milhous and Hume (eds), *English Theatrical Documents*, p.2.

72. Pepys, *Diary*, I, p.297; II, p.5.

73. Milhous and Hume (eds), *English Theatrical Documents*, p.31.

74. Pepys, *Diary*, IX, p.247; XI, pp.229–32.

75. Cited in Foss, *Age of Patronage*, p.105.

76. Pepys, *Diary*, I, p.295; IV, p.2; IX, p.2; XI, pp.443–5.

77. Misson, *Memoirs and Observations*, pp.219–20.

78. Milhous and Hume (eds), *English Theatrical Documents*, p.61.

79. Sorbière, *Voyage to England*, p.69. Magalotti (ed), *Travels of Cosmo the Third*, p.191.

80. Pepys, *Diary*, II, p.44; IX, pp.149, 157.

81. Pepys, *Diary*, VII, p.271.

CHAPTER 5
POPULATION & PLAGUE

1. John Graunt, *Natural and Political Observations … upon the Bills of Mortality in C.H. Hull (ed), The Economic Writings of Sir William Petty*, Cambridge: CUP 1899, pp.349–51.

2. Graunt, *Natural and Political Observations*, pp.354–5.

3. John Cordy Jeaffreson (ed), *Middlesex County Records: Volume 3: 1625–67*, 1888, pp.202, 234, 248.

4. Pepys, *Diary*, I, p.303.

5. Maurice Exwood and H.L. Lehmann (eds), *The Journal of William Schellinks' Travels in England 1661–1663*, Camden Soc., fifth series, I: 1993, p.70.

6. Exwood and Lehmann (eds), *Journal of William Schellinks*, pp.86, 176.

7. *Mercurius Politicus*, 21, 22 Nov. 1653. *CSPVen*, 29, p.153.

8. J.W. Willis Bund (ed), *The Diary of Henry Townshend of Elmley Lovett, 1640–1663*, Worcestershire Historical Soc., 1915, I, p.96. Lady Newdigate-Newdegate, *Cavalier and Puritan in the Days of the Stuarts*, London: Smith, Elder 1901, p.168.

9. Pepys, *Diary*, IV, pp.59–60.

10. Hull (ed), *Economic Writings of Sir William Petty*, II, p.363.

11. BL, Thomason Tracts, E352/2 *Orders formerly Conceived and Agreed to be published by the Lord Mayor and the Aldermen of the City of London*, 1646.

12. William Boghurst, *Loimographia*, 1666, cited in Watson Nicholson, *The Historical Sources of Defoe's Journal of the Plague Year*, Boston, Mass: Stratford 1920, p.125.

13. TNA, PC2/58, pp.114, 118.

14. BL, Add MS 10,117, f.139.

15. J.R. Wardale (ed), *Clare College Letters and Documents*, Cambridge: Macmillan & Bowes 1903, pp.64–5.

16. Pepys, *Diary*, VI, pp.128, 133.

17. BL, Add MS 10,117, f.143. Pepys, *Diary*, VI, p.165.

18. Pepys, *Diary*, VI, pp.120, 124, 131.

19. The figures are printed in, John Bell, *London's Remembrancer: or, A true Accompt of every particular Weeks Christnings and Mortality In all the Years of Pestilence*, 1665.

20. Pepys, *Diary*, VI, pp.206–7. G. Huehns (ed), *Clarendon: Selections from* The History of the Rebellion and The Life by Himself, Oxford: OUP 1978, p.412.

21. *CSPVen*, 34, pp.182, 190.

22. Evelyn, *Diary*, pp.479–80.

23. Pepys, *Diary*, VI, pp.186, 187, 192, 204–5.

24. Lambeth Palace Library, Sheldon's Register, ff.206v–7r.

25. *CSPVen*, 34, p.182.

26. Henry Ellis, *Original Letters Illustrative of English History*, second series, IV, London: 1827, p.31.

27. Pepys, Diary, VI, p.224. Thomas Vincent, *God's Terrible Voice in the City*, London: 1667, new edn, Soli Deo Gloria Publications, 1997, pp.37, 38.

28. HMC, *Duke of Portland MSS*, III, 1894, p.292.

29. Pepys, *Diary*, VI, p.189.

30. Ellis, *Original Letters*, p.36.

31. HMC, *Duke of Portland MSS*, III, p.292.

32. Bodleian Library, MS Add. C.303, f.112.

33. LMA, acc.262/43/51,55,63.

34. A. Rupert Hall and Marie Boas Hall (eds), *The Correspondence of Henry Oldenburg*, II, Madison: University of Wisconsin Press 1966, p.449.

35. William Durrant Cooper, 'Notices of the Last Great Plague, 1665–6; from the Letters of John Allin to Philip Fryth and Samuel Jeake', *Archaeologia*, XXXVII, 1857, pp.8, 9. Ellis (ed), *Original Letters*, p.36.

36. George Percy Elliott (ed), 'Autobiography and Anecdotes by William Taswell, D.D.', *Camden Miscellany*, II, 1853, p.10.

37. Vincent, *God's Terrible Voice*, pp.38–9.

38. Vincent, *God's Terrible Voice*, pp.45–6.

39. Nicholson, *Historical Sources*, p.157.

40. J.F. Payne (ed), William Boghurst, *Loimographia*, London: 1894, p.73.

41. R.G. Howarth (ed), *Letters and the Second Diary of Samuel Pepys*, London: Dent 1932, pp.24–5.

42. Pepys, *Diary*, VI, pp.246, 284, 341–2.

43. Thomas Sprat, *The History of the … Royal Society*, London: 1667, p.121.

44. Nicholson, *Historical Sources*, pp.134–5.

45. Bodleian Library, MS Add c.303, f.104.

46. Camden Local Studies Centre, P/GF/CW/1/1 Churchwardens' accounts, 1640–94.

47. Bodleian Library, MS Add c.303, f.122.

48. Henri Misson, *Memoirs and Observations in his Travels over England*, London: 1719, p.219.

49. Edward Gibbon, *The Decline and Fall of the Roman Empire*, 4, London: Everyman 1994, p.418.

50. Misson, *Memoirs and Observations*, pp.3, 221.

51. Hull (ed), *Economic Writings of Sir William Petty*, II, pp.508, 517–18.

52. Robin Gwynn, *Huguenot Heritage: The history and contribution of the Huguenots in Britain*, Brighton: Sussex Academic Press 2001, pp.44–5, 47.

CHAPTER 6
FABRIC & FIRE

1. Pepys, *Diary*, III, p.11.

2. John James Baddeley, *An Account of the Church and Parish of St Giles Cripplegate*, London: 1888, pp.154–5.

3. LMA, GL MS 4069/1, ff.210, 212, 214, 216, 233v; 4069/2, ff.273v, 290.

4. *CSPVen*, 30, pp.25, 40, 54. James Howell, *Londinopolis: An Historicall Discourse or Perlustration Of the City of London*, London, 1657, pp.22, 74, 398. BL, Thomason Tracts E833/4 *Perfect Proceedings of State Affaires*, 12–19 April 1655, p.4601; E833/15 *Perfect Proceedings...*, 19–26 April 1655, p.4616; E833/9 *The Perfect Diurnall*, 16–23 April 1655, p.4311; E833/10 *The Weekly Intelligencer*, 17–24 April 1655, p.184.

5. Evelyn, *Diary*, p.358.

6. Pepys, *Diary*, III, p.296.

7. J.W. Willis Bund (ed), *The Diary of Henry Townshend of Elmley Lovett, 1640–1663*, Worcestershire Historical Soc., 1915, I, p.95.

8. Pepys, *Diary*, III, pp.247–8; V, p.71.

9. BL, Thomason Tracts, E589/16 *Death's Master-Peece*, London: 1650. Joseph Maskell, *Collections in illustration of the Parochial History and Antiquities of the Ancient Parish of Allhallows, Barking*, London: 1864, pp.23–5, 116.

10. *Mercurius Politicus*, 20–27 July 1654, pp.3637–9.

11. *Journal of the House of Commons*, VI, p.346.

12. H.C. Tomlinson, *Guns and Government. The Ordnance Office under the later Stuarts*, London: Royal Historical Soc. 1979, p.116.

13. Evelyn, *Diary*, pp.495, 502.

14. P.D.A. Harvey, 'A Foreign Visitor's Account of the Great Fire, 1666', *Trans. London and Middlesex Archaeological Soc.*, 20, 1959–61, p.83.

15. Pepys *Diary*, VII, pp.267–8.

16. George Percy Elliott (ed), 'Autobiography and Anecdotes by William Taswell, D.D.', *Camden Miscellany*, II, 1853, pp.10–11.

17. Cornelius Walford, *The Insurance Cycoplaedia*, III, London: C&E Layton 1874, p.623. Pepys, *Diary*, V, p.248.

18. Pepys *Diary*, VII, pp.269–70.

19. Pepys *Diary*, VII, pp.269, 271. Harvey, 'Foreign Visitor's Account', p.83. HMC, *MSS of Reginald Rawdon Hastings*, II, London: HMSO 1930, p.369.

20. Pepys, *Diary*, VII, pp.268, 270.

21. G.J.A., 'Fire of London', *Notes & Queries*, 5th series, 1876, p.306. Pepys, *Diary*, VII, p.271.

22. Pepys, *Diary*, VII, p.271. Evelyn, *Diary*, p.495.

23. Elliott (ed), 'Autobiography and Anecdotes by William Taswell', p.11.

24. Printed in Hallam Moorhouse, *Samuel Pepys: Administrator, Observer, Gossip*,

London: Chapman & Hall 1909, p.74.

25. HMC, 14th Report, *Portland MSS*, III, app., p.298. Walter George Bell, *The Great Fire of London in 1666*, London: John Lane, the Bodley Head 1920, p.347.

26. Pepys, *Diary*, VII, pp.271, 277. Evelyn, *Diary*, p.495.

27. Thomas Vincent, *God's Terrible Voice in the City*, London: 1667, new edn, Soli Deo Gloria Publications, 1997, p.60.

28. Elliott (ed), 'Autobiography and Anecdotes by William Taswell', p.11. Pepys, *Diary*, VII, p.277.

29. Harvey, 'Foreign Visitor's Account', p.84.

30. 'Observations, both Historical and Moral, upon the Burning of London', *Harleian Miscellany*, III, London: 1809, p.296.

31. Pepys, *Diary*, VII, p.276.

32. Vincent, *God's Terrible Voice*, p.63.

33. Evelyn, *Diary*, p.495.

34. Vincent, God's Terrible Voice, p.61.

35. Evelyn, *Diary*, pp.497–9.

36. G.J.A., 'Fire of London', *Notes & Queries*, 5th series, 1876, p.306.

37. HMC, *Hastings MSS*, II, p.370.

38. G.J.A., 'Fire of London', *Notes & Queries*, 5th series, 1876, p.306.

39. G. Huehns (ed), *Clarendon: Selections from* The History of the Rebellion *and* The Life by Himself, Oxford: OUP 1978, p.424.

40. HMC, *Hastings MSS*, II, pp.369–71.

41. C.H. Hull (ed), *The Economic Writings of Sir William Petty*, Cambridge: CUP 1899, II, p.507.

42. Vincent, *God's Terrible Voice*, p.69.

43. Evelyn, *Diary*, p.497.

44. Huehns (ed), *Clarendon*, pp.419–20. *CSPVen*, 36, p.297.

45. A. Rupert Hall and Marie Boas Hall (eds), *The Correspondence of Henry Oldenburg*, Madison: University of Wisconsin Press 1965–86, III, p.229. E.S. de Beer (ed), *The Correspondence of John Locke*, I, Oxford: Clarendon Press 1976, p.293.

46. HMC, 14th Report, *Portland MSS*, III, app., p.299.

47. Hall and Hall (eds), *Correspondence of Henry Oldenburg*, III, p.245.

48. Pepys, *Diary*, VII, p.357.

49. Pepys, *Diary*, VII, p.426.

50. Pepys, *Diary*, VIII, p.136.

51. Evelyn, *Diary*, p.510.

52. Pepys, *Diary*, IX, pp.288–9.

53. T.F. Reddaway, *The Rebuilding of London after the Great Fire*, London: Jonathan Cape 1940, pp.247–9.

54. Nikolaus Pevsner, *The Buildings of England: The Cities of London and Westminster*, 3rd edn, London: Penguin 1973, p.64.

55. Pepys, *Diary*, IX, p.392.

56. *CSPVen*, 37, p.55.

57. W.D. Robson-Scott, *German Travellers in England 1400–1800*, Oxford: Blackwell 1953, p.104.

58. Henri Misson, *Memoirs and Observations in his Travels over England*, London: 1719, pp.134–5.

59. Edward Chamberlayne, *The Present State of England*, Second Part, 4th edn, 1673, p.202.

60. John Strype (ed), *A Survey of the Cities of London and Westminster ... By John Stow*, 1720, bk 1, chap. xxviii.

61. C.H. Hull (ed), *The Economic Writings of Sir William Petty*, II, Cambridge: CUP 1899, p.309.

62. Bernard Mandeville, *The Fable of the Bees*, 1772 edn, I, pp.274–5.

63. Cynthia Wall (ed), Daniel Defoe, *A Journal of the Plague Year*, London: Penguin 2003, p.214.

64. Shropshire RO, 3385/2/7, letter to Henry Mitton, 30 May 1676.

65. Corpus Christi College, MS 390/2, f.198.

66. St Thomas's Hospital, Governors' Court book, H1/ST/A1/6 f.20, 11 Nov. 1681.

67. This section is based upon Michael Turner, 'The nature of urban renewal following fire damage in late-seventeenth and eighteenth century English provincial towns', 1981, pp.4–5. I am very grateful to Dr Turner for allowing me to consult his unpublished paper.

68. Pepys, *Diary*, VIII, pp.152, 155.

69. Pepys, *Diary*, IX, p.250.

70. Andrew Yarranton, *England's Improvement by Sea and Land*, London: 1677, p.16.

71. *The Compleat Tradesman ... Composed by N H Merchant in the City of London*, 1684, p.31.

72. Charles W.F. Goss, *The London Directories, 1677–1855*, London: Denis Archer 1932, pp.16–22.

73. Bodleian Library, MS Tanner 42, f.20.

74. Cited in Claire Tomalin, *Samuel Pepys: The Unequalled Self*, London: Viking 2002, p.297.

75. Narcissus Lutterell, *A Brief Historical Relation of State Affairs Affairs*, Oxford: OUP 1858, I, p.7.

76. HMC, *Ormonde MSS*, IV, 1906, p.356.

77. John Pointer, *A Chronological History of England*, II, 1714, p.447.

78. Edward Maunde Thompson (ed), *Correspondence of the Family of Hatton being chiefly addressed to Christopher First Viscount Hatton*, II, Camden Soc. 1878, pp.231–2.

79. Simon Thurley, *The Lost Palace of Whitehall*, London: Royal Institute of British Architects 1998, pp.56–61.

CHAPTER 7
A WASP'S NEST

1. Pepys, *Diary*, II, pp.167, 170. Evelyn, *Diary*, p.786.

2. Tim Harris, *London Crowds in the Reign of Charles II*, Cambridge: CUP 1987, p.83. Pepys, *Diary*, IX, pp.129–30.

3. Harris, *London Crowds*, pp.66–7. John Cordy Jeaffreson (ed), *Middlesex County Records: Volume 4*, 1892, via index, Conventicles.

4. E.L. Radford and Jeremy Lancelotte Evans, 'Quare, Daniel (1648/9–1724)', *ODNB*.

5. Alan Marshall, 'Blood, Thomas (1617/18–1680)', *ODNB*. Evelyn, p.553.

6. Markman Ellis, *The Coffee House: A Cultural History*, London: Weidenfeld & Nicolson 2004, pp.86–100.

7. Jeaffreson (ed), *Middlesex Sessions Rolls: 1683, in Middlesex County Records*, vol.4, p.201.

8. H.C. Foxcroft, *The Life and Letters of Sir George Savile, Bart., First Marquis of Halifax*, London: Longmans, Green 1898, I, p.217.

9. Lady Newdigate-Newdegate, *Cavalier and Puritan in the Days of the Stuarts*, London: Smith, Elder 1901, p.54.

10. Narcissus Luttrell, *A Brief Relation of State Affairs*, London: 1857, I, p.124. J. Horsfall Turner (ed), *The Rev. Oliver Heywood, B.A., 1630–1702: His Autobiography, Diaries, Anecdote and Event Books*, Brighouse and Bingley 1882–4, II, p.285.

11. Evelyn, *Diary*, p.669.

12. *Journal of the House of Commons*, IX, 1802, pp.516–18, 530–1.

13. Evelyn, *Diary*, p.699. Gilbert Burnet, *History of His Own Time*, London: Dent 1979, pp.154–5.

14. *Journal of the House of Commons*, IX, p.576.

15. John Kenyon, *The Popish Plot*, London: Orion 2000, pp.91, 114.

16. R.G. Howarth (ed), *Letters and the Second Diary of Samuel Pepys*, London: Dent 1932, pp.74–5, 83, 86.

17. Tim Harris, *Restoration: Charles II and his Kingdoms, 1660–1685*, London: Allen Lane 2005, p.164.

18. John Miller, *Popery and Politics in England 1660–1688*, Cambridge: CUP 1973, p.161.

19. Cited in Bernard Capp, 'Arson, Threats of Arson, and Incivility in Early Modern England', in Peter Burke, Brian Harrison and Paul Slack (eds), *Civil Histories. Essays presented to Sir Keith Thomas*, Oxford: OUP 2000, p.209.

20. Burnet, *History*, p.167.

21. Harris, *Restoration*, pp.141–2.

22. *Domestick Intelligence*, cited in Harris, *London Crowds*, p.104.

23. Harris, *Restoration*, p.150.

24. Evelyn, *Diary*, p.677.

25. Newdigate-Newdegate, *Cavalier and Puritan*, pp.70, 78.

26. Foxcroft, *Life and Letters of Sir George Savile*, I, p.203.

27. Burnet, *History*, pp.175, 180.

28. Charles Welch, *History of the Monument*, London: Corporation of the City of London 1893, pp.37–8.

29. Cited in Harris, *London Crowds*, pp.180–1.

30. *The Memoirs and Travels of Sir John Reresby, Bart.*, London: 1813, p.251.

31. George Laurence Gomme, *The Gentleman's Magazine Library: Manners and Customs*, London: Eliot Stock 1883, p.128.

32. Evelyn, *Diary*, p.744.

33. Evelyn, *Diary*, p.756.

34. Harris, *London Crowds*, pp.186–7.

35. Newdigate-Newdegate, *Cavalier and Puritan*, pp.209, 218.

36. Lois G. Schwoerer, *The Ingenious Mr. Henry Care, London's First Spin Doctor*, Stroud: Tempus 2004, pp.214–15.

37. Newdigate-Newdegate, *Cavalier and Puritan*, p.96.

38. Evelyn, *Diary*, p.812.

39. Burnet, *History*, p.261.

40. Steve Pincus, *1688: The First Modern Revolution*, New Haven and London: Yale University Press 2009, pp.207–8.

41. Pincus, *1688*, p.207.

42. William Orme, *Remarkable Passages in the Life of William Kiffin*, London: Burton & Smith 1823, pp.87–8.

43. *A Relation of the Proceedings at Charter-House, Upon Occasion of King James II. His presenting a Papist To be admitted into that Hospital*, 1689, pp.1, 4.

44. Burnet, History, p.265.

45. HMC, *Kenyon MSS*, p.192. Burnet, *History*, pp.267, 268.

46. Evelyn, *Diary*, p.888.

47. Henri Misson, *Memoirs and Observations in his Travels over England*, London: 1719 p.243. Evelyn, *Diary*, p.893.

48. Misson, *Memoirs and Observations*, p.242.

49. Cited in Pincus, *1688*, p.325.

50. Pincus, *1688*, pp.230–1. Misson, *Memoirs and Observations*, p.245.

51. Evelyn, *Diary*, pp.889, 891. Pincus, *1688*, p.257.

52. HMC, *Kenyon MSS*, p.207.

53. Stephen Inwood, *The Man Who Knew Too Much: The Strange and Inventive Life*

of Robert Hooke 1635–1703, London: Macmillan 2002, p.389.

54. Burnet, *History*, pp.284–6.

55. Misson, *Memoirs and Observations*, p.249. Luttrell, *Brief Relation*, I, pp.474–5. I. Gadd, 'Hills, Henry, senior (c.1625–1688/9)', *ODNB*.

56. Cited in Pincus, *1688*, p.259.

57. Evelyn, *Diary*, p.895.

58. Anthony Powell, *John Aubrey and His Friends*, London: Hogarth Press 1988, p.205.

59. Foxcroft, *Life and Letters of Sir George Savile*, II, p.35.

60. Cited in Pincus, *1688*, p.248.

61. Burnet, *History*, p.287.

62. Foxcroft, *Life and Letters of Sir George Savile*, II, pp.37n.1, 41, 43.

63. Evelyn, *Diary*, p.895.

64. Cited in Pincus, *1688*, pp.249–50.

65. Misson, *Memoirs and Observations*, p.249.

66. Evelyn, *Diary*, p.902.

CHAPTER 8
THIS SMOKY, OBSTREPEROUS CITY

1. *A Collection for Improvement of Agriculture and Trade*, 20 Dec. 1695, cited in A.S. Turberville, *English Men and Manners in the Eighteenth Century*, Oxford: Clarendon Press 1926, p.438.

2. Ralph Davis, *A Commercial Revolution: English Overseas Trade in the Seventeenth and Eighteenth Centuries*, London: Historical Association 1967, pp.10–11.

3. Joan Thirsk and J.P. Cooper (eds), *Seventeenth Century Economic Documents*, Oxford: OUP 1972, pp.563–4.

4. Lawrence Stone, 'The Residential Development of the West End of London in the Seventeenth Century' in, Barbara C. Malament (ed), *After the Reformation: essays in honor of J.H. Hexter*, Manchester: Manchester University Press 1980, pp.177–8. Bernard Adams, *London Illustrated 1604–1851*, London: Library Association 1983, p.24.

5. Turberville, *English Men and Manners*, p.153.

6. Henri Misson, *Memoirs and Observations in his Travels over England*, London: 1719, p.222.

7. Thirsk and Cooper (eds), *Economic Documents*, p.556.

8. Evelyn, *Diary*, p.977. Narcissus Luttrell, *A Brief Relation of State Affairs*, III, London: 1857, pp.141, 287–8.

9. R.G. Howarth (ed), *Letters and the Second Diary of Samuel Pepys*, London: Dent 1932, p.261. Turberville, *English Men and Manners*, p.391.

10. Luttrell, *Brief Relation*, III, p.499.

11. *Journal of the House of Commons*, X, pp.37–39. The act 1 William and Mary, c.10 abolished the tax.

12. Cited in D.V. Glass, *London Inhabitants Within the Walls 1695*, London Record Soc. 1966, p.xv.

13. ~~Thirsk and Cooper (eds), Economic Documents, pp.791, 808.~~

14. G. Huehns (ed), *Clarendon: Selections from* The History of the Rebellion *and* The Life by Himself, Oxford: OUP 1978, p.451.

15. Daniel Defoe, *A Tour through the Whole Island of Great Britain*, Harmondsworth: Penguin 1971, p.310.

16. Michael Godfrey, *A Short Account of the Bank of England*, in Thirsk and Cooper (eds), *Economic Documents*, pp.708, 711.

17. Luttrell, *Brief Relation*, III, p.503.

18. Evelyn, *Diary*, pp.1009, 1015.

19. Cited in Steve Pincus, *1688: The First Modern Revolution*, New Haven and London: Yale University Press 2009, p.72.

20. *Journal of the House of Commons*, XI, p.494.

21. C.H. Hull (ed), *The Economic Writings of Sir William Petty*, Cambridge: CUP 1899, I, p.64.

22. Evelyn, *Diary*, pp.973, 1009.

23. Ned Ward, *The London Spy*, London: Folio Soc. 1955, pp.262–3.

24. Peter Earle, *The Making of the English Middle Class: Business, Society and Family Life in London, 1660–1730*, London: Methuen 1980, p.150.

25. Elizabeth Hennessy, *Coffee House to Cyber Market: 200 Years of the London Stock Exchange*, London: Ebury Press 2001, pp.9–10.

26. Ward, *London Spy*, p.298.

27. Ward, *London Spy*, pp.300, 314.

28. William Letwin, *The Origins of Scientific Economics: English Economic Thought 1660–1776*, London: Methuen 1963, pp.52–3.

29. Peter Millard (ed), *Notes of me: the autobiography of Roger North*, Toronto: University of Toronto Press 2000, pp.123–6.

30. *The Wren Society*, vol.18, Oxford: OUP 1941, p.18.

31. Paul Slack, 'Perceptions of the Metropolis in Seventeenth-Century England', in Peter Burke, Brian Harrison and Paul Slack (eds), *Civil Histories. Essays presented to Sir Keith Thomas*, Oxford: OUP 2000, pp.161, 175–8. Letwin, *Scientific Economics*, p.59.

32. Thirsk and Cooper (eds), *Economic Documents*, p.176.

33. Charles Davenent, '*An Essay upon Ways and Means*', in Thirsk and Cooper (eds), Economic Documents, pp.806, 809–10.

34. Stone, 'Residential Development', p.194.

35. Evelyn, *Diary*, p.987.

36. James Howell, *Londinopolis: An Historicall Discourse or Perlustration Of the City of London*, London: 1657, p.343.

37. Hull (ed), *Economic Writings*, I, p.41.

38. Misson, *Memoirs and Observations*, p.177.

39. Evelyn, *Diary*, p.942. Ward, *London Spy*, p.257.

40. Cited in David Esterly, *Grinling Gibbons and the Art of Carving*, London: V&A Publications 1998, p.52.

41. François Brunet, *Voyages d'Angleterre*, 1676, cited in Alois Maria Nagler, *A Source Book in Theatrical History*, New York: Dover 1952, p.203.

42. James Anderson Winn, *John Dryden and His World*, New Haven and London: Yale University Press 1987, p.451.

43. Ward, *London Spy*, p.124.

44. Percy M. Young, *The Concert Tradition*, London: Routledge & Kegan Paul 1965, pp.34–5.

45. Ned Ward, *A Compleat and Humorous Account of all the Remarkable Clubs and Societies in the Cities of London and Westminster*, London: 7th edn 1756, pp.301–2.

46. Michael Burden, *Purcell Remembered*, London: Faber & Faber 1995, p.21. Jonathan Keates, Purcell, London: Pimlico 1995, pp.111, 195.

47. BL, Lansdowne MS 1198, f.9. Stephen Porter, 'Composer in residence: Henry Purcell and the Charterhouse', *The Musical Times*, Winter 1998, 14–17.

48. Young, *Concert Tradition*, pp.38–42.

49. Turberville, *English Men and Manners*, pp.162, 356.

50. Ward, *London Spy*, p.159.

51. Evelyn, *Diary*, p.774. Guy de la Bédoyère (ed), *Particular Friends. The Correspondence of Samuel Pepys and John Evelyn*, London: Boydell 1997, pp.182, 198, 235, 256, 285.

Bibliography

Anon, *The Compleat Tradesman ... Composed by N H Merchant in the City of London*, 1684

Anon, *A Relation of the Proceedings at Charter-House, Upon Occasion of King James II. His presenting a Papist To be admitted into that Hospital*, 1689

Anon, 'Observations, both Historical and Moral, upon the Burning of London', *Harleian Miscellany*, III, London: 1809

Anon, *Old Lombard Street*, London: Sir Joseph Causton & Co. 1912

G.J.A., 'Fire of London', *Notes & Queries*, 5th series, 1876

Adams, Bernard, *London Illustrated 1604–1851*, London: Library Association 1983

Andriesse, C.D., *Huygens: The Man Behind the Principle*, Cambridge: CUP 2005

Ashley, Maurice, *Financial and Commercial Policy under the Cromwellian Protectorate*, 2nd edn, London: Frank Cass 1962

Bachrach, A.G.H. and Collmer, R.G. (eds), *Lodewijck Huygens: The English Journal 1651–1652*, Leiden: Leiden University Press 1982

Baddeley, John James, *An Account of the Church and Parish of St Giles Cripplegate*, London: 1888

Bell, John, *London's Remembrancer: or, A true Accompt of every particular Weeks Christnings and Mortality In all the Years of Pestilence*, 1665

Bell, Walter George, *The Great Fire of London in 1666*, London: John Lane, the Bodley Head 1920

Bennett, Eric, *The Worshipful Company of Carmen of London*, London: Carmen's Company 1952

Bennett, W.L. (ed), *Epistolae Ho-elianae: The Familiar Letters of James Howell*, I, London: Nutt 1892

Bethel, Slingsby, *The World's Mistake in Oliver Cromwell*, London: 1668

Brotton, Jerry, *The Sale of the Late King's Goods*, London: Macmillan 2006

Brunet, François, *Voyages d'Angleterre*, 1676

Burden, Michael, *Purcell Remembered*, London: Faber & Faber 1995

Burnet, Gilbert, *History of His Own Time*, London: Dent 1979

Capp, B.S., *The Fifth Monarchy Men*, London: Faber, 1972

Capp, Bernard, 'Arson, Threats of Arson, and Incivility in Early Modern England', in Peter Burke, Brian Harrison and Paul Slack (eds), *Civil Histories. Essays presented to Sir Keith Thomas*, Oxford: OUP 2000

Chamberlayne, Edward, *The Present State of England*, Second Part, 4th edn, 1673

Chartres, J.A., *The Inland Trade 1500–1700*, London: Macmillan 1977

Clifford, D.J.H. (ed), *The Diaries of Lady Anne Clifford*, Stroud: Sutton 1990

Cooper, William Durrant, 'Notices of the Last Great Plague, 1665–6; from the Letters of John Allin to Philip Fryth and Samuel Jeake', *Archaeologia*, XXXVII, 1857

Davenant: *The Works of Sir William Davenant*, I, London: 1673, reissued London and New York, Benjamin Blom 1968

Davies, Godfrey, *The Restoration of Charles II 1658–1660*, Oxford: OUP 1955

Davis, Ralph, 'English Foreign Trade, 1660–1700', in E.M. Carus-Wilson (ed), *Essays in Economic History*, II, London: Arnold 1962

Davis, Ralph, *A Commercial Revolution: English Overseas Trade in the Seventeenth and Eighteenth Centuries*, London: Historical Association 1967

de Beer, E.S. (ed), *The Diary of John Evelyn*, Oxford: OUP 1959

de Beer, E.S. (ed), *The Correspondence of John Locke*, I, Oxford: Clarendon Press 1976

de la Bédoyère, Guy (ed), *The Writings of John Evelyn*, Woodbridge: Boydell 1995

de la Bédoyère, Guy (ed), *Particular Friends. The Correspondence of Samuel Pepys and John Evelyn*, London: Boydell 1997

Defoe, Daniel, *A Tour through the Whole Island of Great Britain*, Harmondsworth: Penguin 1971

Defoe, Daniel, *A Journal of the Plague Year*, London: Penguin 2003

Dick, Oliver Lawson (ed), *Aubrey's Brief Lives*, Harmondsworth: Penguin 1972

Dietz, Brian, 'Overseas trade and metropolitan growth', in A.L. Beier and Roger Finlay (eds), *London 1500–1700: The Making of the Metropolis*, London: Longman 1986

Donagan, Barbara, 'Ford, Sir Edward (1605–1670)', *ODNB*

Earle, Peter, *The Making of the English Middle Class: Business, Society and Family Life in London, 1660–1730*, London: Methuen 1980

Elliott, George Percy (ed), 'Autobiography and Anecdotes by William Taswell, D.D.', *Camden Miscellany*, II, 1853

Ellis, Henry, *Original Letters Illustrative of English History*, second series, IV, London: 1827

Ellis, Markman, *The Coffee House: A Cultural History*, London: Weidenfeld & Nicolson 2004

Endelman, Todd M., *The Jews of Britain, 1656 to 2000*, Berkeley and Los Angeles: University of California Press 2002

Esterly, David, *Grinling Gibbons and the Art of Carving*, London: V&A Publications 1998

Exwood, Maurice and Lehmann, H.L. (eds), *The Journal of William Schellinks'*

Travels in England 1661–1663, Camden Soc., fifth series, I: 1993

Firth, C.H. and Rait, R.S. (eds), *Acts and Ordinances of the Interregnum, 1642–1660*, 2 vols, HMSO 1911

Foss, Michael, *The Age of Patronage: The Arts in Society 1660–1750*, London: Hamish Hamilton 1971

Foxcroft, H.C., *The Life and Letters of Sir George Savile, Bart., First Marquis of Halifax*, London: Longmans, Green 1898

Gadd, I., 'Hills, Henry, senior (c.1625–1688/9)', *ODNB*

Garfield, James A. (ed), *Clarendon Historical Society*, series II, Edinburgh: 1884

Gibbon, Edward, *The Decline and Fall of the Roman Empire*, 4, London: Everyman 1994

Glass, D.V., *London Inhabitants Within the Walls 1695*, London Record Soc. 1966

Gomme, George Laurence, *The Gentleman's Magazine Library: Manners and Customs*, London: Eliot Stock 1883

Gordon, Alexander, rev. Jane Baston, 'James, John (d. 1661)', *ODNB*

Goss, Charles W.F., *The London Directories, 1677–1855*, London: Denis Archer 1932

Greaves, Richard L., 'Venner, Thomas (1608/9–1661)', *ODNB*

Gwynn, Robin, *Huguenot Heritage: The history and contribution of the Huguenots in Britain*, Brighton: Sussex Academic Press 2001

Hall, A. Rupert and Hall, Marie Boas (eds), *The Correspondence of Henry Oldenburg*, Madison: University of Wisconsin Press 1965–86

Hall, Marie Boas, 'Oldenburg, Henry [Heinrich] (c.1619–1677)', ODNB

Harris, Tim, *London Crowds in the Reign of Charles II. Propaganda and politics from the Restoration until the exclusion crisis*, Cambridge: CUP 1987

Harris, Tim, *Restoration: Charles II and his Kingdoms, 1660–1685*, London: Allen Lane 2005

Harvey, P.D.A., 'A Foreign Visitor's Account of the Great Fire, 1666', *Trans. London and Middlesex Archaeological Soc.*, 20, 1959–61

Heath, Helen Truesdell (ed), *The Letters of Samuel Pepys and his Family Circle*, Oxford: OUP 1955

Hennessy, Elizabeth, *Coffee House to Cyber Market: 200 Years of the London Stock Exchange*, London: Ebury Press 2001

Hockliffe, E. (ed), *The Diary of the Rev. Ralph Josselin 1616–1683*, Camden Soc., 3rd series, XV, 1908

Howarth, R.G. (ed), *Letters and the Second Diary of Samuel Pepys*, London: Dent 1932

Howell, James, *Londinopolis: An Historicall Discourse or Perlustration Of the City of London*, London, 1657

Huehns, G. (ed), *Clarendon: Selections from The History of the Rebellion and The Life by Himself*, Oxford: OUP 1978

Hull, C.H. (ed), *The Economic Writings of Sir William Petty*, 2 vols, Cambridge:

CUP 1899

Inwood, Stephen, *The Man Who Knew Too Much: The Strange and Inventive Life of Robert Hooke 1635–1703*, London: Macmillan 2002

Jeaffreson, John Cordy (ed), *Middlesex County Records: Vols 3 & 4*, 1888, 1892

Jusserand, J.J., *A French Ambassador at the Court of Charles the Second*, London: Fisher Unwin 1892

Keates, Jonathan, *Purcell*, London: Pimlico 1995

Kenyon, John, *The Popish Plot*, London: Orion 2000

Latham, R.C. and Matthews, W. (eds), *The Diary of Samuel Pepys*, 11 vols, London: Bell & Hyman 1970–83

Letwin, William, *The Origins of Scientific Economics: English Economic Thought 1660–1776*, London: Methuen 1963

Lutterell, Narcissus, *A Brief Historical Relation of State Affairs*, Oxford: OUP 1858

Magalotti, Lorenzo (ed), *Travels of Cosmo the Third, Grand Duke of Tuscany, through England, during the Reign of King Charles the Second*, London: 1821

Manchee, W.H., *The Westminster City Fathers, 1585–1901*, London: Bodley Head 1924

Mandeville, Bernard, *The Fable of the Bees*, 1772 edn

Manley, Lawrence, *London in the Age of Shakespeare*, Beckenham: Croom Helm 1986

Marshall, Alan, 'Blood, Thomas (1617/18–1680)', *ODNB*

Maskell, Joseph, *Collections in illustration of the Parochial History and Antiquities of the Ancient Parish of Allhallows, Barking*, London: 1864

Milhous, Judith and Hume, Robert D. (eds), *A Register of English Theatrical Documents 1660–1737*, I, Carbondale and Edwardsville: Southern Illinois University Press 1991

Millard, Peter (ed), *Notes of me: the autobiography of Roger North*, Toronto: University of Toronto Press 2000

Miller, John, *Popery and Politics in England 1660–1688*, Cambridge: CUP 1973

Misson, Henri, *Memoirs and Observations in his Travels over England*, London: 1719

Mitchell, R.J. and Leys, M.D.R., *A History of London Life*, London: Longmans 1958

Moorhouse, Hallam, *Samuel Pepys: Administrator, Observer, Gossip*, London: Chapman & Hall 1909

Nagler, Alois Maria, *A Source Book in Theatrical History*, New York: Dover 1952

Newdigate-Newdegate, Lady, *Cavalier and Puritan in the Days of the Stuarts*, London: Smith, Elder 1901

Nicholson, Watson, *The Historical Sources of Defoe's Journal of the Plague Year*, Boston, Mass: Stratford 1920

Niemeyer, A.H., *Travels on the Continent and in England*, London: Phillips & Co. 1823

Ollard, Richard, *Pepys: A Biography*, London: Hodder & Stoughton, 1974

Orme, William, *Remarkable Passages in the Life of William Kiffin*, London: Burton & Smith 1823

Payne, J.F. (ed), William Boghurst, *Loimographia*, London: 1894

Pearl, Valerie, 'Social Policy in Early Modern London', in Hugh Lloyd-Jones, Valerie Pearl and Blair Worden (eds), *History and Imagination: Essays in Honour of H.R. Trevor-Roper*, London: Duckworth 1981

P[eter], H[ugh] *Good Work for a Good Magistrate*, London: 1651

Pevsner, Nikolaus, *The Buildings of England: The Cities of London and Westminster*, 3rd edn, London: Penguin 1973

Picard, Liza, *Restoration London*, London: Weidenfeld & Nicolson 1997

Pincus, Steve, *1688: The First Modern Revolution*, New Haven and London: Yale University Press 2009

Pointer, John, *A Chronological History of England*, II, 1714

Porter, Stephen, 'Composer in residence: Henry Purcell and the Charterhouse', *The Musical Times*, Winter 1998, 14–17

Powell, Anthony, *John Aubrey and His Friends*, London: Hogarth Press 1988

Price, Curtis, 'The Siege of Rhodes' in Stanley Sadie (ed), *The New Grove Dictionary of Opera*, 4, Oxford: OUP 1992

Radford, E.L. and Evans, Jeremy Lancelotte, 'Quare, Daniel (1648/9–1724)', *ODNB*

Reddaway, T.F., *The Rebuilding of London after the Great Fire*, London: Jonathan Cape 1940

Reresby, John, *The Memoirs and Travels of Sir John Reresby, Bart.*, London: 1813

Robson-Scott, W.D., *German Travellers in England 1400–1800*, Oxford: Blackwell 1953

Routledge, F.J. (ed), *Calendar of the Clarendon State Papers, IV, 1657–1660*, Oxford: OUP 1932

Rutt, John Towill (ed), *Diary of Thomas Burton esq*, 4 vols, London: 1828

Sachse, William L. (ed), *The Diurnal of Thomas Rugg 1659–1661*, Camden Soc., 3rd series, XCI, 1961

Schwoerer, Lois G., *The Ingenious Mr. Henry Care, London's First Spin Doctor*, Stroud: Tempus 2004

Scott, A.F., *Every One A Witness: The Stuart Age*, London: Scott & Finlay 1974

Sharpe, Reginald R., *London and the Kingdom*, II, London: Longmans, Green 1894

Sheppard, Francis (ed), *Survey of London, vol.36, Covent Garden*, London: LCC 1970

Sherwood, Roy, *The Court of Oliver Cromwell*, Willingham: Willingham Press 1989

Slack, Paul, 'Perceptions of the Metropolis in Seventeenth-Century England', in Peter Burke, Brian Harrison and Paul Slack (eds), *Civil Histories. Essays presented to Sir Keith Thomas*, Oxford: OUP 2000

Sorbière, Samuel, *A Voyage to England*, London: 1709

Spalding, Ruth (ed), *The Diary of Bulstrode Whitelocke 1605–1675*, Oxford: OUP for the British Academy 1990

Sprat, Thomas, *The History of the … Royal Society*, London: 1667

Stone, Lawrence, 'The Residential Development of the West End of London in the Seventeenth Century' in, Barbara C. Malament (ed), *After the Reformation: essays in honor of J.H. Hexter*, Manchester: Manchester University Press 1980

Strype, John (ed), *A Survey of the Cities of London and Westminster … By John Stow*, 1720

Symons, E.M., 'The Diary of John Greene (1635–57)', *English Historical Review*, XLIV, 1929

Temple, R.C. and Ansty, L.M. (eds), *The Travels of Peter Mundy in Europe and Asia 1608–1667*, V, London: Hakluyt Soc. 1936

Thirsk, Joan and Cooper, J.P. (eds), *Seventeenth Century Economic Documents*, Oxford: OUP 1972

Thompson, Edward Maunde (ed), *Correspondence of the Family of Hatton being chiefly addressed to Christopher First Viscount Hatton*, II, Camden Soc. 1878

Thurley, Simon, *The Lost Palace of Whitehall*, London: Royal Institute of British Architects 1998

Thurley, Simon, *Somerset House: The Palace of England's Queens 1551–1692*, London Topographical Soc., No.168, 2009

Thurloe: *A collection of the State Papers of John Thurloe*, 2, 1742

Tomalin, Claire, *Samuel Pepys: The Unequalled Self*, London: Viking 2002

Tomlinson, H.C., *Guns and Government. The Ordnance Office under the later Stuarts*, London: Royal Historical Soc. 1979

Turberville, A.S., *English Men and Manners in the Eighteenth Century*, Oxford: Clarendon Press 1926

Turner, J. Horsfall (ed), *The Rev. Oliver Heywood, B.A., 1630–1702: His Autobiography, Diaries, Anecdote and Event Books*, Brighouse and Bingley 1882–4

Vincent, Thomas, *God's Terrible Voice in the City*, London: 1667, new edn, Soli Deo Gloria Publications, 1997

Walford, Cornelius, *The Insurance Cycoplaedia*, III, London: C&E Layton 1874

Ward, Ned, *A Compleat and Humorous Account of all the Remarkable Clubs and Societies in the Cities of London and Westminster*, 7th edn, London: 1756

Ward, Ned, *The London Spy*, London: Folio Soc. 1955

Wardale, J.R. (ed), *Clare College Letters and Documents*, Cambridge: Macmillan & Bowes 1903

Webster, Charles, *The Great Instauration: Science, Medicine and Reform 1626–1660*,

London: Duckworth 1975

Weinreb, Ben and Hibbert, Christopher, *The London Encyclopaedia*, London: Macmillan 1995

Welch, Charles, *History of the Monument*, London: Corporation of the City of London: 1893

Willis Bund, J.W. (ed), *The Diary of Henry Townshend of Elmley Lovett, 1640–1663*, 3 vols, Worcestershire Historical Soc. 1915

Winn, James Anderson, *John Dryden and His World, New Haven and London*: Yale University Press 1987

Worden, A.B. (ed), Edmund Ludlow, *A Voyce from the Watch Tower*, Camden Soc., fourth series, 21, 1978

Yarranton, Andrew, *England's Improvement by Sea and Land*, London: 1677

Young, Percy M., *The Concert Tradition*, London: Routledge & Kegan Paul 1965

Acknowledgements

In preparing this book on the London that Samuel Pepys knew, I have been very grateful for the efforts of many editors for making so many of the sources available in print, especially Robert Latham and William Matthews, for their edition of Samuel Pepys's diary, and Esmond de Beer, for his edition of John Evelyn's diary.

The staffs of the Survey of London, Warwickshire Libraries and the Library of the Shakespeare Institute in Stratford-upon-Avon quickly and competently dealt with my requests. Dr Michael Turner generously allowed me to draw on his unpublished work on the Southwark fire of 1676, and Stanley Underhill kindly provided illustrations from the collection of Sutton's Hospital in Charterhouse, which he has catalogued.

Jonathan Reeve at Amberley Publishing shrewdly suggested that I should follow *Shakespeare's London* with a book on Pepys's London, once again drawing upon the observations of contemporaries. The opportunity to write a study of the city in which Pepys lived was another irresistible invitation and I am very grateful for his suggestion and assistance. Gillian Tindall and Peter Day very kindly read the text and have made helpful and sensible suggestions, for which I am most grateful.

My wife Carolyn has, as ever, provided great support and encouragement, patiently listening to ideas and opinions, and her uncanny ability to find the right material at the right time from a large pile of unsorted stock has been invaluable.

List of Illustrations

69. © Jonathan Reeve JR1985b61fp992c 16501700.
70. © Stephen Porter.
71. © Stephen Porter.
72. © Jonathan Reeve JR2067b67plxxii 16001650 & JR2068b67pxxii 16001650.
73. © Stephen Porter.
74. © Jonathan Reeve JR1980b21p447 16501700.
75. © Jonathan Reeve JR1899b8fp220 16501700.
76. © Jonathan Reeve JR1898b8fp182 16501700.
77. © Crown Copyright. NMR.
78. © Crown Copyright. NMR.
79. © Stephen Porter.
80. © Stephen Porter.
81. © Stephen Porter.
82. © Stephen Porter.
83. © Stephen Porter.
84. © Crown copyright. NMR.
85. © Stephen Porter.
86. © Stephen Porter.
87. © Stephen Porter.
88. © Stephen Porter.
89. © Stephen Porter.
90. © Stephen Porter.
91. © Crown copyright. NMR.
92. © Stephen Porter.
93. © Jonathan Reeve JR2032b40p31 16501700.
94. © Jonathan Reeve JR1957b10p1405 16501700.
95. © Jonathan Reeve JR2047b41p451 16501700.
96. © Sutton's Hospital.
97. © Jonathan Reeve JR1986b61p1049 16501700.
98. © Jonathan Reeve JR1958b24p1429 16501700.
99. © Jonathan Reeve JR1956b10p1337 16501700.
100. © Stephen Porter.
101. © Stephen Porter.
102. © Jonathan Reeve JR19606b24p1488 16501700.
103. © Stephen Porter.
104. © Jonathan Reeve JR1912b94fp264 16501700.
105. © Stephen Porter.
106. © Stephen Porter.
107. © Stephen Porter.
108. © Stephen Porter.
109. © Stephen Porter.
110. © Stephen Porter.
111. © Stephen Porter.
112. © Jonathan Reeve JR1962b24p1573 16501700.
113. © Jonathan Reeve JR1964b24p1577 16501700.
114 a, b, c, 115, & 116. © Jonathan Reeve JR1984b21p821 16501700, JR1968b24p1581 16501700 & JR1975b24p1590T 16501700.
117, 118, & 119. © Jonathan Reeve JR1971b24p1588T 16501700, JR1967b24p1580 16501700 & JR1976b24p1590B 16501700.
120, 121, 122, & 123. © Jonathan Reeve JR1972b24p1588B 16501700, JR1973b24p1589B 16501700, JR1970b24p1587T 16501700 & JR1966b24p1579 16501700.
124. © Jonathan Reeve JR1963b24p1575 16501700.
125. © Stephen Porter.
126. © Jonathan Reeve JR2034b40p193 16501700.
127. © Stephen Porter.
128. a, b, c, d © Stephen Porter.
129. © Stephen Porter.
130. © Stephen Porter.
131. © Stephen Porter.
132. © Stephen Porter.
133. © Stephen Porter.
134. © Stephen Porter.
135. © Jonathan Reeve JR2053b42p355 16501700.
136. © Stephen Porter.
137. © Jonathan Reeve JR2059b43p264 16501700.
138. © Stephen Porter.
139. © Sutton's Hospital.
140. © Sutton's Hospital.
141. © Stephen Porter.
142. © Crown copyright. NMR.
143. © Stephen Porter.
144. © Stephen Porter.
145. © Stephen Porter.
146. © Stephen Porter.

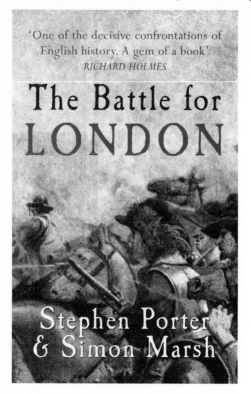

Also available from Amberley Publishing

A.R. MYERS

Chaucer's
London

Everyday Life in London
1342-1400

What it was like to live in London in the time of Geoffrey Chaucer

'A lively panorama' THE INDEPENDENT

Fourteenth-century London was noisy, dirty, and disorderly, but also prosperous, proud of itself and full of life. It was described at the time as a 'mirror to all of England', and indeed it was. The book includes a great deal of familiar streets, buildings and districts but what was going on in them appears very distant, 700 years later.

£9.99 Paperback
33 illustrations (16 col)
208 pages
978-1-84868-338-9

Available from all good bookshops or to order direct
Please call **01453-847-800**
www.amberleybooks.com

Also available from Amberley Publishing

DAVID BRANDON & ALAN BROOKE

Bankside

London's Original District of Sin

The story of historic district on the south bank of the Thames and beyond - the original playground of Londoners, complete with inns, bear pits, brothels and theatres

From a time when London was a collection of discrete districts and villages, here is the long history of Bankside, the metropolis's disreputable and licentious yet vibrant, cosmopolitan underbelly.

£20 Hardback
79 illustrations (41 colour)
304 pages
978-1-84868-336-5

Available from all good bookshops or to order direct
Please call **01453-847-800**
www.amberleybooks.com

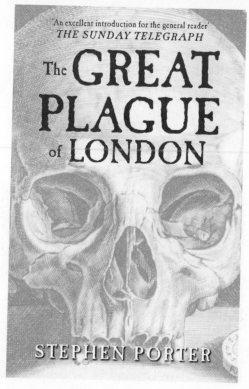

Also available from Amberley Publishing

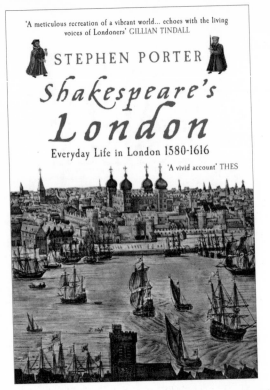

'A meticulous recreation of a vibrant world... echoes with the living voices of Londoners' GILLIAN TINDALL

STEPHEN PORTER

Shakespeare's London

Everyday Life in London 1580-1616

'A vivid account' THES

Everyday life in the teeming metropolis during William Shakespeare's time in the city (c. 1580-1616), the height of Queen Elizabeth I's reign

'A vivid account' THES

'A lucid and cogent narrative of everyday life' SHAKESPEARE BIRTHPLACE TRUST

Shakespeare's London was a bustling, teeming metropolis that was growing so rapidly that the government took repeated, and ineffectual, steps to curb its expansion. From contemporary letters, journals and diaries, a vivid picture emerges of this fascinating city, with its many opportunities and also its persistent problems.

£9.99 Paperback
127 illustrations (45 colour)
304 pages
978-1-84868-200-9

Available from all good bookshops or to order direct
Please call **01453-847-800**
www.amberleybooks.com

Index

Numbers in italics refer to picture numbers